Arthur L. Blumenthal

Harvard University

THE

PROCESS

OF

COGNITION

PRENTICE-HALL, INC., ENGLEWOOD CLIFFS, NEW JERSEY 07632

Library of Congress Cataloging in Publication Data

BLUMENTHAL, ARTHUR L.
  The process of cognition.

  (James Jenkins experimental psychology series)
Bibliography: P.
  Includes indexes.
  1.–Cognition. I.–Title.
BF311.B56   153.4   76-55745
ISBN 0-13-722983-6

Experimental Psychology Series
James J. Jenkins, Editor

PRINTED IN THE UNITED STATES OF AMERICA

10 9 8 7 6 5 4 3 2 1

Prentice-Hall International, Inc., *London*
Prentice-Hall of Australia Pty. Limited, *Sydney*
Prentice-Hall of Canada, Ltd., *Toronto*
Prentice-Hall of India Private Limited, *New Delhi*
Prentice-Hall of Japan, Inc., *Tokyo*
Prentice-Hall of Southeast Asia Pte. Ltd., *Singapore*
Whitehall Books Limited, *Wellington, New Zealand*

CONTENTS

FIGURES

PREFACE

Today, psychologists often observe that cognitive psychology has undergone a "renaissance." In the spirit of that observation, I became wholly involved in comparing current research on central mental processes to similar research that was predominant in experimental psychology at the turn of the century. These comparisons were the initial inspiration for this book, which I offer in response to continuing needs for integrative, introductory reviews of cognitive psychology.

I have not presumed to summarize everything that might come under the topic of cognition as it arises in diverse academic disciplines. Rather, I offer an introduction to unique psychological performance processes that shape the momentary cognitive events of thought, perception, attention, remembering, and emotion. In a recent historical survey of cognitive psychology, Dowling and Roberts (1974) found the most common theme to concern active internal processes that organize immediate experience and behavior. The same theme guided my efforts in the present survey.

A concern for common themes leads to a search for parsimony—for explanations of numerous phenomena as consequences of a few very general processes. Explanatory generalizations are here, as in other sciences, the result of either evolutionary wisdom, logic, general consensus, or empirical observation. Yet the manner of initial discovery and the development of scientific generalizations does not prescribe the best means for teaching them.

This text proceeds by first stating generalizations and then examining their implications in observations and findings. In this way, when students are given an initial structure or a meaningful narrative on which to anchor their learning, they will surely profit, even where that structure is merely tentative. For when armed with well-structured subject matter, students are more able—and more likely—to move on to advanced topics, even if revisions of the basic material should be necessary later.

The goals of parsimony and of pedagogy demand sacrifice. Theoretical unity and the flow of the presentation at times take precedence over the qualifiers that certain specialized researchers may put forth. If in reaching for these goals, I oversimplify or am unduly neglectful of any area, these faults are, I hope, in the service of clarity. Abundant references are provided at the end of the book so that most topics can be pursued to any depth.

I have divided the book into three parts. Part I outlines critical historical and theoretical backgrounds. Parts II and III present a progression of generalities and associated illustrations beginning with elemental processes of immediate experience (Part II), and carrying through to processes of the longer continuity and of the control of human experience (Part III). For the sake of clarity the ensuing chapters should be read in the order presented.

Critical reactions and suggestions that contributed to the preparation of this manuscript came from James J. Jenkins, Doris Aaronson, Sheldon White, Eric Wanner, Henry L. Roediger, W. Edgar Vinacke, James Tweedy, Eric R. Brown, John McConahay, Saul Sternberg, and the Prentice-Hall editorial staff. To them I extend my grateful acknowledgment.

A. L. B.
Cambridge, Massachusetts

So, then, finally, what is psychology about? And the answer I give you is one I got from K. S. Lashley: Psychology is about the mind: the central issue, the great mystery, the toughest problem of all. . . .

Mind then is the capacity for thought, and thought is the integrative activity of the brain—that activity up in the control tower that, during waking hours, overrides reflex response and frees behavior from sense dominance.

D. O. Hebb
Invited Address
American Psychological Association
Montreal, 1973

Part One

HISTORICAL

AND

THEORETICAL

BACKGROUNDS

1

DEFINING COGNITIVE PSYCHOLOGY

At any moment in the course of a day, you or I could find ourselves in a situation something like this: engaging a friend in conversation and, at the same time, dodging traffic on a street corner, struggling to remember items on a shopping list, being distracted by nude figures on a magazine cover, and scratching an itch. If we should pause to reflect, we might wonder how we remain so well coordinated, indeed how we survive, given all the events pushing, pulling, and invading our lives.

Most people manage to survive such tumultuous situations with scarcely a moment's appreciation of their accomplishment. But attempts to explain that accomplishment might well destroy many a psychological theory. Worse, this theoretical Nemesis is not limited to what you might dismiss here as one unusual or extreme example. For in reality, situations like the above resemble more the ordinary state of affairs than the extremity of the human psyche. Indeed, the very complexity of the human organism suggests that the flow of sensations, thoughts, memories, and emotions should ordinarily yield a mass of competing demands upon momentary awareness all the time.

What, then, regulates the stream of human consciousness? The answer to that fundamental question can, with some effort, be glimpsed in the literature of psychology, where it is often hidden in obscurity and just as often ignored. But clearly and certainly, the stream of experience must be endowed with regularity; otherwise, survival itself is threatened. Swarms of impressions and reactions might overwhelm any state of mind, resulting in chaotic and ineffective behavior. Yet most of the time that does not happen. Most of the time our experience is stable and well regulated.

In view of this fact we can see that biological evolution, which has brought about such potential turbulence through the evolved complexity of higher organisms, has at the same time provided a process that survives, indeed controls, what could be a blooming, buzzing confusion of sensations, memories, and emotions. It is the purpose of this text to describe that process.

Descriptions of this process began in earnest about a hundred years ago, when early experimental psychologists set out to explore and unravel the integrative functions of the human brain. Since then, research has run the gamut from simple probes of mental reaction-time to investigations of broad and complex integrations of human thought. Out of this century of research has come the isolation of central psychological processes that help explain many peculiarities of mental functioning. Today, in fact, we have arrived at the position expressed by Hebb in the quotation at the beginning of this text: the integrative activity of the brain is the central control process that, during waking hours, overrides reflex response and frees behavior from sense dominance. Other writers have referred to this central control as "consciousness," "immediate experience," and "attention," or have used more technical terms such as "executive monitor" and "mediator." Regardless of what we call it, the central control process is made possible, first of all, by basic biological capacities. In this text we will be concerned with how the actions of thought, memory, perception, daydreaming, and so forth, develop from those basic capacities.

Today, no single book concerned with "cognitive psychology" can reasonably encompass everything that has passed under that title. Some of the applications of cognitive psychology are highly specialized concerns within developmental psychology, some are specializations within anthropology, or other fields. Therefore, let us here briefly lay down a few ground rules for what will be covered in the following text. At the same time, let us acknowledge that although a text must be limited if it is to be coherent, still no one set of boundaries can possibly satisfy everyone. The important goal, then, becomes an integrated treatment of a reasonably broad area. Perhaps on that basis, at least, everyone can find some satisfaction.

The remainder of this introductory chapter briefly sketches (1) the range of psychological observations to be covered in this text, (2) our focus on central mental processes, and (3) the problem of discovering facts about those processes.

RANGE OF OBSERVATIONS

A century of psychological investigation has provided an overwhelming quantity of data. A broad range of that work is summarized here, but it is limited by the following three points of emphasis: (1) mental process over mental content, (2) mature over immature performance, and (3) functional psychological analysis over neurophysiology. Each of these limitations can be explained briefly.

Mental Process

The study of human cognition traditionally concerns questions of two types: (1) the content of human knowledge and (2) the nature of human mental processes that enable the learning and use of that knowledge. The study of the process of cognition, as in the present text, focuses on the latter question.

Process refers to actions of cognitive performance (perceiving, remembering, thinking, desiring) that depend on the organism's biological performance capacities.

Content refers to systems of knowledge (languages, arithmetic, music, social codes, tools) that the human biological capacities use to extend and enrich experience and behavior. Such systems and devices are learned and passed on from generation to generation. The study and analysis of any one of these systems is the concern of an associated discipline (linguistics, theoretical mathematics, musicology, jurisprudence, cultural anthropology).

Processes of cognitive performance, however, are defined with respect to time: perceiving, remembering, thinking, and desiring are fundamentally temporal processes. (And, thus, *time* is the fundamental variable in much of experimental psychology.) In contrast, the contents of knowledge systems, symbol systems, and rule systems have meaning that is independent of time. That is, the fleeting capacity of memory, the surging waves of emotion, and the variations in sensations all belong to a class of natural phenomena different from that of the learned tools of communication, the instruments for producing music, and the strategies for solving problems.

Certainly, the symbol systems, abstractions, and cultural tools that human beings have created may reflect the capacities of human mental processes. But attempts to draw an identity or even a parallel between the two—that is, between tool and tool-user—often break down. The classic example is arithmetic vis-à-vis the act of adding numbers. Most people can add two- or three-digit numbers in their heads; but they cannot so add ten-digit numbers, because of psychological limitations—limitations which have no representation in the number system, or in the principles of arithmetic.

Similarly, some linguists have emphasized the difference between language as, on the one hand, a system of communication and, on the other hand, psychological capacities that enable human beings to use this system. Essentially the same distinction has been made by certain learning theorists (in particular, Tolman, 1932) who do not wish to confound the "process of learning" with "what is learned." Significant arguments throughout the history of psychology have distinguished psychological actions from the content of those actions (see, for instance, Brentano, 1874; Titchener, 1909; and Bartlett, 1932). Yet we still cannot speak of these two domains as being wholly independent of each. At many points in this text, the content of human knowledge systems and the process of cognition are shown to interact in vital ways.

Mature Performance

This book concerns the psychological performance of mature individuals—those who have passed through the progressive stages of childhood to the point where their human capacities have reached full bloom. It may be that any current state of affairs is not fully understood without knowledge of its developmental history. But the developmental psychologist cannot wittingly study the development of, say, short-term memory until that process is first discovered or conceptualized. Accordingly, this book focuses on the discoveries and conceptualizations of fundamental psychological processes. Any adequate summary of the particular patterns of development of cognitive capacities throughout childhood would require another volume.

Functional Psychological Analysis

Finally, there is the emphasis on psychological over neurological analysis. At many points, the events discussed by psychologists are not visible at the neurological level of study, and the events discussed by neurologists are not visible at the psychological level of study. This is but one instance of distinct levels of phenomena throughout the sciences. Any attempt to provide parallel neurophysiological descriptions of the psychological observations given in this book would represent a by no means certain task of reductionism. It would, at the least, require not only another volume but also both more physiological and psychological knowledge than is presently available.

In general, psychological facts and theories are accepted as those of a biological science. But many psychologists have gone on to assume that a psychological theory is firmly established only when given an explicit physiological basis. The grounding of psychology in physiology, however, is all too reversible: neurological theories should not be retained if they are wholly incompatible with widely observed psychological facts.

Whereas psychology is, and should be, sensitive to the results of neurological and biochemical studies of the brain, by the same token, psychology is, reciprocally, a guide for neurologists because a mental process must be known or conceptualized before it can be intelligibly recognized and understood in neurological analyses. Significantly, it has been neurophysiologists who have stressed this point. Worden concluded, when searching for neurological substrates of the process of attention, that

> it would be most edifying to determine which neural loci are, and which are not, implicated in attention. Unfortunately, to do this without a better behavioral theory [of attention] would border on lifting one's self by one's own conceptual bootstraps. (1966, p. 61)

Efron described how

> the phenomena of consciousness must be understood *before* one can hope to "explain" them in terms of neural action. The

> attempt. . . to reverse this order—to study neural mechanisms underlying perception prior to any adequate definition or conceptualization of perception—is doomed to failure. (1969, p. 171)

In a similar way, this argument applies to the computer simulation of psychological processes. Arguments against the logic of computer simulation claim not so much that machine technology and programming are in a primitive or formative state, but rather that the initial notions of psychological processes are often impoverished.

CENTRAL MENTAL PROCESSES

To the degree that Hebb's central "integrative activity" is dominant in human experience and behavior, the traditional distinctions among memory, perception, and thought are not as great as they have often been described. For these faculties are then all seen as various reflections of one central process of cognitive functioning. When a person solves a puzzle, engages in conversation, or watches a motion picture, he is perceiving, remembering, thinking, and feeling all rather simultaneously.

Yet in scientific investigation, phenomena are usually analyzed into components. Thus, psychologists may be no more able to abandon the traditional separation of psychological faculties than physicists can renounce the separation of elementary particles, or linguists the analysis of sentences into constituents. This fact, however, does not negate the necessity of a central coordination of psychological acts, a point that the cognitive theorist Von Foerster has stated well:

> . . . this reluctance to adopt a conceptual framework in which apparently separable higher mental faculties, as, for example, "to learn," "to remember," "to perceive," "to recall," "to predict," etc., are seen as various manifestations of a single, more inclusive phenomenon, namely, "cognition," is quite understandable. It would mean abandoning the comfortable position in which these faculties can be treated in isolation and thus can be reduced to rather trivial mechanisms. Memory, for instance, contemplated in isolation is reduced to "recording," learning to "change," perception to "input," etc. In other words, by separating these functions from the

totality of cognitive processes one has abandoned the original problem and now searches for mechanisms that implement entirely different functions that may or may not have any semblance with some processes that are, as Maturana* pointed out, subservient to the maintenance of the integrity of the organism as a functioning unit. (1970, p. 29)

Today, this *integrity-of-cognition principle* leads to generalities that apply across the traditionally separate psychological faculties. It implies that input from stimulation, output from memory, and the sheer constructions of imagination all pass through the same experiential level at some point, and that there they are all subject to the same central psychological processes. It is that point, and those central processes, that concern us here.

THE DISCOVERY PROBLEM

There are, however, some traditional objections to the investigation of central mental processes, to the effect that they cannot be discovered and explored scientifically. According to many textbooks, attempts to investigate these processes failed and declined early in the twentieth century. This decline is often laid to the failure of "introspective psychology," a failure imputed most typically to the work of Titchener and his students who were at times accused of studying their private mental experiences in rather casual and idiosyncratic ways. Indeed, many of the fundamental cognitive processes that are found to underlie consciousness are not available to introspection in any straightforward way.

Casual introspection is not used in most current research in cognitive psychology. Nor, in fact, was it used throughout cognitive psychology in Titchener's day. Then as now, investigators with insight and cleverness occasionally devised replicable experiments and found regularities among mental phenomena that others can observe and that furnish useful data. Research in cognitive psychology, as will be shown in this text, has obtained a high level of within-subject and between-subject reliability, and has obtained measures of the capacities of momentary consciousness with the same care that would customarily be devoted to describing an external stimulus.

*H. Maturana, "Neurophysiology of Cognition" in *Cognition: A Multiple View*, ed. P. L. Garvin (New York: Spartan, 1970).

The Problem of Familiarity

To be sure, our inescapable and constant immersion in the processes of perception, attention, and emotion poses peculiar difficulties for the analysis of those events. The immediacy and familiarity of these phenomena can both facilitate and impede psychological research. Advantages exist if observations are sometimes free from the limitations of human sensory systems—as is not the case in the study of events at great distance (astronomy) or of events that are extremely small (particle physics). But a difficulty crops up frequently in the social sciences—that of the overfamiliarity of the phenomena. It is the difficulty of the proverbial fish who is the last to discover the sea. Our mental processes are not immediately obvious, though they may be ever present. Paradoxically, what is continuously present can, by virtue of this fact, often escape detection.

In discussing the evolution of intelligence, Cyril Burt goes a step further to suggest an actual survival value of this limit on self-awareness. He conjectures that the organism who has survived is the one who has perceived only what is necessary for defending itself and its family. Burt then continues:

> For quick and efficient action the universe must appear extremely simple, and man must think of it in simple ways. Day-to-day life must seem so plain and straight-forward that "the wayfaring man, though fool, cannot err therein." Much of his perceptual interpretation his brain automatically supplies of itself. And, were he forced to recognize how incomplete and subjective his picture of life really is, he would hesitate over every action: a race of reflective Hamlets would become extinct with the very first generation. Consciousness itself therefore has to be as transparent as a glass window, so that the man of common sense like the behaviourist, can ignore its very existence. (1961, p. 168)

But human curiosity and the activity of science often move against that disposition and toward the discovery of what has formerly escaped our notice.

In science, the act of observation frequently interferes with the events to be observed. Often, the very occurrence of events can thus be inferred only by means of indirect observations. Yet the history of science is the story of our becoming adept at making inferences about processes that are not directly accessible or easily controlled. The history of experimental psychology is in large part the history of the development of clever techniques and procedures for revealing principles that underlie psychological functioning and for revealing psychological processes that have previously gone unrecognized.

The next chapter presents the foundation of some of the basic notions about cognitive processes. It provides an introduction to and a structure for the more detailed observations and the general principles that are presented in Parts II and III.

2

CONSCIOUSNESS
AND
ATTENTION

Experimental psychologists set out initially to analyze the flow and structure of immediate experience, an undertaking encouraged by the discovery that simple reaction-time measurements could be used to study mental processes. Soon the process of attention emerged in many of the early observations as the central mental process. In this chapter, those beginnings and some of the developments based upon them are outlined in the following three areas: (1) selective attention, (2) levels of cognition, and (3) the temporal basis of cognitive processes.

SELECTIVE ATTENTION

Psychologists in fields as different as sensory psychophysics and psychoanalysis have often noted that there is a unity of focus in all normal human experience and behavior. In the words of James (1890), without selective focusing "experience is utter chaos." Indeed, the immediate events that flow in and around us are manifold and scattered. If our experience and behavior are to avoid being equally scattered, then some control process must select only a few impressions at a time, catching only a small part of the much larger flux.

In modern descriptions, this phenomenon is frequently called the *cocktail party phenomenon*: in a gathering of people where many conversations are in progress at once, we follow only one conversation at a time; our attention may shift, focusing first on one conversation, then on another. This capacity to focus awareness can be directed even to what is vague or abstract, or to what is constructed internally, such as thoughts, sentence meanings, and daydream images, but it is directed to only one object or event at a time. Objects and events around us that do not fall within the scope of our attention are mere transient noise on the periphery of our experience.

The immediate corollary of such a constriction of awareness is *selectivity*. More events and impressions generally bombard consciousness than can be accommodated, so selections must be made. Selectivity, in turn, implies that the organism is purposive, that it is an active, choosing agent. The relative effectiveness of human behavior is the result of a varying ability to "time-share" mental operations, or to alternate attentional focusings purposively and efficiently.

This does not mean that there is one constant capacity of attention. Typical of biological phenomena, attention may expand or contract under conditions of stress, fatigue, or emotion. Then too, some frequently occurring behavior patterns become habitual to the degree that they occur *automatically*; attention is thereby free to turn elsewhere. Still, behavior will not be coordinated, nor will experience be coherent, when all central focus is lacking.

Different Schools of Thought

Even after the above observation, the attentive human mind may still have a difficult time discovering itself, as we noted in Chapter 1. Perhaps for that reason several prominent schools of psychological thought overlooked the faculty of selective attention. In particular, associationist and sensationist traditions in psychological theory seldom considered selective attention. In the eighteenth century, philosophers in those traditions began a search for a Newtonian mechanics of the mind, and in so doing they promoted the frequency, contiguity, and intensity of mental associations as the forces that control and coordinate experience and behavior. Similarly, early advocates of behaviorist psychology took little notice of attention, or, when they mentioned it, rejected it as an intangible mentalism and excluded it from researchable subject matter. Because attention usually implies selectivity, which in turn implies a directive agent within the organism, it conflicted with attempts to base all psychological explanation on external stimulus control.

Inspired by modern physics or by biology, other traditions in psychology have found different models. Gestalt psychology, for one, stressed structure and organization as the controlling variables in experience. The postulates of the Gestaltists concerned the patterns of objects and events, regardless of whether they were inside or outside the organism. Attention was mentioned only occasionally in their work; at times, it was rejected outright. However, they did include notions of a central self- or ego-structure within the organism.

For the Gestaltists, explanations of experience and behavior were to be found in the self-organizing qualities of events and objects. In this sense, the Gestaltists disagreed with the associationists only over the level of description of controlling events—Gestaltists emphasizing configurations of events, associationists emphasizing an analysis into elements. Both often left the perceiving, remembering, and thinking individual in a rather passive state, one in which he would be controlled by these essentially external forces.

Even Titchener's introspective psychology, though clearly acknowledging attention, eventually came to diminish its significance because of Titchener's overriding interest in sensory phenomena. Titchener classified "attensity" together with "hue" and "loudness" as a type of sensory quality.

Because attentional selectivity is inherent in behavior and experience, it is easily taken for granted. Nevertheless, the discovery of attention and of its operational characteristics has inspired a wide variety of investigations that have helped form modern cognitive psychology. Those investigations can be traced back to the beginnings of experimental psychology and to distinctions then made between levels of consciousness.

LEVELS OF CONSCIOUSNESS

Wilhelm Wundt, the reputed founder of experimental psychology, played the dominant role in these beginnings. Wundt was inspired mainly by developmental biology and was unsympathetic to the associationists (see Blumenthal, 1975). In Wundt's system, consciousness first arises when elemental brain processes fall into simple patterns; then primitive perception, feeling, or awareness first occurs. A further sharpening of experience, from vague awareness to clear attention, corresponds to a further increase in mental organization. When attention arises, says Wundt, "creative syntheses" occur. By this he meant that our experience, at its highest level, is fundamentally different from the elemental flux of impressions from which it springs. It is, in essence, an internal construction under the direction of central self-control processes.

Two-level Systems

Wundt's psychology thus divided mental processes into two levels—a central focal level and a peripheral or diffuse level. At the turn of the century, this distinction became known as "the law of two levels" (Titchener, 1908). Figure 1, a simplistic representation of the "law," appeared occasionally in the research literature of that day.

Many related models of attention have been proposed. One, for example, is that of a variable power lens, which exploits the notion of "focusing" so prominent in discussions of attention (Hamilton, 1859; Solley and Murphy, 1960). A similar metaphor, suggested by Hernández-Péon (1964), is that of a beam of light of variable width.

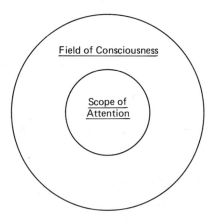

Figure 1. A popular late nineteenth-century conception of the field of consciousness depicting "the law of two levels." One level is attention, the center of voluntary control; the other level is a broader working field of consciousness through which attention moves. Another level was added when Wundt subdivided attention by postulating an "inner or subjective fixation point" within the scope of attention.

In the same spirit as these models is the tuning eye of a radio receiver, which can tune now for high-fidelity reproduction of a large assembly of inputs and now for discriminative concentration on a small selection. Using this and related electronic metaphors, Broadbent (1958) developed the "filter" theory of attention. According to his speculations, information may come into our awareness through any number of parallel channels; but in our cognitive system there is a limited central channel whose capacity is much smaller than the total capacity of the input channels. Between the two is a filter system that has the ability to select one line of input over the others, thereby giving it direct access to the central channel.

Many variations of Broadbent's description of attention were later proposed by his colleagues (see Moray, 1970). The general drift of these revisions is to shift the location of attentional selectivity away from peripheral sensory processes (input channels) and into the center of the cognitive system (the central channel).

Other Two-level Distinctions

Today's theoretical discussions of cognitive processes embrace a variety of distinctions that share, to varying degrees, the conceptual dichotomy of the classical two-level model of Figure 1. Among these distinctions are:

Neisser's preattentive process versus focal attention
Sternberg's field articulation versus scanning device
Norman's rehearsal process versus scanning process
Polyani's subsidiary awareness versus focal awareness
Simon's stimulus information versus noticing system
Broadbent's perceptual system versus selection system
Rapaport's passive thought versus active thought

And there may be others. Neisser also pointed to some further aspects of this separation of two levels of mental phenomena when he noted that

a common thread runs through all the dichotomies. Some thinking and remembering is deliberate, efficient, and obviously goal-directed; it is usually experienced as self-controlled as well. Other mental activity is rich, chaotic, and inefficient; it tends to be experienced as involuntary; it just

"happens." It often seems to be motivated, but not in the
same way as directed thought. . . . (1967, p. 297)

Multilevel Distinctions

In addition to the above two-process, or two-level, descriptions of
mental phenomena, multilevel cognitive systems were also postulated.
Fechner (1860) claimed five levels of consciousness; Baldwin (1889) suggested four levels. And Wundt subdivided attention further by
postulating an "inner or subjective fixation point" within the scope of attention. More significantly, many modern speculations about human
information-processing are multicomponent schemes, in which, for example, attention may be subdivided into a central scanning-process and a
brief buffer-storage, and in which it may be connected to a variety of
memory systems.

Yet the special importance of the original two-level system of
Figure 1 is its theoretical isolation of the notion of attention. No matter
how many component processes are conceived as underlying the process
of cognition, it is those processes described as attentional that are now
shown to make up the central cognitive process.

The Modern Information-processing Model

The style of later twentieth-century analyses of cognitive performance is shown in Figure 2, a multilevel description. This model will be
referred to repeatedly throughout this text, though it is just one instance
of a general descriptive device that has appeared in innumerable variations in recent theoretical writings. The central process that Atkinson and
Shiffrin (1971) here identify as "temporary working memory" (or "short-
term memory") is analogous to Wundt's "field of consciousness," and it
again encloses a "scope of attention" (the "control processes"). In other
versions, short-term memory is sometimes described as more closely associated with long-term memory rather than being separate from it, as
shown here. Nevertheless, it is these central processes that are the
primary concern of this text.

In their original diagram, Atkinson and Shiffrin listed sample tasks
that could occupy the control processes. These were "rehearsal, coding,
decisions, and retrieval." Other theorists have investigated subcompo-
nents of the "control process"—in particular, a "buffer" component and
a "rapid-scan" component (Sperling, 1967). These two subcomponent

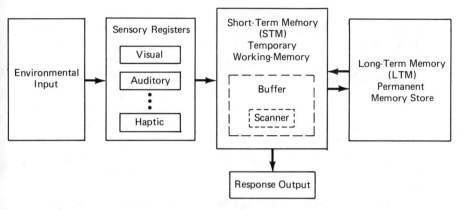

Figure 2. An example of modern flow-chart analyses of cognitive processes. Here, "short-term memory" is analogous to the "field of consciousness" in Figure 1. Among the central control processes, the "buffer" encompasses the scope of attention in Figure 1, and the "scanner" corresponds to Wundt's "inner fixation point." Theoretically, these are central processes, not being limited to any specific sensory modality. In the original diagram, Atkinson and Shiffrin did not present this breakdown of control processes. Instead, they listed typical control-process action: "rehearsal," "coding," "decision," and "retrieval." (Adapted from R. C. Atkinson and R. M. Shiffrin, "The Control of Short-term Memory." Copyright © 1971 by Scientific American, Inc. All rights reserved.)

processes are substituted here for the control-process tasks listed in Atkinson and Shiffrin's original diagram.

The Biological Criticism

Flow-chart diagrams of cognitive processes, as in Figure 2, were originally inspired by models taken from communication engineering. Those models usually show psychological functions (perception, memory, and so forth) as isolated points or boxes along a transmission line. In contrast with this approach are organismic metaphors taken from observations of biological structures and their development. Though often less precise, organismic viewpoints are more likely to emphasize the integration of processes and their variability.

In an influential paper, Craik and Lockhart (1972) criticize the flow-chart analysis of the process of cognition on the grounds that it both oversimplifies and evades significant issues. Whether or not an experience is brought to clear perception or becomes a strong memory depends on an arbitrary degree of processing by a self-controlled and changing organism. Flow-chart diagrams too often suggest a mechanical system in which information merely flows through various stores and filters, one after another, from input to output.

Even though the flow-chart models have been useful in conceptualizing specific mental functions, they have at times led to the error of describing humans as a set of mechanical or electrical elements whose characteristics are inflexible. But, in fact, we are dealing with organic processes that can, as Moray (1967) says, function "now as a store, now as a sensor, now as a calculator, etc." The same central processes of cognition—namely, attention and thought—can be put to many different uses.

Figure 2 reflects both views to a certain degree. It suggests the organismic integration of central mental processes by the embedding of functions within one unit in the center of the diagram. As we shall see, these central processes regulate, or even create, *perceiving, remembering,* and *thinking* at least as much, if not more, than does the input-output flow.

Temporal Characteristics

The central mental processes hypothesized in Figures 1 and 2 have been subjected to innumerable experimental studies and measurements, which have led to further generalizations about their operating characteristics. Immediate experience, for instance, seems to be controlled by a rapid integrative process (the scanner) in a way that makes it unitary, coordinated, and dependent on certain minimal time periods—fractions of a second. There is, at this critical point in the process of cognition, the limitation of "serial processing": at this level, events can be dealt with only one at a time. Thus, when two very brief events fall together within a critical time span of consciousness, either they are fused into one impression, or one event masks the other. The degree of integrative, coordinating activity at this level apparently determines how well an event is perceived or remembered.

These rapid processes, in turn, appear to operate in an attentional field that provides a short delay in the flux of experience (the buffer), a delay in which impressions are held in simultaneous suspension, often called "multiple processing" or "parallel processing." Still other measurements reveal a short-term memory—in essence another type of buffer, but one that is a *postattentive* delay of longer duration. Short-term memory is often conceived as a strong retention of impressions for a short time immediately after they have been scanned (that is, perceived, recalled, or thought of).

Today, the general model of Figure 2 (in many variations) is the object of active study. The time variable is, again, the source of most measurements.

THE TEMPORAL BASIS OF COGNITION

There is a broad and general principle spanning physics, biology, and psychology that describes the universe as being in continual flux and moving steadily toward disintegration or random distribution of energy. This notion, conceived in antiquity, has been formalized in modern science. (In physics it is the second law of thermodynamics.) In nature, however, some forces move counter to dissolution, away from randomness, and toward structure. The appearance and evolution of life is the general example. The construction of momentary perceptions, memories, and thoughts is a more specific example.

Evolutionary Principles

When mental processes are conceived in this latter way, consciousness itself may be seen as the evolved capacity of living systems to cope with relentless flux and change. Imagine an organism for which there exists only immediate sensory events; such a creature would be forever at the mercy of the flux of its surroundings. The natural phenomena in and around us form a kaleidoscope of energies and fluctuations. If awareness of an event could last no longer than the action of some energy on a receptor surface, then, clearly, mental processes would not be stable. There could be no memory. Nor could behavior be organized under the direction of a unitary and enduring set, purpose, or control. Such a capricious existence would be disastrous for most forms of life.

But instead, organisms have the ability to bring about a "time delay" and a temporal integration of experiences, which is surely an important means of their survival. Life is a struggle for stability and persistence. Given fluctuation and change as a primary condition of life, an indispensable further condition must be synthesis or integration, so that the living being can be freed from the haphazard control of its immediate environment, and so that it can find some constancy and stability in the otherwise relentless flux. This is done when the organism forms, preserves, and elaborates its own experiences. An organism possessing this kind of consciousness is better able to survive because it is thus able to compare, to judge, to plan, to predict, and to either elaborate or ignore sensory input. These actions are termed *cognitions*.

The Psychological Present

If there were no delays at all in the flux of experience, then consciousness itself would be a logical impossibility. It would be like an infinitely fine line separating past and future, yet having no duration or temporal extension itself. That predicament is schematized in the following drawing, in which the string of minus signs represents the past and the plus signs the future. James (1890, Vol. 1) called attention to this problem in his discussion of the "specious present" (summarized by Eisendrath, 1971).

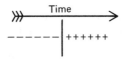

If the psychological present were thus infinitely small, any consciousness of the surrounding world would be an impossibility, for even the fastest scanning device could not then create representations of, or perceive, extended objects. Some extended delay of the otherwise continuous flux is essential.

The psychological present cannot be infinitely brief. It must be some temporal sequence that the organism treats as a unity. This is a rather pervasive principle, and one that will reappear throughout this text. The psychological present is schematized in the drawing below as the time segment within the circle, which symbolizes a minimal "moment of experience." Here, the psychological present is a definite temporal interval where events are temporally integrated—that is, brought together as a unitary experience.

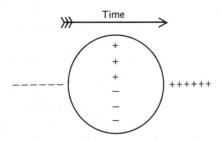

Biological Periodicities

Biological systems show innumerable periodicities of function, and perhaps all biological processes are periodic. Many life processes, whether in the single cell or in the total human organism, reflect regular intermittencies—processes such as heartbeats, brain waves, and sleep-wakefulness cycles. The intervals of these and other biological rhythms range from microseconds to months or years. But the actions of humans and other animals would be chaotic if all these intermittent processes were equally potent in directing experience and behavior. We thus return to the question of one central process. If the living organism is to behave in a coordinated and unified way under the direction of some central control, and if all biological processes are periodic, then the periodicity of that central control-process should be detectable in behavior.

In sensory physiology, a variety of critical periodicities have been observed in the operation of sensory systems. Minute changes in the intervals between extremely rapid stimuli lead to changes in the perceived timbre of a sound. The perception of pitch or of color requires a certain minimal stimulus duration, if only a few milliseconds. These and other critical time spans reflect specific periodicities of mechanisms in sense organs and sensory reception centers in the nervous system. Turning back to Figure 2, those mechanisms may be located conceptually at the level of the "sensory registers" in the information-processing model of Atkinson and Shiffrin (1971).

In the course of further research on the temporal constraints of other psychological performances—of perception, movement, and memory—there have come additional findings that isolate periodicities of purely central integrative mechanisms.

Internal Clocks

A variety of periodicities and biological rhythms have been described in the processes of the central nervous system. But a nagging problem for investigators of this question is their failure to locate an "organ of the time sense"—some internal clockwork that is the source of particular cognitive rhythms. Yet a regular intermittency in a psychological process does not mean that there must be an isolated neurological generator or pathway that controls it. Temporal phenomena in biological systems can arise from greatly complicated arrangements of interacting elements, rather than from a set of individual control units with information flow between them (Oatley and Goodwin, 1971). For example, there are the patterned flights of birds, the coordination in schools of fish, and the synchronized singing of insects. One may conceive, for instance, of a population of quasi-autonomous oscillatory systems, such as brain cells, that entrain upon one another and thereby give the impression that a separate internal clock drives the whole population.

Some early critics considered the findings of consistent temporal patterns in cognitive performance to be mere coincidence. Titchener (1908) and Boring (1942) once conjectured that these patterns are either procedural artifacts or the result of "mystical numerology." Controls against laboratory artifice, however, have long since been carefully observed. And the repeated findings by biologists of critical biological rhythms and periodicities have attracted the interest of some later psychologists, who have pressed further into this area of investigation, as subsequent chapters will show.

Temporal Limits on Human Performance

It follows that the rate of cognitive performance in general (perception, thought, and memory) must be temporally limited in some manner. With a moment's reflection, it should be obvious that human performance is temporally limited and that we all function in approximately similar time frames. We would not be able to understand one another's speech or perceive one another's actions should those of one individual be measured out in microseconds and those of another in hours.

We shall see that just as human sensory systems are "tuned" to narrow ranges along certain energy spectra, so human cognitive activity (perceiving, thinking, and remembering) may be limited temporally to narrow ranges of event-durations and intermittencies. Brecher (1932) and Von Uexküll (1934) showed, in some remarkable observations and experiments, that certain animals other than humans operate perceptually within entirely different temporal ranges. That is, the rates of their actions and perceptions are radically different from the rates of human speech, human music, and human actions in general. Some creatures form perceptions much more slowly, some much more rapidly, than do humans. For a fanciful example, if a Mozart sonata could be made intelligible to a hummingbird, it would likely have to be played so rapidly that to human ears it would sound like a brief buzz. If adapted to the perceptual rate of a snail, it would be so slow as to again lose any coherence for human perception (Brecher, 1932). When we become aware of these differences between ourselves and certain other forms of life, we begin to realize just how much our own experience may be limited by certain periodicities. Those limits are described in Part II, beginning with the next chapter.

Plan of the Following Chapters

Although the research summaries that follow (in the next chapter and throughout the book) derive from long and tedious examination of isolated experimental detail, I have chosen not to present them in that same manner. Instead, a basic structure of general principles, in the form of a few descriptive generalizations, is presented first, followed by selected sets of observations that illustrate these generalizations in several areas of research. Each set of observations is merely an introduction to what is, in reality, a much larger area of research. At the end of each chapter a conclusion section then briefly summarizes these observations and generalizations.

Since cognitive psychology is about processes that are often not directly observable in behavior, offering a single type of indirect observation would provide little information, for it would likely fail to distinguish among central cognitive process, response system, sensory system, and measurement artifact. As illustrated by Garner, Hake, and Eriksen (1956), the researcher must select a variety of experimental demonstrations or observations that converge, ideally, only at the point of isolating the central process. This enables us to study processes that are not uniquely identifiable with any one type of operation or observation.

Part Two

IMMEDIATE

EXPERIENCE

3

RAPID
ATTENTIONAL
INTEGRATIONS

In this chapter we begin an examination of immediate experience with a look at the briefest and most elementary pulse of attention. The simplest act of attention reveals some general principles of cognition. In Figure 2, this central process was represented as the "scanner." The literature of experimental psychology contains an assortment of terms that refer to minimal time requirements for central-process actions of thought, perception, and memory. Examples are "scanning rate," "the psychological moment," "central consolidation time," and "minimal dwell time." Whereas these terms refer essentially to periodicity, others such as the following refer to underlying mechanisms: "serial processor of information," "cortical excitability cycle," "integrator mechanism," "comprehension operator," "identifier," "attentional energy unit," and "central assembly."

None of these terms has become dominant in the sense of describing the whole class of observations. Yet throughout this range of observations, there are close similarities of duration, of variability, and of other characteristics. For consistency and generality, the expression *rapid attentional integration* (RAI) will be used in reference to this class of observations. This term shares the meanings of most of the above expressions.

GENERAL PRINCIPLES

As conceived here, rapid attentional integrations are elemental temporal processes that generate the flow of experience. They are brief pulses of integration that fuse a set of events or impressions into a unitary experience.

In one survey of such processes, Stroud (1955) observed a temporal limit or constant in a variety of perceptual and performance tasks. Reaction times, sequential perceptions, and other sequential performances were found to be limited by a fastest rate of about ten per second (100 milliseconds per event). In another review of research, White (1963) showed that when several separate events occur within about 100 milliseconds, they are preceived as one unitary event.

Summarizing many other investigations of this periodicity, Harter (1967) lists perceived simultaneity, subjective counting and rate judgments, intermittency of corrective movements during tracking, perceptual masking, discontinuities in motor behavior, apparent movement of intermittent stimuli, and temporal information-processing in general as all reflecting the same temporal characteristics. He concluded that "the critical periods of time at which the above phenomena occurred ranged from 50 to 200 msec, the most common value being 100 msec."*

The idea of a series of "psychological presents" might, however, suggest a sequence of "snapshots" of experience. But the critical intervals found here do not resemble photographic exposures; they are active information-processing intervals, within which the temporal ordering of events may be critical in determining various qualities of experience, such as the pitch of a tone or the apparent movement of an object.

Yet arguments have arisen over whether minimal information-processing intervals should be conceived as discrete time-quanta, so that

---

*In modern philosophy a parallel line of study is the analysis of human experience into temporally and logically minimal units, which Carnap (1928) called "elementary experiences," Whitehead (1929) the "actual occasion process," and Goodman (1969) "concreta."

the apparently smooth stream of consciousness is actually a chain of psychological "moments," or whether the stream of consciousness is a continuous traveling wave, a moving average of events that are experienced. The traveling wave is seen as having a specific time-width. Some data favor one view, some the other (Stroud, 1955; Shallice, 1964; and Allport, 1968). Although these alternatives may have important theoretical implications, they will not be advanced here. The phenomena of attentional integration can still be described without the resolution of this quantum-versus-wave issue.

Neurological speculations. Do such intermittencies or waves reflect the brain's fundamental operation of assembling and integrating immediate experience? This question has been discussed ever since the discovery that the brain generates rapid electrical waves. And yet we still cannot single out any obvious, simple neurological structure or process that would explain many seemingly related psychological observations. But that, again, is not an uncommon situation in the relationship between psychology and neurology. Often, what appears as a simple, unitary psychological process is the result of the interaction of any number of complex, diverse, and derivative physiological mechanisms (see Uttal, 1971). As we noted in the previous chapter, an assembly of quasi-autonomous systems may entrain upon one another and thereby give us the impression that a separate internal clock drives the whole population. A general RAI function would likely represent what are, at the physiological level, many different processes.

Nevertheless, one research tradition has long sought to establish a connection between the brain's 100-msec electrical wave (the alpha rhythm in EEG recordings) and various psychological performances. But the alpha rhythm, recorded from the surface of the scalp, readily changes or disappears during waking states. It is usually present during relaxed or meditative states, but often disappears during active problem solving, though even this generalization is far from consistent. Simple reaction-times, at least, are strongly correlated with variations in the rate of these brain waves.

Derived from such investigations are speculations about the mechanisms that may determine a basic rate of brain function. There are fundamentally two hypotheses: *cortical excitability cycles* and *cortical scanning mechanisms* (both reviewed by Harter, 1967). The cortical excitability hypothesis originally concerned the temporal regulation of incoming sense data. Both the spontaneous alpha rhythms and the evoked cortical potentials are thus conceived as reflecting a cyclic fluctuation in the threshold for the cortical response to incoming impulses.

The cortical scanning hypothesis comes from the observation that the cortex is divided into layers. Impulses, it was proposed, descend from outer layers to inner layers, and thus they are averaged or integrated over time by a scanning mechanism, a process that may be reflected in the brain's alpha rhythms. The actual mechanism of scanning may be the activation of successive cortical layers in a 100-msec sweep up and down through the cortex. Control of the sweep may reside at lower brain-stem levels.

An alternative to this vertical-sweep hypothesis, proposed by Wiener (1948), suggests a horizontal scan: the alpha rhythm is viewed as a sweep across the cortex, rather than from inner to outer layers. Wiener's proposal used the analogy of the horizontal scanning of the electron beam that maintains an image on a television screen.

Summary generalizations. Looking now to functional psychological descriptions, we may advance some generalities describing rapid attentional integrations in order to help introduce further observations. These following generalizations have appeared in a variety of forms and terminologies in associated psychological research, much of which is described later in this chapter:

> Rapid attentional integrations form immediate experience; the integration intervals vary from approximately 50 to 250 msec, with the most common observation being about 100 msec.

> Temporally separate events included in one integration are fused in experience to form a unitary impression; when those events are structurally different or incompatible, some may be omitted rather than fused.

What these generalizations may lack is an adequate indication of the constructive power of this elementary integrative process. Integrations or "fusions" at this central level are not merely summative but are also selective, constructive, creative, and synthesizing, which is apparent in the experimental illustrations that follow.

Gestalt structuring. To elaborate the notion that structure and compatibility play a role in these integrations, it may be said that this rapid central process follows the course of least complexity, or of least effort. The school of Gestalt psychology, though not concerned specifically with attention, described the developments of perceptions and other experiences as following courses of least effort. The cognitive "laws" proposed by the Gestaltists are statements that integrations favor simplicity over complexity, regularity over irregularity, unity over disunity, consonance over dissonance, and the like.

In turn, these statements are all reflections of a more universal Gestalt principle, the "law of *Prägnanz*" (translatable as "compactness" or "conciseness"), which states that psychological organization will always be as concise, simple, and unified as immediate events permit. That is to say, psychological organization will take the course requiring the least effort or energy in the achievement of the spatial and temporal stability of experience.

Variability. Considering the duration of these elemental acts of integration, they should, like all biological phenomena, show a certain degree of temporal variation. As Harter (1967) noted, variations in this process are often found within the range of 50 to 200 msec.

Several stimulus and subject parameters should then be kept in mind for the remainder of this chapter. Most notably, *there is an inverse relation between length of integration interval and intensity of events that occupy RAI*, as if slightly more time is allowed for low-intensity stimuli or weak memory-images. The earliest observation of this was in simple reaction times. The stronger a stimulus, the more rapid the identification (Berger, 1886; Piéron, 1914; McGill, 1961). Nerve conduction, it should be noted, is more rapid with stronger stimulation.

Other sources of variation are more speculative. Greater task demands or increased information loads may hurry and thus shorten reactions (as in the case of decoding an auditory message and simultaneously attempting to track a visual input). Rapid switching between two trains of activity may thus force an increase in the rate of attentional action. But information load, when considered as the amount of information packed within one processing interval, may also have the opposite effect: it may "stretch" the processing interval and slow performance. In addition, the effects of practice, expectancy, attitude, habituation, fatigue, and age may affect the briefest psychological functions, just as they affect other biological functions.

OBSERVATIONS

The data selected here as illustrations of rapid attentional integrations fall into the following seven categories:

1. time-intensity relations
2. central masking
3. apparent movement
4. temporal numerosity and simultaneity

  5. refractory period and prior entry
  6. memory scanning
  7. stroboscopic disturbance

In the remainder of this chapter, each of these phenomena is described briefly. Each one provides an example of a rapid attentional integration that controls immediate experience.

Time-Intensity Relations

Some of the earliest studies of human perception yielded the discovery of a regular relation between the *duration* of brief stimuli and their experienced *intensity* (Swan, 1849; Exner, 1868). This effect of time on intensity occurs only for time spans of around 100 msec, allowing for the usual variability. Yet there is no experience of time differences among events this brief; that is, stimuli of sub-100-msec durations are all experienced as the same temporally—as lasting around 100 msec.

Bloch's Law. In 1885, Bloch became the first to propose a law to describe this relation. This law's original and most familiar form is *intensity × time = a constant* in the critical period of approximately 100 msec. To illustrate this relation a light whose duration is 40 msec will appear identical to a lower-intensity light whose duration is 80 msec. This is perhaps the simplest demonstration of an elementary process of temporal integration.

In the physics of inanimate light-sensitive substances, a similar relation is known as the Bunsen-Roscoe Law. But this law differs in not being confined to a critical time interval: a light-sensitive substance changes continually as long as it is exposed to light. A variation unique to the psychological time-intensity relation was pointed out by Broca and Sulzer (1902): in many observations, there is a peaking at around 100 msec in the activity that converts duration into intensity experience; this is then followed by a slight decline in experienced intensity. This action suggests an internal pulse of temporal integration.

One of the best graphic descriptions of the time-intensity relation was provided by Stevens (1966). Figure 3 is his plot of data, originally gathered by Raab (1962) for the easily tested case of visual brightness. In these tests, observers estimate the relative brightness of brief flashes of light. The data show the Broca-Sulzer effect, or the peaking of integrative action. Moreover, they show the most extreme degree of variation that might occur in the critical interval as a result of extreme changes in stimulus intensity.

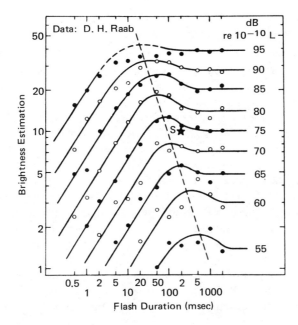

Figure 3. Illustration of both the time-intensity relation and the range of variation in length of integrative period as a function of stimulus intensity (from 55 to 95 dB). For the median stimulus-intensity, the integration interval is 100 msec. The results were obtained from the matching of numbers to the brightness of flashes of various durations; nine different intensities of light were used. Measures of light intensity are often expressed on a scale of "luminance" (L). Stevens has transformed luminance into another energy scale, "decibels" (dB), which is more readable in the present context. Each point is the geometric mean of the judgments of 18 observers. The star *S* designates the standard stimulus, called 10. Relative to this standard, observers estimated the brightness of other stimuli, presented in irregular order. The peaking (humps in the curves) at the end of the integration interval is the Broca-Sulzer phenomenon. It may reflect the oscillation of an intrinsic integration process. (From Stevens, 1966; reprinted by permission of The Psychonomic Society, Inc.)

Originally, investigators assumed that Bloch's Law was solely the result of sensory-cell dynamics, which do show various types of time-intensity reciprocity. However, sensory systems leave much of this phenomenon unaccounted for. One indication of the higher nervous system location of this summative process is that if two brief flashes of light stimulating separate retinal locations, one in each eye, occur within a critical time span, they will produce the summative effect in experienced intensity (Bouman, 1955a, 1955b). The perceiver experiences a single light, the intensity of which varies as a function of the summed durations of the two flashes. The summation of these two inputs must occur at a level of the nervous system much deeper than that of the retina.

Other sensory modes. The same perceptual synthesis occurs when other senses are involved. For example, separate sound bursts within a 100-msec interval, one to the left ear and one to the right, may be integrated and summed to a louder tone (Schenkel, 1967). Surveying many studies of auditory time-intensity relations, Port (1963) and Fidell et al. (1970) found the estimates of the critical period to cluster again, around 100 msec. In a broader review of auditory data, Zwislocki (1969) concluded, "There is compelling evidence that the linear temporal summation takes place in the central system. . . ." He found the critical interval to be 100 msec for sounds of medium intensity. Figure 4 presents Zwislocki's summary of several sets of data concerning observers' comparisons of brief sound bursts of varying intensities and durations. These data yield an equal-loudness contour that again reflects the time-intensity reciprocity for the critical 100-msec interval.

The same temporal integration interval has been found in form perception. Wever (1927) found that the perceptual experience of figure-ground relations develops over a similar time course. Leibowitz and

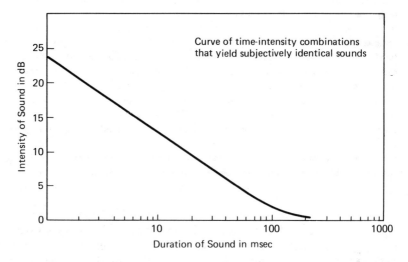

Figure 4. The time-intensity relation for auditory stimuli (broad-band noise). Short bursts of sound of varying durations and loudness levels are perceived as being the same. High-intensity sounds of brief duration match low-intensity sounds of longer duration just for durations within about 100 msec. (Based on Zwislocki's summary of four earlier investigations; by permission of American Institute of Physics ©1969.)

Bourne (1956) and Boynton (1957) showed the 100-msec time dependency in the development of pattern and shape percepts. Piaget and co-workers (1958) found that the perceptual distortions of optico-geometric illusions must develop over a minimal presentation time of around 100 to 200 msec in order to have their full effect. That is, the full effect of the perceptual distortion of lines or figures by means of biasing contexts doesn't take effect until the end of this time interval.

Central Masking

Often, when two brief stimuli occur sequentially within the interval of an RAI action, then, rather than fusing, one will be omitted from immediate experience and prevented from being known to later consciousness. Such "masking" effects have a long history of research, only a small sample of which can be cited here.* It was the considerable contribution of Turvey (1973) to distinguish central from peripheral masking in a series of careful experiments. Anatomically, this distinction would not arise easily; peripheral nervous structures appear to merge gradually into central ones, so at this level of observation, the distinction is not at all clear. However, peripheral sensory masking and central cognitive masking obey different laws.

The rule that determines central masking is known as *stimulus onset asynchrony* within a critical interval (Kahneman, 1968), which is to say that central masking may occur when the time between the onsets of two events is less than a critical interval. The rapid integration process usually begins with the onset of some stimulus event and then leads to the identification or recognition of that event. During the integration interval, however, this process is at times susceptible to disruption by certain other events.

Figure 5 is Turvey's (1973) data from visual stimuli showing a critical interval of nearly 100 msec after stimulus onset in which cognitive events are susceptible to masking. If the separation between two stimulus onsets is less than about 10 to 15 msec, peripheral masking is activated. In distinction to *critical intervals*, which determine central masking, relative *stimulus energies* determine peripheral masking. With peripheral masking, two inputs are fused at the sensory level so that there is only one event to deal with centrally. This accounts for the particular form of

---

*Visual masking effects in which two stimuli of similar geometrical form mask each other when presented in spatially adjacent rather than overlapping positions have also been called *metacontrast*. See the historical review by Alpern (1952).

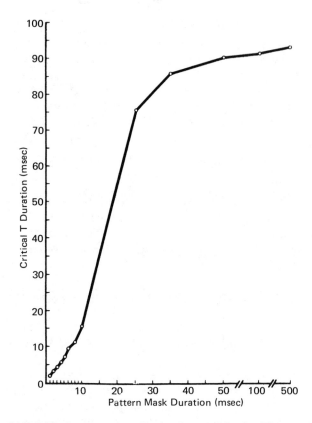

Figure 5. Critical durations necessary for visual target stimulus (T) to evade masking by immediately following stimulus. Critical duration may also be called critical onset-onset interval. Target stimuli were a set of letter trigrams (three consonants each). Masking stimuli were an abstract pattern of lines presented at various durations. Below about a 10 to 15-msec onset separation, peripheral masking occurs where the duration of the following stimulus determines masking. At longer intervals up to about 90 msec, central masking occurs where the duration of the following stimulus is largely irrelevant; instead, onset-onset intervals between two stimuli determine masking. Averages were obtained from 6 observers. (From Turvey; copyright 1973 by the American Psychological Association. Reprinted by permission.)

Figure 5, which encompasses both peripheral masking, at intervals of about 10 msec and less, and central masking, at longer intervals up to about 90 msec.

With peripheral masking, the longer or stronger stimulus dominates, regardless of order. Thus, "forward" masking, where the first stimulus prevails over the second, is as likely here as "backward masking" where the second stimulus prevails. In the combining of inputs into one sensory representation, the features or contours of the weaker stimulus are likely to be overshadowed by the greater energy of the dominant stimulus.

Forward masking is a rare or doubtful occurrence at the central level. To quote Turvey's distinction of peripheral and central actions:

> When two successive stimuli compete for the services of peripheral systems, the greater energy event wins; on the other hand, when two stimuli compete for the services of the central decision process, the victor is likely to be the one that arrives second. (1973, p. 39)

In the central attentional process, the integration (that is, construction, identification, or recognition) of the first event may be interrupted and lost as this limited serial process switches to the integration of the second event.

Practice does not significantly overcome susceptibility to peripheral sensory masking, yet extended experience will lower the critical intervals somewhat for susceptibility to central masking (Schiller, 1965; Schiller and Wiener, 1963).

Other sensory modes. In research with auditory stimuli, Studdert-Kennedy and associates (1970) showed the masking of the first consonant-vowel syllable in a rapid sequential presentation of two syllables, one to each ear. Békésy (1971) obtained masking with simple tones in an open field (presented to both ears). Again, this occurred only when the onsets of the two stimuli were separated by not more than about 100 msec. Demonstrations of masking with cutaneous stimulation appear in Halliday and Mingay (1961) and Rosner (1961). Here a tactile stimulus on one forearm disrupts the experience of an earlier sensation delivered to the other forearm, again, when the onset-onset interval is within about 100 msec.

Significantly, central masking is strongest when the masking stimulus is structured, patterned, or meaningful—that is, when it is an event that requires constructive or structuring activity in the central process. A flash of white light or a field of random noise is less likely to mask at the central level. Yet these forms of stimulation are effective masks at the short-interval peripheral level.

Conversely, a highly structured first stimulus can be more resistant to masking. Mayzner and Tresselt (1970), in an instructive example, masked a five-letter nonword stimulus with another five-letter nonword.

They then replaced the first stimulus with a five-letter meaningful word; masking did not occur with the same after-coming nonword, which means, perhaps, that the attentional integration of the word stimulus was occupied with the additional semantic context (that is, it was a more intricate or active integration), and thus was less susceptible to central masking.

Two temporally separate events that are highly similar or compatible in some structural sense will often fuse in the central integration rather than mask one another. Presumably, whatever integration occurs, it is the one requiring the least effort. For example, Day (1968) presented pairs of words, one to each ear, some of which were relatively compatible in terms of articulatory phonetics and some of which were not. A compatible pair was *tease* and *she's*, whose initial phonemes are acoustically close; in this case, listeners heard the word *cheese*. A relatively incompatible pair was *blue* and *hurt*, in which case listeners did not hear a fusion (such as *blurt*), but heard only one of the two words, or sometimes both separately.

Apparent Movement

The phenomenon of apparent movement yields some of the most startling experimental demonstrations of the RAI process—indeed, some of the most popular effects—for it is the same critical integration period-icity that was exploited in the invention of commercial cinematography. Before turning to the more esoteric laboratory demonstrations, let's consider first the everyday phenomenon of motion pictures, which demonstrates most of the generalizations listed at the outset of this chapter.

Motion pictures. When two nearly identical pictures are shown in rapid enough succession and some objects in the second picture are spatially displaced from their location in the first picture, observers will experience a single picture in which those objects appear to move. One of the pictures may enter only the left eye, the other only the right eye, illustrating that the movement illusion does not depend somehow on the interaction of receptor cells in close proximity in the eye.

The motion picture projector presents a rapid sequence of still pictures with a black interval between each. During that interval, the light is cut off while the pictures are changed; if the light were not cut off, we would see a terrific blurring and streaking, caused by the movement of the pictures as they were being changed. A popular, but hasty, explanation of how motion pictures work lays everything to an after-lag of retinal sensation. But such an after-lag, as a moment's thought shows, can bridge only a temporal gap, not a spatial gap. It would only strengthen our perception of a sequence of still views.

The motion in moving pictures occurs because, at one level of comprehending the environment, the brain integrates impressions in time-blocks slightly longer than the alternation rate of the individual still pictures. The integrative process just begins to react to the first picture and then, in the midst of its constructive activity, it shifts to the second one. With the stimuli separated spatially, a compromise construction yields the impression (a fusion) of one object in motion between two locations—the integration of spatially separate occurrences into a unitary impression. Possibly, the two spatially and temporally separate events activate central masking effects so that spatial-location information is lost or reduced, which, in turn, enhances the illusion of a moving object.

In early silent films, individual pictures followed one another every 60 msec (16 pictures per second). This rate is about the same as the rate at which auditory pulses begin to be heard as pure tone, or at which repeated tactile stimuli begin to be felt as smooth vibration. In all these cases, separate events are integrated by RAI into a unitary impression. Yet in all these cases, sensory systems transmit impulses at a much faster rate; that is, these integrations do not occur at the periphery of the nervous system.

The critical frame-rate for motion pictures varies slightly from individual to individual. Infants can integrate motion at much slower event-rates (Gantenbein, 1952). Complexity of operations, one of the above-mentioned sources of RAI variability, is heightened with the addition of sound to motion pictures. Because in the earliest sound films the illusion of motion broke down for some viewers, the frame-rate was then increased in order to maintain the illusion of smooth motion. The standard rate then became 24 pictures per second, or a new picture approximately every 45 msec. The coordination of, and response to, both visual and auditory events apparently forces the integration process to react more rapidly, thereby necessitating an increase in the critical frame-rate for motion.

Among the subject parameters of RAI variability suggested previously are the perceiver's states of expectancy and habituation, which may influence the illusion of motion. Jones and Bruner (1954), for instance, showed that a visual object usually associated with motion (the figure of a runner) can be set into cinematic movement more readily than an unfamiliar abstract figure.

Apparent movement demonstrates the constructive power of the RAI process. These constructions are not merely a perceptual filling-in of space between stationary objects, for the moving perceptual impression may change in color, size, shape, number, or other qualities, thereby resolving such differences as may exist between events that alternate within the RAI interval.

Consider now the more typical laboratory demonstrations of apparent movement in which the motion-picture illusion is reduced to its essentials. The paradigm arrangement involves two spatially separate flashes of light in a sequence rapid enough that there is an experience of only one light moving between the two locations (Wertheimer, 1912). If the onsets of the two lights are a mere few milliseconds apart, the lights are seen as flashing simultaneously, with no movement. It seems the impression (or integration) of one of the lights must be developed to a certain degree before the other light occurs in order to produce the illusion of movement. Kolers (1972) has reviewed in great detail a long and prolific tradition of vision research that grew from Wertheimer's classic studies of apparent visual movement.

Other sensory modes. In 1855, Czermak discovered apparent motion in the sense of touch. Analogous to the visual situation, two separate points on the surface of the skin, when stimulated alternately within 100-msec intervals, will give rise to a feeling of only one stimulus that appears to move back and forth over the intervening body surface. Benussi (1916), Burtt (1917a), and Whitchurch (1921) made detailed studies of the remarkable similarities between apparent tactile movement and apparent visual movement. Sherrick (1968) found that brief stimuli presented alternately to the two hands can evoke the feeling of one object in space moving between them Again, this integration is the simplest way of fusing the two impressions so that they are experienced as a unity.

In the auditory realm, alternating sound sources can provoke the impression of a single sound moving back and forth in space (Burtt, 1917b). Another auditory manifestation is the "trill threshold" (Miller and Heise, 1950), which involves the alternation at 100- to 200-msec intervals of two tones of different pitch. In this situation there is seemingly only one tone that varies in pitch up and down the frequency range between the two stimulus pitches.

At slower rates, say 500-msec intervals, two separate and discrete tones appear to alternate. The critical temporal interval for the trill experience becomes greater as the two sounds are increasingly separated, one becoming higher and the other lower in pitch. At some degree of separation, the "trill motion" will break down. Here, the RAI process behaves in what seems to be the same manner as it does in apparent visual movement, in which increasing spatial separations of two alternating lights force the lengthening of the RAI interval within certain limits; then, with extreme separations, the integration process breaks down and visual movement no longer occurs.

Occasionally, and strangely, apparent movement is reported when different stimuli are alternated between different sensory systems. Galli (1932) alternated a brief light and a brief sound, producing what was described as the fused motion of "a luminous sound or an audible light." Observers varied in their descriptions of what they experienced: one person reported "a light tunnel which grows longer or shorter as a sound passes through it"; another merely reported that "something moves between the sound and the light." These observations were later replicated by Zapparoli and Reatto (1969).

Perception of causality. To conclude this account of apparent movement, consider a closely related perceptual effect that is another reflection of a critical 100-msec integration interval. It is the perception of physical causality as studied by Michotte (1963). When a moving object *A* collides with a stationary object *B*, and *B* is immediately set into

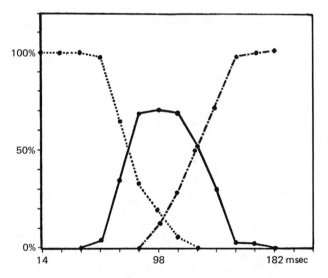

Figure 6. Type of perceived causality as a function of the time interval separating the motion of object *A* from that of object *B*, where *A* collides with *B*. Breakdown of type of perception according to time interval separating the two movements: dotted line = "immediate causation"; continuous line = "delayed launching"; dots and dashes = "two independent movements." Averages are from three subjects. (From *The Perception of Causality* by A. Michotte, ©1963 by Methuen & Co., Ltd., Basic Books, Publishers, New York.)

motion, it then appears that *A* has caused *B* to move, or that motion is imparted to *B*. Imagine, for example, one billiard ball colliding with another.

The impression of "causation," however, may occur just as realistically when there is no real action of one object on another. Michotte controlled the motion of the stimuli so that when *A* collided with *B*, he delayed *B* for various intervals before allowing it to begin to move. The impression of causation continued until the delay between the motion of *A* and that of *B* exceeded about 100 msec. Only beyond that critical interval did *A* reliably appear to stop, and *B* subsequently but independently appear to move, as if under its own power. The appearance of causality then changes to that of two separate events as the temporal interval exceeds 100 msec. With the delay at or near 100 msec, viewers sometimes report a third experience, a "delayed launching" effect: only some of the action of *A* appears involved in setting *B* into motion. Figure 6 illustrates Michotte's findings as well as the range of temporal variation in the integration process.

Temporal Numerosity and Simultaneity

In sending or receiving Morse code, human operators cannot perform beyond a certain transmission rate, again roughly 100 msec per dot or dash (Woodworth, 1938). Beyond that limit, the auditory experience changes, and items in the sequence appear to mask one another or to blend together. Early experimental determination of this "temporal separation threshold" came from Wundt's laboratory (Weyer, 1898, 1899), where it was studied with visual, auditory, and tactile stimuli. These data illustrate, in a simple way, that the pace of cognitive performance is no faster than the central integration process.

Apparent temporal numerosity is an experience of intermittency that does not match the true intermittency of repetitive stimuli. If a rapidly flashing light is observed for a short time in which either 10, 20, or 30 flashes occur, then the number of flashes seen will not exceed that allowable by the rate of integrations, 10 per second on the average (see White, 1963). This is so even though the peripheral visual system is capable of much more rapid response rates, up to at least 40 or 50 per second.

Flicker phenomena. The above temporal numerosity illusion has long been known under the name of *flicker phenomena*. Rapidly flashing lights, from about 10 to about 50 flashes per second, often appear to fluctuate in intensity at approximately 100-msec intervals—hence, a "flickering" light. This results from the fact that the intermittency of extremely rapid sequential events is detectable only at the boundaries between separate attentional integrations (approximately every 100 msec). Brief interruptions in a stimulus that occur *during* a 100-msec attentional integration are not represented in experience because sub-100-msec events that fall within the integrative process-interval are summed together into a perceptual unity.

Beyond about 50 flashes per second, the peripheral visual system can no longer respond as fast as the flash rate of the light; also at that point, the flicker sensation ceases and the light appears to be continuous. That point is termed the *flicker-fusion frequency*.

The flicker intervals will vary when the brightness of the light is changed; flicker is faster with brighter lights. This is a case of the usual shortening of integration intervals induced by increased stimulus intensity, as described previously.*

The suggestion that visual flicker is the effect of a central integration process leads us naturally to the question of similar effects with repetitive events in other sensory systems. Auditory "flutter," one such case, has been known for some time. Békésy (1936), Miller and Taylor (1948), and Pollack (1952) measured this phenomenon as a 100-msec variation experienced in low-frequency sounds. White (1963) observed the same type of intermittency effect with tactual stimuli, as well as with visual and auditory stimuli.

Other observations. These examples of numerosity mostly concern very simple stimuli—visual flashes and auditory pulses. Lawrence (1971), however, contributed observations with more complex stimuli—words. In his tests, subjects estimated the number of words presented in rapid visual sequences at rates from 4 to 16 per second. Later, they also named the words they saw. Degree of underestimation increased, of course, with increasing rates of presentation. The maximum *average* counting rate was between 6 and 7 words per second, and the number of words that were namable agreed closely with this. Although Lawrence's observers reported that each word perceived was clear and distinct, they were generally surprised to learn that their count of words seen was often well below the number actually presented. In this case some items were obviously suppressed or centrally masked rather than fused.

Allport (1966, 1968) described perhaps one of the most dramatic of examples: *apparent simultaneity*—a phenomenon observed in the

---

*In motion picture projection when the rate of successive pictures is about 24 per second, an annoying flicker may occur, especially with high screen-brightness. But modern commercial projectors interrupt the light once between each picture and twice during each single picture, thereby producing an intermittency rate that is well over the flicker fusion frequency.

appearance of stroboscopically illuminated moving objects. At flash frequencies below about 10 per second, a moving object is seen as a number of replicas of itself in rapid succession and spread out along the course of movement. But when strobe-light frequency exceeds about 10 flashes per second, the object appears as a number of replicas *coexisting* in time and spread out along the course of movement; these replicas, then, are seen as a unitary configuration of multiple objects in motion as a unit.

For a moving object, Allport used a white line forming a radius on a black turntable that could be rotated at various speeds. When the frequency of the strobe flash is below 10 per second, the appearance is that of a succession of radial lines spaced equally around the turntable (Figure 7a). When the flash frequency is increased to about 10 per second, then one radial line is seen in smooth motion. When the flash frequency is increased further, then more than one line appears, forming a "fan" of simultaneous radii that rotates as a unit (Figure 7b). The number of simultaneous radii depends on flash frequency. The arc of the fan spans about 100 msec on the average. Reduction in the intensity of the light increases the apparent width of the fan (again, change in the length of the processing period is inversely related to intensity). The eyes of all observers were fixated on the center of the turntable to prevent attempts to track the motion of the fan with the eyes; such eye movement could alter the illusion.

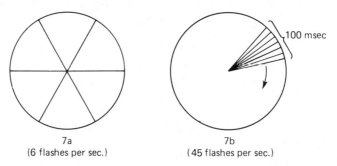

7a
(6 flashes per sec.)

7b
(45 flashes per sec.)

Figure 7. Simulation of perceptual experiences where a radial line on a rotating turntable is illuminated stroboscopically as the turntable rotates at a speed of one revolution per second. In Figure 7a, with the frequency of the strobe flash less than 10 per second, the line is seen as a number of stationary lines appearing *one after the other* and spread evenly along the course of movement. In Figure 7b, with the flash frequency greater than 10 per second, a "fan" of *simultaneous* lines emerges and rotates as a unit. The number of lines in the fan increases with increasing flash frequency; the width of the fan varies inversely with flash intensity. (Adapted from Allport, unpublished doctoral dissertation, 1966)

Allport noted that the sequence of lines in the illusory fan are not retinal afterimages. If they were, they would have a different time course, less intensity, and a certain coloration. Allport measured the observers' perceptions by having them match an adjustable real fan to the width of the illusory perceived fan. It was then easy to estimate the interval of temporal simultaneity from the arc of the adjusted real fan.

Refractory Period and Prior Entry

If, when the RAI process is occupied in its brief integrative action, another event immediately occurs that requires a separate reaction, that reaction is systematically delayed. Because the minimal act of integration requires a certain time, that time must pass before the integration of, or reaction to, a second event can begin. This phenomenon has been called *the psychological refractory period.*

In the earlier literature, there is confusion over what this interval is. More recent summaries (such as Davis, 1956, 1957) conclude that a decrease in the interval between two stimuli below about 200 msec begins to produce a proportional delay of the reaction to the second stimulus. The two stimuli may be in the same or different sensory modes. In the first investigations, two stimuli were presented in rapid succession and a response was made to each, the second response being systematically delayed. But the same delay was then observed where a response was made only to the second stimulus. Thus, the delay cannot be attributed to the difficulty of executing two responses in a short amount of time.

These observations coming mainly from British psychologists resulted in a formidable array of complex theories. Theorists have divided sharply over explanations based on "central refractoriness," "response conflict," "expectancy," and "single channel operation" (see reviews by Smith, 1967a and Tolkmitt, 1973). Kantowitz (1974) suggested that the refractory effects are closely related to central masking (discussed earlier in this chapter).

As other observations of central integrative actions would lead one to expect, the refractory period decreases as stimulus intensity increases (Koster and van Schuur, 1973; Smith, 1967b). Hence, the delay of a response to a second stimulus is greater following a weak first stimulus than following a strong first stimulus. Again, the RAI interval lengthens for low-intensity events.

Prior-entry phenomena. Another set of observations is occasionally related to refractory-period findings, and again illustrates a "single-channel" operation of the central control process. These are observations that involve the simultaneous presentation of two stimuli, typically in separate modalities to lessen the chances of fusion. In this situation, one of the two signals may be subjectively displaced in time: the displaced impression appears to happen later than its true occurrence.* Sometimes, when a person attends to (or expects) the second of two rapidly successive events, central integration can reverse their order in perception. James (1890) wrote of the surgeon who would see blood before his knife penetrated the skin and of the blacksmith who would see sparks before his hammer hit the iron.

The investigation of such temporal-displacement illusions is perhaps the oldest topic in experimental psychology. Early astronomers first encountered these illusions in their attempts to determine the times at which stars pass over meridian grid-lines in telescopes (Bessel, 1823). Their measurement procedure was simply to read the time in seconds from a clock, and then, while watching a star, to count additional seconds by listening to the strokes of a pendulum, thereby noting the exact time of the star's passage across a meridian. But troublesome discrepancies, in fractions of seconds, became notorious. Tests with artificial stars showed the transit to be signaled as much as 70 msec too early, or 250 msec too late.

This problem was also the topic of Wundt's first psychological experiment, in 1862, which he called the "complication experiment." His subjects were to observe a pointer moving over a calibrated arc when, at a certain instant a click would sound; the subjects then had to indicate the pointer's position at the time of the click. Reported position, again, was displaced from the true position of physical coincidence. The direction of displacement, ahead or behind, depended on whether the observers anticipated the sound or the pointer. In other words, if the sound was not expected, it was experienced as occurring later in time than it actually did. Wundt found these displacements to be as great as 100 msec. His students then carried out a prolific array of replications and variations of this test, and similar effects were found with stimulus combinations in other sensory modalities.

Memory Scanning

Simple reaction-time has often been a powerful device for making inferences about central cognitive processes, and the earliest experimental psychologists were quick to develop this tool. Slight delays in

---

*Both this phenomenon and the refractory effect require a preattentive, buffer-storage capacity to hold delayed input for later processing, which is described in the next chapter.

responses have been used to estimate the status of memories or the depth of mental computations.

In some remarkable experiments, Sternberg (1970) established a set of stimulus items (either digits, letters, or faces) in the immediate memories of his subjects. He then presented a single probe item, and subjects were to indicate as rapidly as possible whether the probe item was contained in the memory list. In other tests, subjects were to recall or to recognize the precise location of specified items in the memory list ("context recall" and "context recognition"). The procedure in the context recognition tests was as follows:

> On each trial the subject attempted to memorize a list of from three to six different digits, presented visually one after another. To increase accuracy, the list was actually presented twice, with a recall attempt after the first presentation. The test stimulus was a pair of simultaneously presented digits that had appeared successively somewhere in the list. The subject's task was to decide whether the left-to-right order of the pair was the same as its temporal order in the list, or reversed. He made his response by pulling one of two levers. (1970, p. 49)

The subject's task was thus to scan his immediate memory for the desired information. The amount of time required was directly proportional to the number of items in the memory list. For each item added to the list, reaction times grew by a constant amount, which fell within the range of the usual RAI intervals (see Figure 8). Further, Sternberg noted that the more intense the "image" that is impressed into memory, the less the integration time per item in the scanning of that memory—which again, is the familiar intensity-induced variation in the RAI process. Very simple items (digits) were identified at an extremely rapid rate relative to the usual integration intervals. With more complex items such as faces identification is somewhat slower.

Sperling (1963) once postulated an even more rapid item scan—at a rate of one item every 10 msec. His findings came from very brief exposures of arrays of numerals or letters, in which one additional letter was identified for every additional 10 msec of exposure of the array. Neisser (1967) points out, however, that this may reflect not a scanning mechanism of unusual speed but only the operation of the time-intensity relationship (reviewed above, pp. 34-37). Longer exposure times in this very brief range simply lead to more fully developed perceptions. With a slightly longer exposure of the stimulus array, the items will be slightly

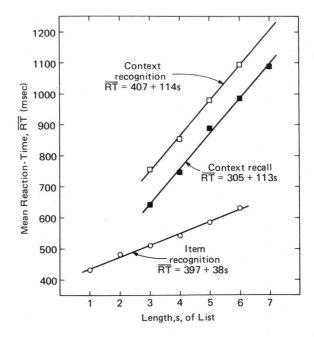

Figure 8. Comparison of reaction-time averages from context-recognition, context-recall, and item-recognition tasks involving lists of items (digits) held in immediate memory. *Context recognition*: times required to recognize the order of a pair of items from a memory list of varying length; average reaction time increased by 114 msec for each increase of one item in the length of the list. *Context recall*: times required to recall the item that followed an individual item from a memory list; average reaction time increased by 113 msec for each increase in the length of the list. *Item recognition*: times required to indicate whether or not an individual item was contained in a memory list; average reaction time increased by 38 msec for each increase in the length of the list. Averages are from 6 subjects for context recognition and recall, from 8 subjects for item recognition. (From Saul Sternberg, "Memory-Scanning: Mental Processes Revealed by Reaction-time Experiments" in John S. Antrobus (ed.), *Cognition and Affect*, p. 53. Copyright © 1970 by Little, Brown and Company. Reprinted by permission.)

more legible and the chance of making correct identifications is therefore greater.

   Reaction time and semantic structure. Human knowledge, or long-term memory, is generally conceded to be arranged in organized structures, presumably hierarchical structures. Such structures are the relationships between the concepts and items of memory. Figure 9 diagrams such a structure: "Fish," for example, is a conjunction of the

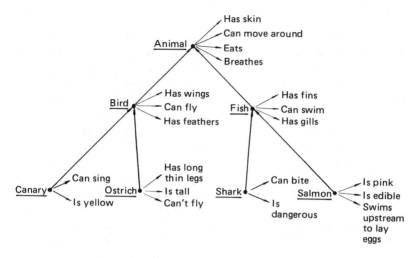

Figure 9. The hierarchical structure of a portion of semantic memory. (From Collins and Quillian, 1969; reprinted by permission of Academic Press, Inc.)

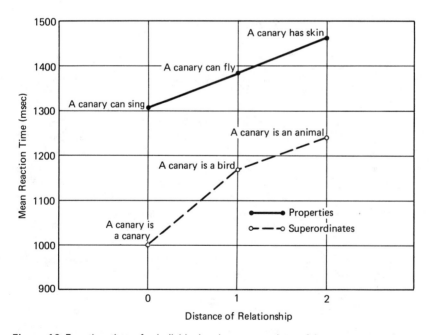

Figure 10. Reaction times for individuals who answered true-false statements about the relations between items in semantic memory. In the statements, the semantic distance between items was varied. Averages from 19 subjects. (from Collins and Quillian, 1969; reprinted by permission of Academic Press, Inc.)

properties "has fins," "can swim," and "has gills." With semantic structures such as these in mind, Collins and Quillian (1969) devised an experiment in which people were to classify as true or false individual sentences that referred to items in a particular semantic structure. Collins and Quillian suspected, correctly, that the speed of the true-false judgments would be related to the degree of search through a semantic structure, a search that would be required in order to arrive at a judgment. A "zero-order" memory scan would be involved in the following redundant predication: "A canary is a canary." A sentence involving a slight separation in the semantic hierarchy, and thus a slight memory scan, would be "A canary is a bird." A relationship that is further removed would be indicated by "A canary is an animal." Figure 10 shows the average reaction times in which such relationships were judged as true or false. According to Collins and Quillian, each additional step in the scan through the hierarchy of semantic memory required, on the average, an additional 75 msec.

Stroboscopic Enhancement

The final set of demonstrations in this chapter concerns an artificial "driving" of the central integrative process that results in "overactive" integrations and leads to exaggerated or hallucinatory experience. Apparently, the amplitude of the rapid attentional integrations can be boosted when they are entrained for a prolonged time with an external intermittency. This yields a striking—even potentially dangerous—demonstration of the constructive power of the rapid integrational process.

The simplest example of this effect is sensory-enhancement phenomena, the most common of which is *brightness enhancement:* at flash frequencies around 10 per second, a light appears brighter than at other flash frequencies or than when it is constantly lit (Bartley, 1939). In the Broca-Sulzer phenomenon (shown previously in Figure 3), there is an indication of the slight enhancement of subjective brightness for a single 100-msec flash, which may reflect the peak in a single RAI action. It may be this same peaking action that is accentuated by a long train of stimulus pulses at 100-msec intervals.

Stroboscopic hallucinations. But there are much more exaggerated effects of RAI enhancement. In 1823, Purkinje gave the first accounts of these effects—complex illusory cognitions evoked by a prolonged train of intermittent stimuli. These cognitions occur most readily in response to a uniform, pulsing sensory field whose rate of pulsation is at or near 10 per

Figure 11. Copies of line drawings of hallucinatory visualizations made by subjects immediately after prolonged stroboscopic stimulation at flash frequencies ranging from 6 to 20 per second. (From Smythies, 1959b; reprinted by permission of Cambridge University Press.)

second. Such a condition is easily arranged for vision by the placing of a strobe light with a flash rate of 10 per second behind a large diffusion screen. After a period of exposure to the flashing screen, most people will experience complex patterns, shapes, images, or movements; still others will experience a cognitive "blanking" or a sense of paralysis. In some cases, the hallucinatory activity will spread from visual experiences to other areas of experience. Even various emotions have been evoked, ranging from unpleasant to pleasant affect and erotic sensation. There is one report of subjects hearing "illusory conversations" but not being able to grasp the content or meaning of them (O'Flanagan et al., 1951).

Smythies (1959a, 1959b, 1960) described in detail the characteristics of these phenomena as well as the history of their discovery. In his experiments, flash frequencies were varied from 6 to 20 per second. Within this range, a sudden, slight change in rate would occasionally increase hallucinatory experiences. The degree of structure in these strange experiences, as reported by Smythies' subjects, varied from simple blotches in the flashing field, to a variety of geometrical patterns of increasing complexity, to fully formed natural scenes, such as an aquarium containing a school of fish and a mountainside covered with brightly colored vegetation. Figure 11 contains several drawings made by Smythies' subjects of the types of geometrical patterns they experienced.

It must be warned that prolonged subjection to this form of undifferentiated sensory intermittency can produce undesirable aftereffects. For instance, some normal individuals have exhibited epileptic patterns in this situation (Walter, 1953).

Because two persons seldom see the same stroboscopic hallucination, some students of human personality have become interested in the diagnostic possibilities of this phenomenon. General types of stroboscopic hallucination may correlate with recognized personality types (Freedman and Marks, 1965). The induced strobe patterns may thus reflect, and indeed exaggerate, individual differences or biases in cognitive constructive capacities.

CONCLUSIONS

The wide range of phenomena that were reviewed in this chapter have been classed together here because, at the least, they all fall within a common temporal range. But more than this, they are *microgenetic processes*—elementary processes that generate immediate experience.

To summarize and to comprehend all this data, it is useful now to think of a *central, integrative cognitive process*. This is a single-channel process under a narrow time constraint that is reflected in all the above elementary actions of attention—actions that perhaps reflect the brain's fundamental and time-limited excitability cycles or scanning mechanisms. In these actions the brain selects, sums, integrates, constructs, or elaborates the mass of sensations and memories, and it initiates behavior—all at very rapid speeds.

The following summary generalizations given earlier in this chapter help organize many of these observations:

> Rapid attentional integrations form immediate experience; the integration intervals vary from approximately 50 to 250 msec, with the most common observation being about 100 msec.
>
> Temporally separate events included in one integration are fused in experience to form a unitary impression; when those events are structurally different or incompatible, some may be omitted rather than fused.

Within the varying but brief integration interval, there is a reciprocity between time and the intensity of experience, as shown many times above. When more than one stimulus occurs in the course of one of these brief attentional pulses, there is still only a unitary experience; several stimuli are then experienced as one, either through their fusion, or the masking of one another, or their temporal displacement. The very rate at which cognition (perception, memory, or thought) can proceed is ultimately limited by the time constraints on this process. Different temporal intervals may govern similar integration processes in certain other animal species.

Like all biological events, this process is not fixed at a specific time interval, but rather varies within a certain range of intervals. When greater energy is present (as with intense stimuli), then the process of integration is more rapid. The complexity (or information load) of experiences or of stimuli may slow the integrative actions, just as practice, habituation, expectancy, fatigue, and age may cause this elemental psychological process to vary.

Gestalt principles are observed in these constructive actions. There is, for instance, a general tendency for rapid attentional integrations to develop in those directions that require the least energy or least effort and, accordingly, to move toward simplicity in the formation of experience. This reflects a more general biological tendency—to conserve energy is to conserve life. When other things are equal, or when there are no other constraints or demands, then simplicity prevails over complexity, regularity over irregularity, unity over disunity, and consonance over dissonance in the brief formations of immediate experience.

A problem that will be taken up in the following chapters concerns the question of how the continuity of everyday experience arises out of these intermittent microgenetic events. The study of a single pulse of rapid attentional integration may be highly artificial with respect to ordinary human experience, which certainly must be built up from long trains of these elemental actions.

With a continuous recycling of integrative actions, we could say that "movement" is ever present in normal human experience. It is a movement that may be analogous to visual *nystagmus*, the constant vibration of the retina of the eye. Continual fine-grain retinal movements ensure that visual receptor cells do not receive unchanging stimulation (they respond only to changes in energy). If images are stabilized on the retina by stopping these minute movements, then momentary blindness occurs. A similar operation may hold for cortical (cognitive) processing. Cortical cells, like retinal cells, may require some rapid fluctuation (the rapid scanning) in order to maintain proper cell function and to maintain enduring images and cognitions.

Other processes are surely required in the organism for any adequate account of the continuity of our daily experience. The following chapters are concerned with those other processes.

4

BUFFER
DELAYS

This short chapter describes another component of the central cognitive process schematized in Figure 2. This component is a *buffer*—a brief delay of the flow of experience for durations that are short and yet significantly longer than the rapid attentional integrations. Such delay-processes are necessary in order for any information-processing system to operate effectively. As we noted in Chapter 2, some early psychologists conceived of a similar process as the "scope of attention." More recent descriptions use the terms "iconic storage," "echoic storage," "stimulus trace," "sensory store," "very short-term store," "immediate memory," "buffer," "channel capacity," and "field of centration."

Although there is some consistency in the use of these terms, the reader should be forewarned that there is by no means unanimity of usage. Haber (1970), for example, uses "iconic storage" in the sense of a buffer delay, but he uses it to describe the apparent endurance of a 10-msec stimulus for 100 to 200 msec, which is seemingly an illustration of the RAI process reviewed in the previous chapter. Rather than run afoul of terminology, we must examine the content of any individual investigation and only then decide what process is under consideration. For the sake of consistency and generality, the term *buffer* appears throughout the present chapter.

GENERAL PRINCIPLES

The array of sensory stimuli and the reverberations from memory present human thought and awareness with a mass of impressions that might, and indeed at times do, confound human experience and action. One minimal defense against this cognitive overload is a buffer process—a brief *pre*attentive delay of input. This is necessary in any information-processing system whose capacity, or speed of processing, differs from the capacity for information reception. A buffer will delay the rush of events and thus render them more available for further synthesis or analysis—that is, for further processing.

In reviewing periodicities in immediate cognitive actions and perception, Aaronson (1967) distinguished buffer delays from rapid attentional integrations (in her terms, "Stage 1" versus "Stage 2" processing). The following is a simplified summary of her findings:

1. Perceptual structuring in Stage 1 (the buffer) is at a low level; impressions are "unidentified sensations" or "direct representations" of physical attributes of stimuli.
2. Impressions can attain permanence through Stage 2 integration (RAI). However, some initial information may be sacrificed in this integration.
3. Stage 2 (RAI) is a system of very limited capacity; it can receive items only in series (one at a time), additional items being delayed until this "single channel" is free.

Periodicity. Many investigators have succeeded in measuring Stage 1 buffer delays with a variety of stimuli and with a variety of procedures. Several examples are included in the observations in this chapter. The periodicities generally range from about a half-second to almost two seconds, the modal estimate being about three quarters of a second (750 msec). Estimates vary partly because of differences in measurement criteria. Some measures are of the period of complete information preservation—that is, the period before there is noticeable decay of impressions. Other measures are of the time to total decay. Estimates also vary because the processes of buffer delays are themselves variable within a limited range.

Békésy, in particular, has argued for the theoretical status of this delay process as a function of the central nervous system that is not correlated with peripheral or circulatory systems. In his view, it is this buffer periodicity, varying around 750 msec, that represents "the conscious present" (Békésy, 1931, 1960, 1967).

Process characteristics. Any anatomical localization of a general buffer process remains uncertain, even though this process serves important functions as a fundamental component in discussions of human information-processing. A buffer-delay process could have multiple neurological representations in a variety of neural systems, and these might involve both central and peripheral mechanisms.

After Aaronson's influential paper on periodicities in cognitive performance, other investigations showed that mental impressions at the level of buffer delays have only the gross properties of segmentation, location, movement, brightness, size, color, and shape. Buffer delays are now often called "literal storage" or "precategorical storage" (Neisser, 1967; Broadbent, 1971), and the higher attentional process (RAI) is viewed as being able to select or ignore events in the buffer delay only on the basis of the above gross dimensions, not on the basis of derived properties, such as the meanings attached to symbols. For example, in tachistoscopic analyses of buffer impressions—analyses in which attentional integration is curtailed by a rapid cutoff of stimuli—letters are not distinguishable from numbers, words, or nonsense syllables. The derived properties, such as meaningfulness, are the contributions (or constructions) of the central integration process.

Broadbent (1958, 1971) suggests that by virtue of a limited level of representation at the buffer-delay stage (in his terminology, "the short-term store"), there may be a low level of attentional selectivity operating here. But in contrast with the central integrative actions, buffer delays are more like snapshots than like information-processing intervals. And they are always quite transient, being lost permanently if not subjected to the "fixing" power of attentional integration. The buffer representation is also unaffected by repetition or practice (shown in experiments by Turvey, 1967). But practice clearly does affect the central attentional integration process.

All the above observations of buffer delays concern the perception of sensory input. We might ask whether the same process is involved with inputs from memory, which the model in Figure 2 would allow. As Freud (1900) speculated, the mechanisms of consciousness may have "two sensory surfaces," one that interfaces the immediate environment and one that interfaces memory. But this is obviously a difficult notion to verify, since memories cannot be manipulated and measured as easily as external stimuli. Nevertheless, some of the observations cited below at least suggest a central cognitive periodicity, that of the typical buffer duration, that is independent of any particular sensory process.

Summary generalizations. The following generalities summarize many of the above observations and help introduce the more specific examples to be considered in the remainder of this chapter.

> Preattentive buffer delays are delays of inputs to experience at a simple or unstructured level of representation prior to incorporation into central attentional integrations; these delays vary from about 0.5 second to about 2.0 seconds, with the most common observation being about 0.75 second (750 msec).
>
> In contrast to the one-track unifying process of rapid attentional integration, buffer delays maintain many separate events simultaneously.

OBSERVATIONS

Some classic findings that reflect the characteristics of buffer delays are illustrated below. They are taken from the following four areas of observation:

1. duration of buffer images
2. the indifference interval
3. rhythm and time-order errors
4. anticipation in performance

Duration of Buffer Images

It is a common observation that in a very brief presentation of an array of stimuli, observers will claim enigmatically to see more than they can report afterward. Numerous accounts of this observation appear in the earliest psychological research literature. The more significant modern investigations are those of Sperling (1960) and Averbach and Sperling (1961), which were inspired partly by Wundt's (1899) work. Wundt had made the following three observations:

1. The effective stimulus duration is not identical with the duration of the stimulus source, but also reflects the duration of an internal mental delay.
2. The relation between accuracy of a perception and stimulus duration depends on pre- and postexposure fields (which may induce what we now call masking).
3. These delays are determined by central processes rather than by sense-organ aftereffects.

Wundt described tests in which observers were shown arrays of simultaneous stimuli so large that it was not possible to report them all after a single brief exposure. Immediately following the presentation, however, observers were told to report only some small part of the array. If the instruction was given soon enough, the observer's report of stimuli was nearly perfect, regardless of which part of the matrix was requested. This showed that the entire momentary set of stimulus impressions is cognitively available for a brief time after stimulus exposure, but not long enough for the observer to attend to (or integrate) all the items. From this fiinding we can infer the existence of a brief, large-capacity buffer-delay.

Sperling found that the accuracy of the partial report in these situations decreases in a predictable manner as the time between stimulus-offset and partial-report signal increases. In his initial tests, observers received a 50-msec simultaneous visual presentation of three rows of four letters each. The observers then reported only one of the three rows, not knowing in advance which one. The presentation was followed at various intervals by an instruction tone (high, medium, or low in pitch) indicating that either the top, middle, or bottom row was to be reported. The pre- and postexposure visual field was also varied between light and dark. Generally, if the delay between exposure and instruction tone is longer than about one second, a partial report will be little better than a whole report.

The results of one of Sperling's further examinations of this phenomenon are shown in Figure 12. In these tests, the instruction tones that prompted the selection of items from the buffer image were location instructions (they signaled "upper right," "lower center," and so forth). Yet any segmentation of the items in terms of one of the characteristic buffer parameters (for instance, "the red item," or "the big item") will yield similar results. In addition to location, other features that have been

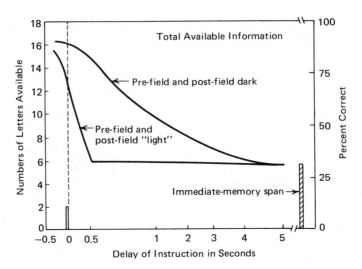

Figure 12. Buffer storage decay rates for one observer and two kinds of stimulus presentation. Stimuli were 18 letters. Exposure duration was 50 msec. Any one of 6 different tonal combinations was presented at various poststimulus intervals as the "instruction" to report certain letters. (The fraction of letters reported correctly in these partial reports is multiplied by the number of letters available in the buffer.) In one type of presentation, letter exposure was preceded and followed by a totally dark visual field, which yields the best buffer storage but which can also produce persisting retinal afterimages that may improve the reporting of stimuli. In the other type of presentation, the exposure was preceded and followed by a field of white light, which eliminates retinal afterimages but which might also have some masking effects on the stimuli. (From G. Sperling, "A model for visual memory tasks," *Human Factors,* 1963, *5,* 19-31, © The Johns Hopkins University Press.)

used for this quick partial report of buffer images are movement, brightness, size, color, and shape.

For another example, Bliss and his associates (1966) arranged a Sperling-type partial report technique for tactual rather than visual stimuli by delivering brief bursts of air to many different points on the surfaces of fingers. Again, subjects were unable to report accurately all the points of stimulation. But when an instruction signal followed, indicating that only one specific area of sensation was to be reported—either fingertip, middle-finger, or lower-finger—then accuracy was higher. Again, this improvement occurred only if the partial-report signal followed within about one second.

Treisman (1964) and Norman (1969) observed buffer-storage times with auditory stimuli by presenting simultaneously two independent signals, one to each ear. Listeners can attend to only one ear at a time. If the signal in the unattended ear is not attended to within 1.0 to 1.5 seconds after its occurrence, then it is lost to the listener and cannot be recalled.

Darwin, Turvey, and Crowder (1972) designed an auditory test, analogous to the Wundt-Sperling visual arrangement, in which subjects listened to three sets of mixed letters and digits presented simultaneously from three loudspeakers. The entire auditory presentation was, again, quite difficult to report. Yet with postpresentation signals instructing the subjects to report a particular subset of the whole, the resulting partial reports again were quite accurate if the report signal was presented within an interval similar to the interval Sperling found.

Manifestations of buffer delays are not difficult to observe in everyday performances. One such performance is the act of reading aloud. In this case there is an "eye-voice span," which is the distance in terms of time, letters, or words, that a reader's eyes may move ahead of his voice in scanning written material. In terms of time, Geyer (1966) showed that the voice cannot follow eye-fixations on the written text by more than about one second and still maintain fluent reading. It is as if the input is limited to approximately one-second chunks; no more time can be taken for the rapid integrative scans of the input because the input will have decayed after one second.

Finally, a well-known investigation by Posner and his students (1969) gives us a more subtle measure of buffer-image durations. When people are shown two letters of the alphabet, one after the other in rapid succession, and then asked whether the second letter is the same as the first, the response "same" is 80 to 100 msec faster if the letters are visually identical ("A" and "A") than if identical only in name ("A" and "a"). With the impression of the first letter held in a buffer delay, comparison with a visually identical second letter is more rapid because only a direct match of images is required; no categorizing or attaching of meaning to the stimuli is necessary. This greater speed of image matching for visually identical letters disappears, however, when the delay between them extends beyond the furthest extent of buffer-delay times—that is, beyond about 1.5 seconds. The buffer delay of the first stimulus impression has by then faded, so no immediate image-matching can occur.

The Indifference Interval

A strange psychological phenomenon involving short time-intervals is the temporal *indifference interval* (also known as the *indifference* point, or *indifference zone*). This observation, made first by Vierordt (1868) and commented on repeatedly since then (see James, 1890, and Woodrow, 1951), is that people consistently overestimate intervals or durations that are less than about 750 msec, and they underestimate ones that are somewhat longer. The "indifference point" is the point that separates under- and overestimates. It may be an artifact of an intrinsic buffer delay. That is, short events may be prolonged subjectively by the holding action of buffer processes and slightly longer events may be constricted subjectively by the same process. Békésy (1931) suggested this when he noted the same periodicity in the perception of fading tones that decline rapidly to threshold level; lapses in the auditory experience occur at about 750- or 800-msec intervals as the tone nears threshold intensity. Figure 13 contains some introspective descriptions of the experience drawn by Békésy's subjects.

Because the time of onset of the stimulus decay was arbitrary with respect to circulatory fluctuations or to possible cyclical changes in sense-organ sensitivity, these experiences are more likely a reflection of central control processes. Békésy (1967) also pointed out that the same interval is

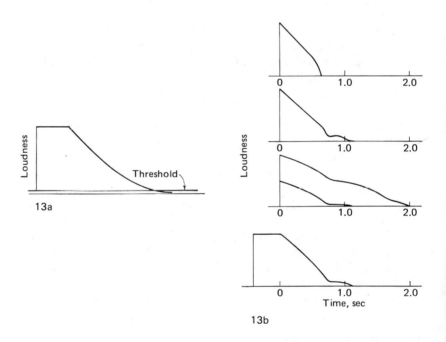

Figure 13. Decay of the loudness of a tone. Figure 13a is the approximate form of the loudness function of the stimulus. Figure 13b is the form of perceived loudness decay drawn by several subjects. The interruption in the smooth course of loudness decay occurs at about 0.75 second (750 msec). (From Békésy, 1931; also appearing in Békésy, 1960, and in Békésy, 1967. Reprinted by permission of McGraw-Hill Book Company and by Princeton University Press.)

fundamental in the sequencing of speech and in other motor rhythms and that it underlies musical rhythms. It is a response interval that is most typical of the rate of "fast" motor behavior that is voluntary, whether it be finger tapping or walking.

Rhythm and Time-Order Error

The first experimental investigations of rhythm perception were those of Dietze (1885), Meumann (1894), and Bolton (1894). They all provided observations on the illusion of apparent rhythm: with perfectly even and unaccented beats, most people experience a subjective rhythm in which every other beat appears to be stressed. This is most likely to occur when beat separation falls into intervals of about 750 msec.

The experience of rhythm, whether illusory or real, breaks down when beat separation goes beyond about two seconds. If beat separation is less than 750 msec (but not less than about 100 to 200 msec), then the illusory rhythm usually involves more complicated patterns, such as 3/4 or 4/4 time.

Apparent rhythm also occurs with repetitive visual stimuli (Miner, 1903; Koffka, 1909; Ruckmick, 1917; Fraisse, 1948). When viewing a rapidly flickering light—say at ten real or apparent flashes per second—for long periods of observation, observers have reported seeing a slower illusory rhythm imposed on the rapid pulsations: the flickering light appears divided into phrases of about six to eight beats each, or 750-msec groupings.

Phenomena of apparent rhythm are also found in a sequence consisting of only two stimuli. Such phenomena are known as *time-order errors*. The length of the pause between two brief and faint stimuli can influence the relative prominence of the two successive perceptions. "Prominence" refers to either apparent duration or apparent intensity. Two brief events that are equally intense and separated by 750 msec will appear equally prominent. But if the interval is slightly less, say 500 msec, then the first stimulus may appear more prominent. If the interval is greater than 750 msec, say 1,000 msec, then the second event may appear more prominent (Stott, 1935; Philip, 1940, 1947; Tresselt, 1944a, 1944b).

Anticipation in Performance

Wundt (1903) described the 750-msec interval as the "optimal association time." He observed that paired events become associated in the mind of a learner most efficiently when they are separated by no more than that amount of time. For then, presumably, the two events are together in one buffer image, rather than each being in a separate buffer image. Associations between events are thus facilitated when they belong to the same transient image; this permits the RAI process to fuse or integrate them more readily.

In many cases of Pavlovian conditioning, an optimal interval between presentation of conditioned stimulus (CS) and unconditioned stimulus (UCS) results in the most efficient development of the conditioned response. This interval is in the sub-750-msec range, and is generally about one-half second (Fraisse, 1963). That optimal interval shows in diverse forms of conditioning in which both stimulus delivery and response measurement can occur rapidly. For example, it is found in the conditioning of hand withdrawal (Wolfle, 1932; Spooner and Kellog, 1947), eyelid reflex (Kimble, 1947; McAllister, 1953), and respiration (Kappauf and Schlosberg, 1937). When the conditioned stimulus is made more complex than the very simple stimuli customarily used in these experiments, the optimal CS-UCS interval is longer, approaching one second (Czehura, 1943). Thus, as a sequencing of two stimuli, classical conditioning may follow Wundt's observations on the optimal interstimulus time for associations to take place.

The same critical interval is found in reaction-time investigations in which the warning signals that precede test stimuli are most effective in bringing about rapid response when they lead by 750 msec (Woodworth and Schlosberg, 1954; Botwinick and Brinley, 1962; Aiken and Lichtenstein, 1964). In a related test, Oléron (1952) had subjects reproduce auditory tones immediately after hearing them, and found that reactions began about 750 msec after the offset of the test stimulus. Similarly, the time required to organize complex perceptual identifications is generally the same 750 msec (Ross and Fletcher, 1953; Shepard and Teghtsoonian, 1961).

CONCLUSIONS

Within and around the human organism are innumerable fluctuating energies and events. Yet the process of attention is fundamentally a single-channel process, where only one event is dealt with in one narrow span of time. All other events, at that point in time, might then be lost from awareness were it not for buffer processes that briefly delay many inputs or potential impressions so that the scanning attentional integration can still encompass them.

The buffer delay is a holding of simultaneous raw inputs in a crude form (for example, simple physical properties of stimuli) prior to any structuring or elaborating activity of the more rapid integrations. These delayed events are quite transient and are lost permanently if not subjected to the fixing power of attentional integration. Such delays are probably necessary in any information-processing system where the rate and number of input events differ from the speed and the capacity of the information processor.

Summary generalizations were given above to help organize the different observations and measurements of buffer processes. Those generalizations are again as follows:

> Preattentive buffer delays are delays of inputs to experience at a simple or unstructured level of representation prior to incorporation into central attentional integrations; these delays vary from about 0.5 second to about 2.0 seconds, with the most common observation being 0.75 second (750 msec).

> In contrast to the one-track unifying process of rapid attentional integration, buffer delays maintain many separate events simultaneously.

In addition to all the above observations of both rapid attentional integrations and buffer delays, many other regularities, oddities, illusions, and measures reflecting these processes may be found in the literature of experimental psychology. Yet the organization of successive events into perceptual unities and intervals is a characteristic of our experience so primitive that we are hardly aware of it. It is fundamental to our perception of sequence, of rhythm, of the sounds of language, and surely of many other aspects of the flux of experiene.

Momentary experience, however, is still a seemingly continuous process. And it is likely that both the buffer delays and the rapid attentional integrations are engaged in a recycling and reinstatement of impressions over longer periods of time. In the next chapter, our examination of cognitive performance proceeds to a wider span of immediate experience—that of short-term memory.

5

SHORT-TERM MEMORY

This chapter describes a cognitive capacity that lends some basic, though minimal, continuity to experience. In Figure 2 it is labeled "temporary working memory" and "short-term memory." Fechner (1860) first discussed this capacity; he called it the "memory afterimage," distinguishing it from sensory afterimages. Exner (1879) rephrased Fechner's term as "primary memory image," and James (1890) shortened this to "primary memory," a term that is occasionally used today.

In the twentieth century, variations of these terms have proliferated. They include "short-term memory," "active memory," "temporary working memory," "surface memory," "operational memory," "short-term store," and "immediate memory." This profusion of labels may lead to confusion, for these terms have not always been applied consistently. But the most common expression for the component of cognition described in this chapter is now *short-term memory* (STM).

GENERAL PRINCIPLES

The above expressions all describe another type of buffer capacity, yet one fundamentally different from the brief delays reviewed in the previous chapter. The latter were clearly delays of impressions prior to or coordinate with the rapid integration process, whereas short-term memory is a *post*attentive delay of experiences, in the sense that it follows some action of attentional integration. It is the temporary holding of impressions just perceived, identified, or recalled. The result of this holding action is the simultaneous availability of a sequence of previous experience, as though the original stimulating conditions were still present. And further, short-term memory is a longer delay, on the order of 10 to 15 seconds.

Early notions of this cognitive capacity came from anecdotal accounts concerning, for example, the ability to count clock strokes from the beginning after a number had already passed, and the ability to recover the whole of a sentence whose beginning had been neglected (Fechner, 1860). James (1890) saw short-term memory as a possible mechanism for providing a continuous link between the fleeting "psychological present" and permanent memory. Today, perhaps our most common experience of short-term memory is with telephone numbers. A number that has just been read or heard must be dialed fairly soon if not written down or continually rehearsed; otherwise, it is lost.

In the course of later physiological investigations, several scientists suggested that short-term memory can be observed at a neurological level as a fading electrical reverberation within the brain (see, for example, Hebb, 1949; Glickman, 1961; Konorski, 1967). Long-term memory is then usually considered to be some relatively permanent change that perhaps takes place in the molecular structure of brain cells.

The function of STM. It is easy to argue for the biological usefulness of a short-term-memory component in the process of cognition. With this capacity, actions and thoughts can be held for monitoring or restructuring. Performances with complexly interrelated sequences, such as speech, music, and problem-solving tasks, usually require the delay of the full interpretation of certain early elements until decisive later elements occur.

For examples of this type of STM function, consider that the intended meanings of very many of our sentences in natural language remain ambiguous until the final phrase or word is uttered. For example, consider this sentence: "The shooting of the prime minister was upsetting to his wife and children, who had thought he was a better marksman." Upon hearing the first half of that sentence, a listener might develop the interpretation that the prime minister has been shot. But short-term memory allows us to hold our interpretations of sentences in a tentative state so that we can go back and revise them, as we most likely must do in the above example. Early constituents are stored temporarily in STM so that interpretation may remain in a labile state until the end of the expression. Thus, a sentence can be perceived as a simultaneous whole on the basis of the interrelation of all its parts held together in one immediate representation.

Newell and Simon (1972) described how the short-term memory process provides a general "back-up capacity" that permits the correction of immediately previous misperceptions, or the reanalysis and reintegration of immediately previous experiences of any type. Accordingly, this process serves a place-keeping function in larger contexts and sequences. The milieu of motives, patterns of thought, and ambient impressions in short-term memory thus supports (or detracts from) the central motif of momentary thought and experience. Fraisse depicted this aspect of short-term memory in an apt introspection:

> When I listen to speech, I perceive the clause being pronounced by the speaker, but I interpret it in accordance with all the preceding sentences which I no longer perceive and of which I have only retained a general idea. When I listen to music, I perceive again and again a short, rhythmic structure, but this is integrated with a melodic whole to which it owes its affective resonance. (1963, p. 88)

In general, STM is observed as a temporal constraint on *recall* capacity and not as a constraint on *recognition* capacity, recognition being a distinct and powerful long-term-memory ability (see Chapter 8). An object briefly seen can soon be totally unavailable to recall, yet days later its recurrence may be recognized immediately.

Interference versus decay. The question that underlies most recent STM research concerns the mechanism of the particular duration of short-term memory. Today, there is still no unanimity concerning this issue, but there are two fundamental points of view. One considers STM in the context of traditional learning theory and appeals to notions of interference or response competition. The other is conceptually closer to the study of perception (or of imagery) and appeals to notions of the decay of images and traces.

The learning-theory view attributes the brevity of short-term memories to their interference or replacement by other items that may have preceded or followed those to be recalled. The perception-imagery view holds that impressions disintegrate with the sheer passage of time if they are not reinstated by attentional refocusing or rehearsal. It is, of course, not unusual to live with more than one explanation of a phenomenon. And it may be that both of these processes determine the duration of STM.

Brown (1958) first suggested the time-decay position to modern psychologists. Keppel and Underwood (1962) disputed this theory by arguing for the alternative interference position, and the debate has continued ever since. It is universally recognized that variables other than elapsed time may affect retention. Yet some theorists have claimed that elapsed time per se does not affect retention at all, and that the retrievability of a memory is solely a function of how much interference has occurred at the time of recall. The classical statement of this view is that of McGeoch (1932).

To Melton (1963, 1970) and Murdock (1972), a short-term-versus-long-term distinction appears extravagant. If all memory loss is the result of interference, why divide memory into two processes when the same laws govern both? Yet distinct STM periodicities and peculiar STM phenomena continue to appear. (See, for instance, Waugh and Norman, 1965; Atkinson and Shiffrin, 1968).

Tulving (1968) and Norman (1968) suggest that short-term memory should not be considered as a memory phenomenon at all, but rather should be viewed as an immediate cognitive process that is best understood through investigations of attention. In the context of human experience and behavior, a process that endures a mere few seconds hardly seems worthy of the designation "memory." Traditionally, memory concerns events that are not available to immediate experience but that must be reconstructed from the past. Short-term memory has this immediate availability; thus it may be better understood as a component of the central processes of immediate experience than as a type of memory.

Further, with its central position in the general theory of cognitive performance, STM surely must have a broader function than that of a simple early stage of memory. As several recent theorists have suggested, it more generally provides the working background of consciousness (Atkinson and Shiffrin, 1971; Lindsay and Norman, 1972). More than merely holding events for rehearsal, STM maintains a context for mental operations, which brings some continuity to the stream of thought.

Summary generalizations. The following generalizations stem from the work of many of the investigators cited above and serve to introduce many of the observations of STM that follow.

Short-term memory is a *postattentive* delay that holds impressions immediately accessible to consciousness for a limited period; unless attentionally reinstated, these impressions decay over an interval that varies from approximately 5 to 20 seconds, with the most common observation being about 10 seconds.

Short-term memory provides a working background or directive context for the integrative operations of attention.

OBSERVATIONS

Because short-term memory is a central process, STM periodicity is reflected in diverse areas of human performance. Selected demonstrations are described below in the following four areas:

1. decay of impressions
2. memorization and retrieval
3. speech rhythms
4. attention waves

In view of the controversy that has accompanied the revival of STM research in the mid-twentieth century, all of these observations might be interpreted, each in a unique way, without reference to a central STM process. But such an accounting would yield, at the least, an inordinately complex and unparsimonious description.

Decay of Impressions

One early experimental psychologist, Daniels (1895), devised a very simple experiment that presaged many observations and tests of short-term memory in the 1960s. Daniels simply questioned how the duration of impressions in STM (in his terms, "the field of consciousness") could be measured independently of the confounding action of focal attention. Attentional refocusing (often called "rehearsal") can maintain impressions in immediate awareness indefinitely, thereby obscuring any intrinsic STM periodicity. Daniels presented a simple stimulus (three digits) and at the same time prevented the subject from refocusing it after the initial presentation. To accomplish this, the experimenter first set the subject to reading passages of prose aloud and rapidly. Then the experimenter called out the three digits while the subject continued reading. The reading task, of course, occupied the subject's attention and prevented him from repeating the digits to himself (that is, from refocusing them). At certain intervals (either 5, 10, 15, or 20 seconds), the subject was interrupted in his reading task and asked to recall the digits. In this way, Daniels showed that unrefocused digit impressions decay steadily over a period of 10 to 15 seconds. Beyond that they are no longer accessible to facile immediate recall.

Independently, and much later, Peterson and Peterson (1959) used a very similar technique, one that has played a large role in the later revival of research on STM. For their stimuli the Petersons used three conso-

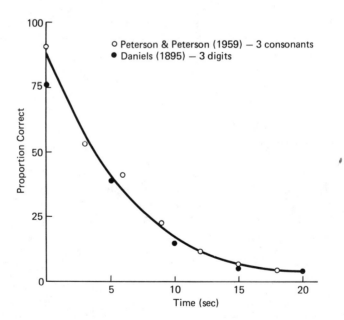

Figure 14. Decay of short-term-memory impressions. The proportion of items recalled correctly from short-term memory is shown as a function of time. Data are from Daniels (1895) and Peterson and Peterson (1959). In both tests, subjects were engaged in activities that prevented rehearsal during the time intervals.

nants and rather than reading aloud, their subjects counted backwards by threes from some large number. The results of the 1895 and 1959 investigations, which are plotted together in Figure 14, are identical.

As we noted previously, one explanation of this curve is interference from competing items (rather that sheer passage of time). In this vein, some investigators have shown that the greater the number of items attended to immediately after the appearance of some target item, the more rapid that target item will decay from STM (Conrad and Hull, 1966; Norman, 1966).

Similar decay rates have also been found with very different types of stimulus presentations in other modalities: visual presentations (Phillips and Baddeley, 1971), tones (Wickelgren, 1969), touch (Gilson and Baddeley, 1969; Sullivan and Turvey, 1972), and kinesthesis (Pepper and Herman, 1970).

An example of the STM periodicity in what may be a somewhat more familiar setting comes from Eriksen and Johnson (1964), who presented a faint tone to people engaged in reading. At varying intervals after the tone, the readers were asked if a tone had occurred. Their accuracy of reporting whether the tone had been sounded declined as the interval between the tone and the attempt to recall it increased. Accuracy depended on being asked about the tone's presence within about 10 seconds of its occurrence.

Everyday experiences. Preventing attentional refocusing, as was done in most of the above demonstrations, is, of course, an artificial or at least uncommon situation in everyday mental performance. This is happily so, for some refocusing indeed seems necessary if thoughts are to be stored effectively in long-term memory. Otherwise, we would often experience a sudden inability to retrieve the thoughts and impressions that have just passed. However, such an experience does at times happen in natural settings. The following illustration of this phenomenon should be familiar to most readers: When listening to rapid conversation, an individual may think of a relevant comment or interjection but not act upon it at that moment. Instead, he or she continues listening. In such a sequence of events, this listener's intended comment may become hopelessly lost. So when it is finally time to speak, the individual unfortunately is left with only a vague awareness that some brief thought had just occurred to him and had set him to respond.

In studies of daydreaming and mind wandering, Singer described similar happenings:

We have all had the experience of having a sudden, original combination of associations yield a potentially creative solution, whether to an unimportant puzzle or a serious problem, and then, because we are suddenly distracted by noises or conversation, of being unable to recapture the idea because we did not have sufficient time for reverberation and sustained attention. (1966, p. 124)

Tulving (1969) and Saufley and Winograd (1970) studied the effect of distraction on input to memory under experimental conditions in which subjects were shown and asked to remember lists of common words. Some lists contained a famous name (such as Aristotle, Washington, Beethoven, or Moses). With fast rates of list presentation (one word every second), the probability of recalling the word immediately preceding the famous name is consistently lower. Famous names apparently can dominate attention to the detriment of refocusing on the preceding item. As presentation rates are slowed, this effect disappears, for there is then ample time for attentional refocusing—in this case, rehearsing earlier words in the course of receiving the list.

Perhaps certain emotional states of an individual can interfere with attentional focusing, and thus, in turn, with the input to long-term memory. Luborsky (1973) systematically studied the occasional occurrence of this phenomenon in psychiatric interviews, labeling it "momentary forgetting." Further descriptions of these emotional effects are taken up in Chapter 7.

Memorization and Retrieval

Is the STM delay truly a necessary step in the establishment of permanent memory? The attentional activities of recycling, organizing, and co-integrating impressions might not be possible without a critical short-term delay. And this attentional activity might be required for stable long-term storage.

Cognitive activities that ensure the passage of experiences from the psychological present into the psychological past and enhance their later recall are generally called *mnemonic* techniques. These techniques amount to the analysis of experience into structured or interrelated impressions.

To quote Craik (1971), "Transferring an item to secondary (that is, long-term) memory may comprise the integration of the item with the body of past learning—the formation of associations, images, and stories." A typical mnemonic technique is the active associating of to-be-remembered items with well-established memories, such as the visual memory of objects in a familiar room. Such "associating" would mean the actual imaginal visualization of an item in combination with familiar imagery. For example, to remember items on a shopping list, one might visualize a bunch of bananas hanging in the bedroom window, a container of milk sitting on the bedroom desk, and so on. Later recall is initiated by first thinking about (or imaging) the familiar room. Those thoughts give the attentional scan a structured point of entry into long-term memory and thus an easier retrieval of the shopping-list items.

Obviously, this imaginal activity demands considerable performance from attentional-integration processes—performance that would ordinarily not occur if one were merely to remain passive in the face of changing experience. Perhaps all memories are established only to the degree that they have been the object of attentional activity. From this point of view, a psychology of education should be concerned with the development of attentional processes and with attention control.

Baddeley and co-workers (1969) suggest that immediate memory is crucial for mnemonic functions because it holds impressions for a brief time so that attention can be free to scan related memories, integrate images, and form associations. When impressions fade from short-term memory, they are no longer directly accessible to attention. And, though perhaps not completely lost for later retrieval, they now require some greater effort (a search of permanent memory) to return them to focal attention.

Some studies of rote learning in fact show critical time-spans for mnemonic activity (rehearsal). Up to certain short intervals, recallability improves rapidly as a function of initial learning time. Ebbinghaus (1885) found this time to be 10 to 12 seconds of rehearsal per item (nonsense syllable). With other kinds of items, Hovland (1938) found 10 seconds per impression; Underwood and Schulz (1960), 13 seconds; and Bugelski (1962), 9 seconds. These, again, are typical STM durations.

Within these critical time-spans, attentional processes can search out related permanent-memory configurations and integrate new impressions with them. The chance of retrieving impressions at will improves, presumably because it is easier to locate an item in the vastness of permanent memory when that item is part of a large, integrated memory configuration.

Retrieval. The same periodicity may be just as critical in the act of retrieving long-term memories as it is in storing them. Buschke (1967) thus described a temporary memory-activation that arouses reference information or that provides access to the content of long-term memory. Lindsay and Norman (1972) used a spotlight metaphor (illustrated in Figure 15) to describe this act of retrieval.

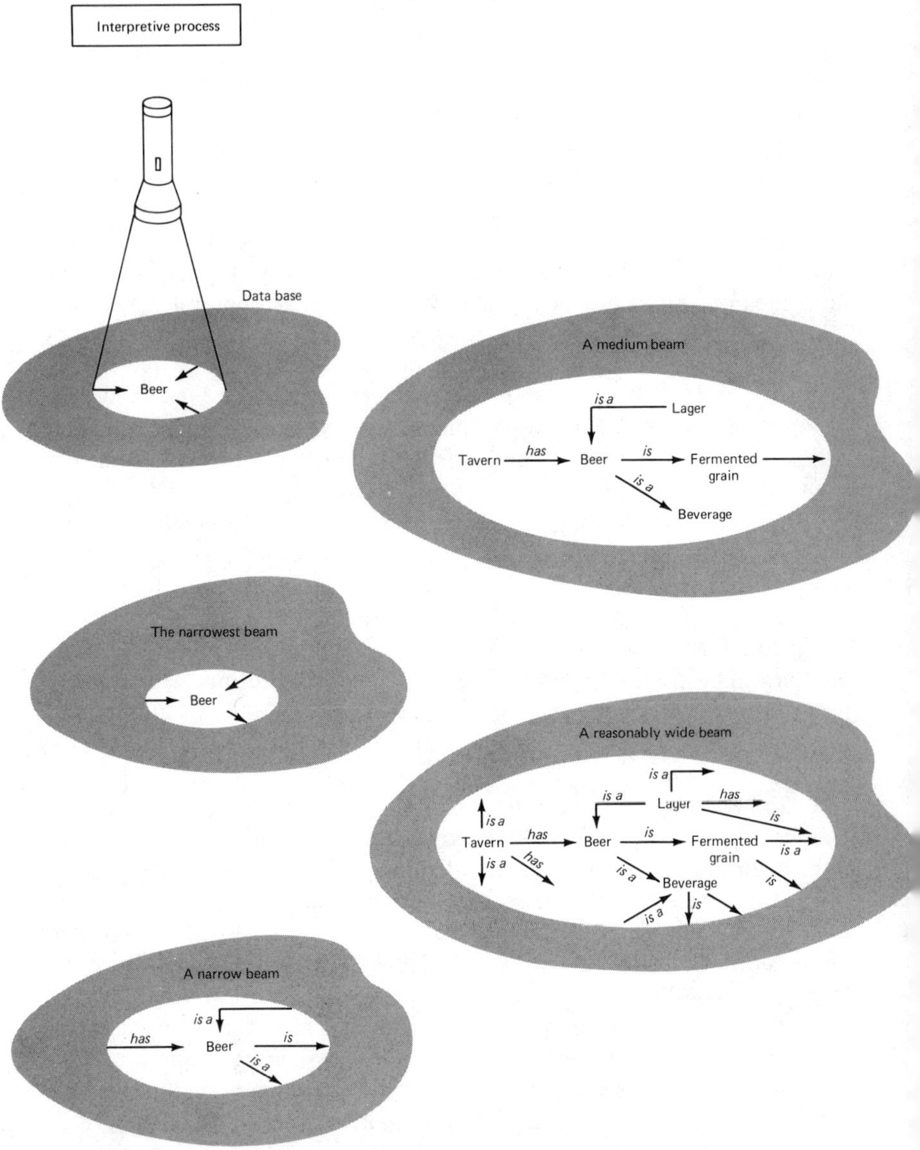

Figure 15. The spotlight metaphor used by Lindsay and Norman (1972) to illustrate the arousal of working memory (STM) from permanent memory. In their discussion of networks of permanent-memory associations, Lindsay and Norman used this descriptive device to show segments of the permanent-memory trace ("the data base") aroused by "interpretive processes of immediate consciousness." In the present example, the concept aroused from memory is "beer." The breadth of the STM arousal can vary, as indicated by the differences between "narrow" and "wide" beams. (Reprinted by permission of Academic Press, Inc.)

In the retrieval of long-term memories, STM holds the temporary activation of some part of the larger permanent storage. Presumably, this activation is the direct effect of the attentional scanning process being directed toward long-term memory. In any case, these activations are fleeting arousals, so they must be subjected to the continued action of attentional processes if they are to be stabilized in consciousness. Otherwise, they soon dissipate as the memory search moves on.

Speech Rhythms

Immediate cognitive processes are obviously involved in the rapid planning and execution of utterances. Speech-planning activity at the level of central attentional processes is done according to the structural schemes or the rules of a language. This involves the analysis of semantic content (thoughts, images, percepts, affects), the selection of words, and the arrangement of these words in grammatical patterns. In spontaneous speech, all this must occur at very high speeds. The rapid temporal processes of human cognition are well suited to carry out this performance.

Much of modern psycholinguistic research has focused on the nature of the structural scheme of language rather than on the language performance per se. A notable exception, however, is the work of Goldman-Eisler and her students, who have indirectly provided another demonstration of STM periodicity in human performance. Their concern is with spontaneous natural language performance, such as the spontaneous speech of unconstrained conversation. Certain patterns of hesitation in these language acts reflect the underlying cognitive planning process (Goldman-Eisler, 1968).

Some hesitations (pauses) are associated with the structuring of the surface sound-pattern of speech; they usually occur at phrase boundaries as very brief pauses. Hesitations of a very different character are associated with the content selection and the planning or organizing activity of the central control process. These generally longer pauses can occur at any point in the course of an utterance. Often, they take the form of vocalized "ahs," "ums," and "ers."

Does the content planning indicated by this latter type of pausing occur sporadically during spontaneous speech, or does it reveal any regularity? Henderson and his associates (1966) answered that question. By analyzing speech-pause rates, they found that there are periods of high hesitancy (frequent pauses) that alternate in a certain regularity with periods of low hesitancy (fluent speech). Further, the amount of pausing in the hesitancy phase is correlated with the amount of speech production in the subsequent fluency phase; that is, the more time spent planning, the greater the subsequent fluency.

Henderson's data show the time of the average hesitancy-plus-fluency cycle to be 18.0 seconds. Figure 16 is one especially clear record of the alternations between the hesitancy and fluency phases. Because these cycles fall within this particular temporal range, they would seem associated not only with cognitive planning but also with the intrinsic temporal constraint of short-term memory. If not thus constrained, a speaker would be able to plan spontaneously any amount of speech and then produce a period of fluent speech of any length, which obviously does not happen. Typically, high-hesitancy planning periods occupy some several seconds and are followed by fluency periods of about 10 seconds.

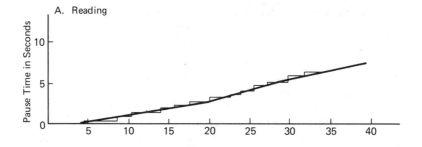

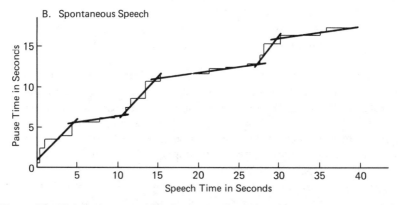

Figure 16. High-hesitancy and low-hesitancy alternations in spontaneous speech for one subject. The speech sequence was fed into a signal detector that translated signals into impulses. The signal-detector output was then fed into a pen-oscillograph, which gave a visual record. (From Henderson, Goldman-Eisler, and Skarbek, 1966; reprinted by permission of Kingston Press Services, Ltd.).

On the basis of a semantic (or content) analysis of spontaneous speech, Butterworth (1975) suggests that these fluency alternations have an intracycle semantic consistency. Short-term memory holds the results of immediately previous thought and planning "in mind," as it were, while the central attentional processes shift to the task of transforming that STM content into the linguistic code. Changes of semantic theme or topic thus tend to be coordinated with the high-hesitancy phases, which is to say that topical changes reflect the change of content held in short-term memory.

Of course, the rhythm of ordinary speech can be distorted or interrupted by the demands of a conversational situation or by other potentially competing activities. Everyday speech is often disturbed by false starts, by indecision, or by other speakers who compete for the same audience. Speech will not be smooth when a speaker is unsure of what to say or is under stress. A failure to maintain fluent, articulate speech has probably been experienced, painfully, by most people.

Attention Waves

Images, schemes, plans, thoughts, and even daydreams obviously do not have a life that is strictly limited by STM duration. They may be recycled or reprogrammed over indefinite intervals. Still, cognitions and cognitive activities are continually subject to change, drift, and fading in relation to the periodicity of short-term memory. Consequently, the difficulties of prolonged and concentrated thought or of prolonged attention to one item of experience are familiar to most people. The effort required to maintain one subject of thought for problem solving over extended lengths of time is a familiar difficulty. A normal tendency toward mind wandering is always present—it always threatens the goals of the thinker and the problem solver. But even though we must often fight it, mind wandering can, at some unsuspected time, lead us to the hidden solution of a problem.

Periodic fluctuations in the orientation of attentional activities are so-called *attention waves*. They have been studied most often in the simplified situation of attempting to maintain attention continuously on a very faint stimulus, one that is barely above the sensory threshold. This is a difficult task and requires continual high-level concentration. What usually occurs is a periodic fade-out of the stimulus, that is, of the experience of the stimulus. In other cases, attention waves are observed as fluctuations in the experience of ambiguous perceptual configurations (reversible figures, figure-ground alternations, and so forth).

Fluctations in the sensitivity of receptor organs do, of course, occur, but they are generally of much briefer duration than attention waves and have been inadequate to account for them. Hence, explanations have progressively been forced from peripheral-sense-organ dynamics back to central-nervous-system dynamics.

Guilford (1927) reviewed many early measurements of attention waves, measurements in which the observed intervals separating the brief fade-outs appeared remarkably similar regardless of the modality or task involved. In 1938, Woodworth summarized these findings with the conclusion that the average attention-wave duration is about 10 seconds. Shortly thereafter, however, this line of research was brought to a close, largely because of lack of agreement on just what phenomenon was being studied, and because sufficient experimental support had never been achieved for a popular assumption that attention waves are caused by fluctuations in blood pressure (Woodworth and Schlosberg, 1954).

Throughout most of that research history, attention waves were not often associated with short-term memory. Yet short-term memory, as we already noted, seems to include the functions of maintaining local goals and of placekeeping; it may thus support or detract from the central motif of momentary thought and experience. As the momentary background of ambient thoughts and impressions decays, control over attention to the stimulus may lapse. Even the instruction, "attend to the faint stimulus," is itself an item in short-term memory and is subject to decay. Especially with a threshold-level stimulus, any diversion of attention by a daydream (the radical replacement of STM content by different memory impressions) can easily lead to the lapse of attention to the appointed task.

Such fluctuations of experience are common in everyday life, where they may be even more dramatic than in laboratory investigations. For example, sometimes attention "wanders" (is not held by immediate goals, contexts, interests) and a person will claim not to have heard long stretches of a previous conversation, even though the words were clearly audible.

Blocking. A related phenomenon, called "mental blocking," is usually observed as brief lapses in performance during prolonged and monotonous work, most commonly where performance involves a sequence of repetitive responses. The "block" is reflected in an occasional extra long reaction time, and the reacting person may then have the outward appearance of distraction.

Bills (1931, 1935) provided the first systematic investigations of this effect, although he did not relate his findings to attention waves or to short-term memory. Rather, he suggested that the function of the block is to allow momentary fatigue to dissipate. The blocks (momentary lapses) that he observed occurred with a rhythmic regularity—three or four times per minute, which is in the range of estimates of STM periodicity.

In highly repetitive tasks, according to Bills, these blocks may be seen as part of a more pervasive "wave" that is sometimes detectable in behavior. They may be seen when responses tend to group together toward the center of the interblock interval, yielding a wavelike pattern in repetitive activity. Errors in performance are then more frequent at or near the occurrence of the block. And even when a total block does not occur at the expected interval, this wave pattern and distribution of errors may still be detected in the behavior sequence. Bills was unable to find a correlation of the blocks with breathing rate or with fluctuations in blood pressure. More precise measures of the occurrence of such blocks were provided later by Bertelson and Joffe (1963). (See Figure 17.)

Stroud (1955) observed blocking frequencies in the simple response of tapping a key in phase with repetitive auditory tones that were alternated between left and right ears. The input to one ear was controlled by the key, so that if the tapping went out of phase, the input to that ear was

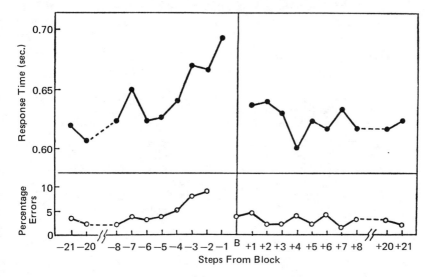

Figure 17. Some characteristics of the lapse, or "block," in repetitive behavior: reaction time and percentage of errors before and after a block. The task consisted of pushing one of four keys in response to the appearance of one of four figures on a numerical indicator. The abscissa gives the number of steps from the block. The ordinate gives the reaction time in seconds (black circles), and the percentage of errors (open circles). The averages are from 28 individuals. (From Bertelson and Joffe, 1963; by permission of Taylor and Francis Ltd.)

cut off. With the tapping rate set at one tap per second, subjects rarely performed beyond 20 to 30 seconds without some sort of lapse. In connection with these observations, Stroud suggested the notion of a "moment train," a coherent sequence of rapid attentional integrations on the order of, say, 100 RAIs at a time, all focused on one experience or performance. The coherence of this sequence—that is, the continued focusing of RAIs on one area of experience—may show the effect of the STM context in which the train of attentional integrations is embedded.

Mental programs. The brief temporal gaps in the continuity of human performance are presumably occupied by the reorganization or reorientation of the direction of the cognitive process—a changing of the contents of short-term memory. This changing is similar, perhaps, to the changing of a program in a computer: a person pursues a given program, plan, set, or schema as long as it is available in STM. When that STM representation decays, either the person will "reset" the line of thought or perception on another program, or may recycle the same program.

The controlling programs or schemata are often the longer temporal integrations that have been aroused from permanent memory (see Chapter 8). When these programs or schemata are activated and held in STM, they directly influence ongoing cognition. This is not to say that a given configuration of short-term memory must have absolute control over the course of cognition. More likely there are always competing or interfering representations. Neisser came to a similar conclusion:

> ...a hundred or a thousand "thoughts" appear briefly and are gone again even when we are primarily engaged in purposeful activity. The extent to which these fleeting thoughts are developed, and are permitted to interrupt the main direction of mental activity, varies from person to person and from time to time. For the most part, they are immediately forgotten, like the dreams they so strongly resemble. Occasionally they interrupt ongoing activity, and we recognize a "mental block," a "lapse of attention," or a "Freudian slip." (1967, p. 298)

CONCLUSIONS

The events of immediate experience do not come and go without a trace. If they pass through the focus of attention, they remain for a brief time in highly accessible form on the "fringe" of consciousness. This delaying action of short-term memory makes possible a working background and a directive context for the stream of experience. It allows a back-up capacity for the revision of immediately previous experience. It simultaneously holds momentary goals, patterns of thought, and ambient impressions. Therefore, this capacity has considerable survival value for the organism.

Unless reestablished by rehearsal or refocusing, the STM contents decay steadily over time, either as a result of interference and replacement by other items of experience, or as the simple fade-out of an image. Perhaps it is inappropriate to consider this process as a true form of *memory*, when it is, in fact, another type of short buffer delay of immediate experience. But STM is still important for the successful operation of long-term memory, because it permits time for the relating, comparing, and associating of items in immediate experience with items in long-term memory. In this way, our experiences can be stored systematically in permanent memory and thus made easier to recall at some future time.

Many sequential activities (for example, speech) reflect cycles of activity that seem related to an underlying STM periodicity. Even immediate goals may fluctuate because of this periodicity in mental capacity. Hence, the task that faces many a thinker or problem-solver is to overcome a drifting or fading of thoughts and to maintain them, holding them in view, until a problem is solved.

Earlier in this chapter some generalizations were advanced to help summarize STM observations. They are, again, as follows:

> Short-term memory is a postattentive delay that holds impressions immediately accessible to consciousness for a limited period; unless attentionally reinstated, these impressions decay over an interval that varies from approximately 5 to 20 seconds, with the most common observation being about 10 seconds.

> Short-term memory provides a working background or directive context for the integrative operations of attention.

In the next chapter we turn to the phenomena of *cognitive spans,* which are further complications and interactions of short-term memory, buffer delays, and rapid attentional integrations.

6

COGNITIVE SPANS

There are some very general limitations on human performance that may be classed together as *cognitive spans*. They are derivative effects of the processes described in the previous three chapters, where they have been suggested in a number of observations. (The eye-voice span, for example, was described in Chapter 4, in the discussion of the duration of buffer images.) In the literature of psychology, such limits are widely known as "memory span," "attention span," "apprehension span," "perceptual span," "span of absolute judgment," "central computing space," and "channel capacity." They are observed most often as limits on the number of impressions, items, or distinctions that can be grasped at once, held in mind briefly, or used as a basis for making judgments.

These limits vary within a narrow range now commonly known as "the magical number 7 plus-or-minus 2," following Miller's (1956) description.

GENERAL PRINCIPLES

Limits on the number of events that pass through the stream of experience at any one moment were long ago recognized as a "human engineering" problem. For example, when devising a touch alphabet for the blind early in the nineteenth century, the French physician Braille found it hopeless to use a system based on a configuration of more than six tactile points. The letters in the Braille alphabet now each derive from a six-point configuration: ∷ ; examples are ∷ (q), ∵ (d), and ∴ (v). Any system based on a configuration of nine points, ⋮⋮⋮ , is impractical, for the letters can then be identified only by the counting and spatial comparison of the individual points. With a six-point base, each pattern is easily recognized as a whole with one pass of the fingers.

The discussion of such limits by the philosopher Hamilton (1859) was one of the first observations to catch the interest of early psychologists. Hamilton described the results of his attempts to estimate the quantities of various clusters of marbles after "brief glances" at them. The result was accurate judgments up to a limit of six or seven. Later, in another influential report, Jevons (1871) replicated Hamilton's test in a more sophisticated way with many more trials, and strongly confirmed Hamilton's findings.

From that time to the present, manifestations of all kinds of this performance limit have been reported. Such observations received prominent attention during the era of Wundtian experimental psychology (Wundt, 1891, 1892; Müller and Schumann, 1894). By the 1930s, findings from a great variety of human performances were available and many were reviewed by Blankenship (1938). For some years thereafter, however, these findings were lost sight of by most experimental psychologists. But in the rush of new data-gathering after the Second World War, this psychological constant cropped up again in the study of human skills. Miller's (1956) review of that later evidence led to the more recent recognition of cognitive spans.

The importance of these findings is that widely diverse performances all show the same, or very similar, limiting conditions. Without external aids, only about six or seven unrelated events can be reproduced, no more than six or seven distinctions can be kept in mind at once, and no more than that many parts can be identified in a briefly presented stimulus pattern. Then, too, there are seven primary colors, seven notes in the musical scale, seven days in the week, and a preponderance of "sevens" elsewhere in human history, according to Miller. Musical phrases and poetic verses contain no more than six measures or feet, while larger musical groupings and poetical stanzas are seldom of more than four or five phrases or verses. The troubling question, however, is whether all this is a pernicious coincidence perpetuated by tradition, or whether it reflects basic psychological performance capacities?

When the observations of these spans were not a coherent part of any theoretical system in psychology (which was the case particularly in the 1940s and 1950s), they were often considered to be merely some strange "Pythagorean coincidence," to use Miller's words. But with later developments in the general theory of cognitive processes, these old observations have again become relevant.

Temporal basis. Anticipating later work, a few early cognitive psychologists suggested the direction in which to look for explanations of cognitive spans. The following statement by Ward is an example:

> The comparatively constant span of prehension is doubtless closely connected with certain other psychical constants, such as the range of the psychical present, and of the primary memory image, the tempo of movements of attention, etc. (1918, p. 223)

Again, *time* is the fundamental and limiting variable in the performance of living systems. And time-constrained central processes should naturally result in information-processing limits. On the one hand, the relation of the buffer delay to the speed of rapid attentional integrations should obviously constrain performance. That is, in any single focus of attention, the number of impressions that can be identified is limited by the time that the buffer keeps them available to the RAI process. Performance with sequential events, on the other hand, should be limited by STM duration, as shown in the previous chapter.

Summary generalizations. The above observations can be summarized with the following two generalities:

> The number of simultaneous impressions that can enter consciousness is limited by the ratio of buffer-delay time to rapid-attentional-integration time.

The number of sequential impressions that can be grouped together in momentary consciousness is limited by their duration in short-term memory.

Here it must be reemphasized that whatever is called a "memory item," "impression," or "item of experience" is arbitrary. These are whatever can be focused by attention as a unitary percept, cognition, or thought— including an external object, a group of objects, an abstract concept, or general subject matter. As we noted in Chapter 2, the breadth of the attentional integration determines this "unit of experience."

OBSERVATIONS

In general, instances of cognitive spans fall into three categories, which will be identified here as:

1. simultaneity span
2. sequentiality span
3. absolute-judgment span

The limit on the identification of simultaneous events (the *simultaneity span*) is often termed "perception span." The limit on immediate reproduction of sequential events (the *sequentiality span*) is often termed "immediate-memory (or short-term-memory) span." The limit on the accuracy of identifying the place of an isolated event or stimulus on some scale or in some context is the *absolute-judgment span*. The remainder of this chapter gives further demonstrations of each of these three spans.

Simultaneity Span

The number of briefly occurring simultaneous items that can be identified depends on buffer-delay times and on attentional-integration times. Integrating one item at a time, the attentional process can identify items only as long as the stimulus information is held by the buffer delay. Thus, we have the following relation:

$$\text{simultaneity span} = \frac{\text{buffer-delay time}}{\text{item-integration time}}$$

Substituting the most common estimates of the duration times of the processes in this relation (from Chapters 3 and 4), the following result is obtained:

$$\text{simultaneity span} = \frac{750 \text{ msec}}{100 \text{ msec}} = 7.5 \text{ identifications}$$

Obviously, this span varies as the two underlying processes vary in their durations. Schlegel (1929) was the first to discover that this span varies with changes in stimulus intensity. The more intense the stimuli, the greater the perception span (or simultaneity span). As we observed frequently in Chapter 3, increased intensity reduces the time of rapid attentional integrations, and according to the above formula, that should yield a larger cognitive span for simultaneous items. In other cases, the span may be affected by item complexity or by observer states, such as arousal, habituation, and fatigue.

Hunter and Sigler (1940), in an often-cited experiment, showed precisely how the differences in numbers of dots that observers can count (or perceive) in a brief visual presentation vary as a function of stimulus intensity. Their data are shown in Figure 18. As exposure time is increased beyond the region of 75 to 100 msec, the number of reportable simultaneous stimuli for stimuli of moderate intensity increases approximately by one for each additional 75 msec of exposure time—that is, time enough for another attentional integration. To utilize the present descriptive model, this increase in reportable stimuli follows a pattern somewhat like this:

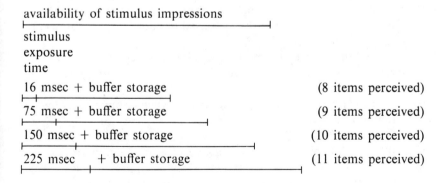

The curves in Figure 18 also reflect the familiar time-intensity reciprocity for events less than 75 to 100 msec in duration (see the discus-

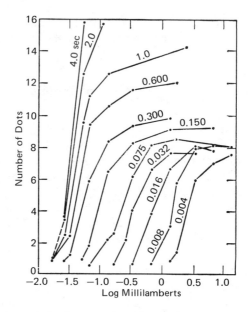

Figure 18. Numbers of simultaneous dots visually discriminated 50 percent of the time at different stimulus intensities (millilamberts) and different exposure times. The number attached to each curve is the exposure time. The averages are from 2 subjects. (From Hunter and Sigler. Copyright 1940 by the American Psychological Association. Reprinted by permission.)

sion of Bloch's Law in Chapter 3, in the section on time-intensity relations). Thus, to perceive six dots in a 32-msec exposure, the stimulus intensity must be about −0.3 log millilamberts. To perceive six dots in a 16-msec exposure, the intensity must be raised to about 0.1; for 8 msec, to over 0.2; for 4 msec, to 0.5.

Because there is a large amount of information represented in Figure 18, it is perhaps not easy to decipher. A simpler illustration of the same time-intensity relation is shown in Figure 19, gathered a generation later by Averbach (1963). Notice the change in performance once the exposure duration exceeds approximately 80 msec.

As early as 1887, Jacobs observed that simultaneity spans vary slightly with differences in item *complexity:* greater complexity yields lower spans. In Chapter 3, it was suggested that more complex events may lengthen the duration of the rapid-attentional-integration process. Figure 20, based on Cavanagh's (1972) review of data, illustrates this relationship, and it shows that item integration-time, or processing-rate, is inversely related to cognitive span. Note also that *familiarity* of items may be involved in this relationship: nonsense syllables and random

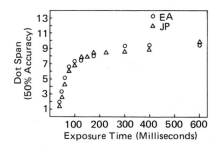

Figure 19. Number of dots discriminated in simultaneous presentations as a function of exposure time. The averages are for 2 subjects ("EA" and "JP"). Dot presentations were followed by a 500-msec visual-noise stimulus (a much larger field of dots) for the purpose of controlling the availability of the first stimulus array. (This likely induces some classical masking effects at the briefest exposure times.) The difficulty of discriminating larger numbers of dots from this following array may, according to Averbach, have contributed to a lower rate of growth of dot span at the longer exposure times (400 to 600 msec) when compared with similar exposure times in Hunter and Sigler's tests (Figure 18). (From Averbach, 1963; reprinted by permission of Academic Press, Inc.)

This experiment was replicated by Lorinstein and Haber (1975), who found that after the first 60 to 70 msec, the number of dots counted increased at the rate of one additional dot for every additional 60 msec of exposure to the array.

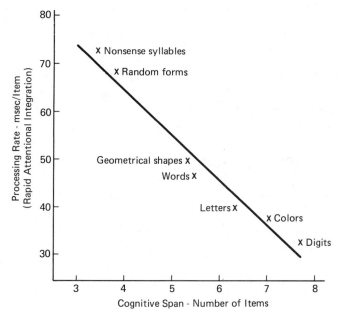

Figure 20. Correlation of attentional-integration rates with simultaneity spans for items of differing complexity. Averages are from 45 separate investigations. (Adapted from Cavanagh, 1972.)

forms are novel, whereas words, letters, colors, and digits are not. The latter yield longer perception spans.

Sequentiality Span

After hearing a list of unrelated words read at a rapid rate of speech, we are generally unable to repeat more than about six or seven of them, unless we have some supplementary memory aids. This finding is general for almost any type of item.

One of Wundt's favored experimental demonstrations of mental processes involved the presentation of sequences of auditory beats from a metronome. With the beats separated by intervals of from one half to three quarters of a second, it is difficult not to project an apparent rhythm on to the sequence so that every other beat is accented (as was described in Chapter 4). Thus, every two beats in a sequence of beats may appear grouped as follows:

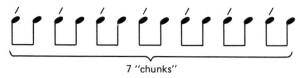

7 "chunks"

(The accent marks above every other note indicate a stress.) Only about seven of these two-beat phrases (in modern jargon, "chunks") can be recognized immediately—that is, recognized instantly as being different from a slightly longer or slightly shorter sequence (Dietze, 1885).

With a more complicated rhythm and a faster beat rate, the following sequence may be recognized and discriminated:

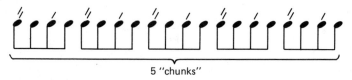

5 "chunks"

Here there are twenty beats in all, but they are divided into five phrases, or chunks, which fall within the STM duration. Similar sequentiality spans occur widely in human performance. For instance, a similar sequentiality pattern appears in almost every line of the works of Shakespeare:

Shall Í compáre thee tó a súmmer's dáy.

More systematic and frequent observations of sequential STM limits have been made as part of an enormous compilation of research on verbal learning. For example, after one hearing of a sequence of unrelated digits, letters, or words read at a rapid rate of speech, most people cannot repeat accurately any sequence longer than about six or seven items unless they use mnemonic schemes to organize items into groups or structures (Woodworth, 1938). There is, again, some variation that corresponds to differences in complexity of individual items; for example, the usual span for digits is slightly greater than that for words (Hayes, 1952; Pollack, 1953).

Another persistently studied performance that reflects the sequentiality span is paired-associate learning—the task of pairing one set of items with others from memory. For the sake of parsimony this is included under the third category of cognitive spans, described in the next section.

Absolute-Judgment Span

Absolute judgment is the identification of the magitude of some simple stimulus—for instance, the brightness of a light, the loudness of a tone, or the curvature of a line—whereas *comparative judgment* is the identification of some relation between two stimuli both present to the observer. Absolute judgment involves the relation between a single stimulus and some information held in short-term memory—information about some former comparison stimuli or about some previously experienced measurement scale. On that basis, an observer identifies or rates a single stimulus (for example, "about two pounds in weight" or "sounds like middle C").

The number of accurate discriminations that can be made in this way along a single sensory dimension is extremely limited. This limit is the absolute-judgment span. On the average, people can make such judgments accurately for only about six musical pitches (Pollack, 1952), about five loudnesses (Garner, 1953), or about 10 to 15 positions on a line (Miller, 1956).

In recent investigations, this limit has been viewed as deriving from the sequentiality (or short-term-memory) span. In judging an isolated item, there is no external context or scale immediately present; hence, a person must rely heavily on memory and on the amount of STM imagery that can be retained in the course of making judgments. To make the judgment, a person must compare an immediate impression with memory impressions of similar stimuli.

Several demonstrations suggest that absolute judgment reflects STM duration. When the pace of presentation of individual items to be judged is progressively slowed, the number of correct identifications becomes less (Siegel, 1972), as if the STM context necessary for judgments fades with the passage of time. When a sequence of stimuli to be judged becomes increasingly numerous and diverse, STM capacity becomes inadequate for the task or is increasingly overburdened, so that the number of correct identifications declines (MacRae, 1970). Absolute judgments are also affected by the discriminability of the segments of the STM image. Thus, judgment improves as spacing along a subjective scale is increased (Hartman, 1954).

As Leshowitz and Green concluded, "Clearly, the [absolute-judgment] limitation must be on the memory for the various categories or some interaction between retrieval and comparison of sensory images" (1974, p. 178). This limit involves the difficulty of holding many distinctions in mind long enough to scan and compare them. And that is a type of short-term memory difficulty, the same type of difficulty that may be encountered in spontaneous speech production (noted in the previous chapter).

Perfect pitch. In some situations, absolute-judgment limits can be extended through practice. But this can be done only with great effort, especially when the stimuli lack meaning. It is most difficult to organize a mnemonic structure or context for a stimulus (such as a tone or a light) that is so simple that it provokes a minimum of associations (memories, images).

The most celebrated example of overcoming this limit is the "perfect pitch" (or absolute pitch) that occurs among many musicians. In the typical case, about 45 notes presented in random sequence are identified correctly by an individual with this ability (Attneave, 1959). For some years, the possibility of learning perfect pitch was incompatible with theories of learning as well as of absolute judgment; this ability was assumed to be the mysterious inborn gift of musical geniuses (Seashore, 1938). But on the contrary, musical pitches afford opportunities for mnemonic organization. They are structured into octaves, and on most instruments the tonal qualities of notes vary from one octave to another. These and possibly other memory images provide the basis for mnemonic techniques that lead to perfect pitch, as was indeed shown in the early days of experimental psychology and again recently (Stumpf, 1883; Boggs, 1907; Cuddy, 1968; Brady, 1970).

Paired associates. Siegel and Siegel (1972) showed that the task of paired-associate recall methodologically parallels that of absolute judgment. In both cases, a person identifies randomly presented, isolated items by giving some predetermined response, such as "middle C" for a note sounded on a piano, or the name "John" for a certain face. But the more complex items found in most paired-associate-learning tasks are not limited to one sensory dimension. Accordingly, they are rich in associations that readily suggest mnemonic structures and so facilitate recall. The seven-item immediate-memory limit (often observed on the first attempt at recall) is easily overcome through practice on subsequent trials.

CONCLUSIONS

Ultimately, what counts as an item of experience depends upon the relative breadth or narrowness of the focus of attention at any given moment. The number of distinct impressions that can pass through the stream of experience at a given moment is subject to the temporal constraints of rapid attentional integrations, buffer delays, and short-term memory. Those constraints limit the number of impressions, distinctions, or ideas that can be grasped at once, held in mind briefly, or used as a basis for making judgments. Taken together, these limits may be termed "cognitive spans."

The relation of the buffer delay to the speed of rapid attentional integrations yields a simultaneity span—a limit on the number of simultaneous events that can be identified. It is often called the "perception span." Performance with sequential events is limited by STM duration and yields a sequentiality span—a limit on the numer of events in a series that can be reproduced immediately. This is also called the "immediate-memory span," or the "short-term memory span."

The limit on absolute judgment is a limit on the ability to place some isolated item on an abstract scale, or to match it with some previous item from memory. This limit may be considered a special case of the limitations on short-term memory, and hence, a special case of the sequentiality span.

Two summary generalizations were given earlier in this chapter to help organize observations on cognitive spans. Again they are as follows:

> The number of simultaneous impressions that can enter consciousness is limited by the ratio of buffer-delay time to rapid-attentional-integration time.

> The number of sequential impressions that can be grouped together in momentary consciousness is limited by their duration in short-term memory.

This concludes Part II and the description of immediate information processing. If our mental life were limited by these brief processes to a mere string of brief, disconnected cognitive events, it would indeed be chaotic, and our survival would be doubtful. But inherent in these processes of immediate experience are the means for longer temporal integration—that is, for continuity in our experience and actions. These means are the topic of Part III of this text, which begins with the next chapter.

Part Three

THE CONTROL

OF

IMMEDIATE

EXPERIENCE

7

EMOTION

Emotional experience is an essential aspect of the process of cognition and must be considered in any adequate description of it. In common language, emotional states are "affects," "emotions," "feelings," "sentiments," "moods," "attitudes," or "values." Of course, each of these terms has a somewhat different usage. The first two, affect and emotion, are perhaps the most rudimentary in discussions of the process of cognition. At one time, *affects* referred primarily to elemental experiences, whereas *emotions* referred to global and complex experiences. But that distinction is not consistently followed today.

The emotional augmentation of experience links enduring needs and dispositions to the psychological present. It can direct the course of cognition—the retrieval of memories, the structuring of thoughts, or the formation of perceptions. In this way, emotion contributes to the longer continuity of human experience.

GENERAL PRINCIPLES

As one of the components in the integration of human experience, emotion is fundamentally different from perceptual information. It is not information about external objects, or about our memories of them as such; rather, it is information about our impulsive reactions to them. These reactions are, as we shall see, connected to the most central cognitive functions, and so emotional reactions may generalize across modalities and across the mental functions of perceiving, thinking, and remembering. There is no set of emotions that is associated with only one type of mental function. The variety of emotional experiences is obviously large, if not infinite.

Heated debates about emotion were prompted by the speculations of James (1884) and Lange (1885). This well-known episode in the history of psychology began when these men suggested that visceral reactions, or certain bodily states ("trembling," "crying," "fleeing"), either color or wholly determine emotional experience. Critical studies by Cannon (1927) downgraded that proposal on the basis of physiological observations. For example, emotional behavior occurs in the absence of these visceral reactions, and when these reactions do occur, they are often the same for different emotions. Then too, emotional experience arises more rapidly in response to an emotion-provoking situation than do visceral reactions.

Another line of early theoretical speculation suggested that emotion is an integral and fundamental part of every mental act. For instance, Sherrington conjectured that "Mind rarely, probably never, perceives any object with absolute indifference, that is, without 'feeling.' In other words, affective tone is the constant accompaniment of sensation" (1900, p. 974). McDougall argued that, "The emotional qualities have, then, a cognitive function; they signify to us primarily not the nature of things, but rather the nature of our impulsive reactions to things" (1923, p. 326).

Primal qualities. According to classical Wundtian theory, emotion is the primary source of all experience and is the primordial form of consciousness, both in the life of the individual and in the historical evolution of living organisms. This view finds some support in the observation that the parts of the nervous system that are associated primarily with emotional reactions are, in an evolutionary sense, the oldest parts and among the earliest structures to develop in the fetus. Wundt went further to propose that the underlying condition of all immediate experience is always an affective state, whether in acts of memory, acts of perception, or acts of thought. The following quotation from Krueger, a student of Wundt's, elaborates this notion:

> . . .isolated sensations, perceptions, memories, clear ideas, firm decisions—in brief, all organized experiences—split off from diffuse emotional tendencies and always remain dominated by them. These experiences always remain embedded in the emotion which fills in gaps, as it were, and forms the common background of all experience. Emotion is the maternal origin of all other types of experience and remains their most effective support. . . . When there is a change in experience, the emotion also changes, either alone or together with other experiences, determining their course. (1928; translated by Arnold, 1968, p. 99)

As living organisms evolved, according to these speculations, parts of the primordial, affective sense split off and became the specialized and localized sensory systems. This could have happened when certain qualities of feeling (that have evolved into our experiences of colors, sounds, tastes, and so on) became signals for the presence of events that are critical to survival. Yet a primordial core remains, producing emotional reactions to central cognitive events and playing a crucial role in the integration and flow of consciousness. Aristotle, in his *De Anima*, had described this core of affect as the "common sense." Certain later psychologists and physiologists called it the point of "the unity of the senses" (Hornbostel, 1927; Sherrington, 1900; Werner, 1934). A more extended modern statement of this line of thought appears in Langer's review (1967).

Modern cognitive psychology, however, has been heavily influenced by metaphors based on communication engineering, metaphors that are devoid of reference to emotion. In the information-processing model that was shown in Figure 2, p. 19, the sources of input to the central cognitive processes are clear, but there is no representation of the source of emotional qualities. Formerly, it was easy to accept this limitation by citing fundamental differences between emotion and other forms of human cognition. It was often assumed that either the two are wholly separate domains, or that emotions are breakdowns or disorganizations in the functioning of mental and behavioral processes, or that they are conflicts that occur within the cognitive system.

But modern cognitive psychology has increasingly found these latter accounts to be inadequate (Arnold, 1970). Breakdowns, disorganizations, and conflicts may certainly yield emotion; yet emotion is also found in normal, smooth functioning. Moreover, it has been shown experimentally that emotional reactions can play a basic role in normal cognitive processes.

Emotion and motivation. Theorists have often treated emotion and motivation as the same. There are, however, logical differences. We use the term "motive" to indicate the connection of our thoughts, impressions, and memories with other things we *do*. "Emotion," however, is a term that we use to indicate experiences that *come over us* but that do not necessarily goad us to action.

Emotions obviously can function as "amplifiers" of needs and motivational states. Amplification, a notion stressed by Tomkins (1962), means that certain elements of experience that have motivational significance in the immediate attentional integration will be accented or augmented by an infusion of emotional reactions. These reactions are apparently the special contribution of the central integrative process, and occur in the course of its constructive activity.

Centrally generated affective qualities of experience are observed no less at the highest (that is, the most abstract) levels of cognitive performance. Bruner, Goodnow, and Austin (1956) noticed this in their studies of thinking and concept formation:

> One characteristic of cognitive activity, whether at the level of instrumental activity or in the playful realms of chess, is that it has associated with it some rather unique affective states. The sense of tension that occurs when we cannot "place" somebody, the frustration we have been able to induce in subjects serving in tachistoscopic experiments when exposure levels were too low, the malaise of the trained mind faced with a seemingly causeless effect—all of these are as characteristic of frustrated cognitive activity as desire is of blocked sexual activity. (1956, pp. 16-17)

On the positive side, there is the sudden impulse of pleasure, joy, relief, or excitement that is often felt at the moment of the solution of a problem or of the resolution of a conflict. It seems clear that these affective qualities may remain in short-term memory, providing a context for and an influence on immediately subsequent cognitions. It also seems clear that we can refocus or rethink the events that provoked these qualities, thereby recycling and extending the affective state.

Emotional content. Must there always be some memory, perception, or thought carrying or provoking emotional experience? Can experience never consist of emotion alone? The majority of writers on this topic appear to say yes to the first question and no the the second (Titchener, 1908; Harlow and Stagner, 1933; Leeper, 1970; and many others). To experience pleasure, then, it would be necessary to have images, thoughts, or perceptions of which pleasurable emotional reactions are an integral part. Yet decisive studies of this question are lacking.

Perhaps a weaker form of this position would be safer at the present time; it could be phrased as follows: to experience emotion a person's central cognitive processes, which produce perceptions, memories, and thoughts, must be functioning. Regardless of the point at which emotional reactions occur in the course of rapid attentional integration, they still depend on that process as their basis.

Among the sparse data that bear on this question, the following findings by Schachter and Singer (1962) stand out: If emotional reactions do occur but their relation to the other aspects of cognition is not maintained, there will be no continuing emotional experience. For instance, the artificial arousal of emotion-associated reactions (tremor, flushing, palpitations) by an injection of adrenalin will not by itself sustain emotional experience. To do so, it must be integrated with other items of attention, such as threats or jokes, in which case the adrenalin reactions may be integrated with, and thereby strengthen, the emotional qualities of experience.

The emotion system. How, then, should emotional quality be described? What is the range and structure of emotional experience? We describe most sensory experiences, aside from their intensity and duration, in terms of dimensions or qualities that are unique to each, such as the primary colors, or the fundamental tastes—salt, sour, bitter, sweet. Can some analogous approach be followed in the description of emotional experience?

We recognize some emotional experiences as being related to others; for example, we distinguish groups of pleasant emotions from unpleasant emotions. This suggests that a general system underlies them. There is some tradition of agreement on rudimentary dimensions of emotional experience, and this agreement has withstood changes of theoretical orientation as well as of method and measurement. Most descriptions of emotional quality proceed from a framework consisting of a small set of rudimentary bipolar dimensions.

Each dimension is, in one way or another, considered an internal process that contributes in varying degrees to momentary emotional reactions. Each may be activated differently by the flow of the contents and structures of experience. The following are the three most commonly cited emotion dimensions, in the order of their historical appearance and of their support in the research literature.

The first is the *hedonic* dimension. To almost everyone who has studied emotion, it seems natural to identify a bipolar dimension of *pleasantness-unpleasantness*. In structuralism, psychoanalysis, Gestalt psychology, behaviorism, and social psychology, this dimension appears variously as:

pleasure versus pain
positive versus negative affect
approach versus avoidance behavior
positive versus negative reinforcement
high versus low evaluation

In the fundamental effort of living systems to strive for self-preservation, constancy, stability, and structure, anything that reduces chaos and disorder, or that helps the organism maintain its integrity (including the integrity of consciousness) may be a source of pleasant affect. Neurologically, much has been written about pleasure centers located in the brain's limbic system.

A second dimension contributing to emotion, and one that is also widely observed, is the *arousal* system. It has been described by the following bipolar expressions:

high versus low arousal
activity versus passivity
excitation versus depression
high versus low activation

Neurophysiologists have studied the reticular activating system of the brain stem as the source of this dimension.

A third frequently observed dimension is somewhat less consistently named. Here, it will be called the *attentiveness* dimension. It has also been identified with the following terms:

concentrated versus relaxed attention
high versus low control

expectancy versus resolution
high versus low potency
dominance versus submissiveness
vividness versus vagueness
tension versus relaxation

Notice that in this analysis *attentiveness* is not the same as *arousal*. Thus, high arousal does not necessarily determine highly focused attention. For example, consider deep meditation, in which an individual attains states of very low arousal by means of extremely intense and highly focused attention (Kasamatsu and Hirai, 1966; Ornstein, 1972). Osgood's description of this dimension is as follows: "The potent direction is characterized by tight, controlled, deliberate states. . .while the impotent direction is characterized by loose, uncontrolled, unintentional states" (1969, p. 195).

In early theoretical psychology, the claims for these systems or dimensions came largely from introspective observation and associated logical arguments. Later techniques of quantitative analysis (factor analysis, cluster analysis, multidimensional scaling) confirmed earlier speculations. These techniques are now applied to judgments and ratings of felt emotion, the emotional content of words, attitudes, facial expressions, social relations, aesthetic impressions, and affective impressions of simple stimuli.

It was Wundt who originated the tridimensional system in the 1890s by arguing against the view that emotion is adequately described solely in terms of the hedonic dimension. His reasoning was simply that the qualities of emotional experience are much too rich and varied to be ordered along one dimension alone; to describe emotion in terms of solely one dimension would be like describing visual sensations only in terms of brightness, with no reference to color. Wundt further realized that we cannot simply arrange emotions into ordinary language categories and subcategories (many arbitrary schemes had been tried before). Rather, there must be an underlying scheme separate from the arbitrary terms and linguistic histories of language. Wundt therefore sought a system of cognitive dimensions of emotion that would be analogous to the dimensions of sensory systems, which are independent of language.

Supporting data. Undertaking an ambitious research program, Wundt hoped to find indicators of each of the three affective dimensions in patterns of physiological response, such as patterns of respiration and pulse. Yet convincing data apparently eluded him. The fatal blow, however, was the opposition of Titchener and his students, who were unable to find Wundt's three dimensions in their characteristic introspections (Titchener, 1908; Ruckmick, 1936).

Years later, in a far-removed time and place, Schlosberg (1954) and Osgood, Suci, and Tannenbaum (1957) independently rediscovered the Wundtian tridimensional structure by using new techniques of quantitative analysis. Schlosberg found the same three systems to underlie facial expressions of emotion. Osgood and his associates studied human attitudes by means of a rating scale constructed from bipolar adjectives (good-bad, strong-weak, and so on) and named it *the semantic differential*. Here again, Wundt's three factors emerged and accounted for the greater part of the variance in measures of human attitudes.

According to Osgood, the "semantic differential technique measures certain affective features of total meaning, closely related to the dimensions of emotion or feeling, which appear to be universal in the human species" (1969, p. 194). The three dimension, he claims, may be "the common coin of metaphors. . .and the psychological basis of synesthesia and of aesthetic communication" (ibid. p. 197). Osgood's students have replicated the finding of the three factors in twenty different language communities.

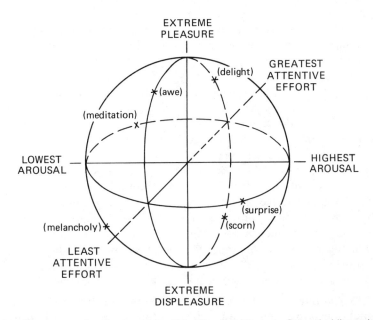

Figure 21. Schematic representation of the Wundt-Schlosberg-Osgood tridimensional model of emotional quality. The three bipolar dimensions are pleasure versus displeasure, high versus low arousal, and greatest versus least attentive effort. Also shown in lower-case letters in parentheses are examples of typical placements in this system of six affective states.

Other investigators approached the issue of emotional dimensionality by means of other measurement situations and techniques, with the following results: Abelson and Sermat (1962), Block (1957), and Shepard (1963) confirmed the finding of the first two dimensions. Bales (1970), Engen et al. (1958), Gladstones (1962), Royal and Hays (1959), Stringer (1967), Wedin (1972), and Yoshida (1964) produced similar findings of three-dimensional systems. Davitz (1969) found four factors, and Frijda (1969) found six; in these cases, it appears that one or more of Wundt's original three factors is subdivided.* Figure 21 is a schematic representation of the Wundt-Schlosberg-Osgood tridimensional analysis. Within the "emotion space" of the tridimensional system, each emotion is theoretically describable as a unique point in that space.

Summary generalizations. The following two generalities summarize many of the above notions about emotional experience and help explain the more specific observations that follow:

Emotion arises from reactions of the rapid-attentional-integration process in the course of its integrations of immediate experience.

There are at least three systems (or dimensions) of fundamental reaction that form emotional experience. These have been called, among other terms, "the hedonic," "the arousal," and "the attentiveness" systems.

OBSERVATIONS

Results from the following areas of investigation have helped us describe the nature of the emotional aspects of cognition:

1. synesthesia
2. the experience of pain
3. reactions to music
4. visceral-cognitive integrations
5. enhancement and repression

*A summary of yet another set of factor-analytic investigations—all of which concern aesthetic judgments—is found in Berlyne (1974).

Synesthesia

Synesthesia is the curious phenomenon of having the same affective reaction to sensations from different sensory modalities. On this basis, certain sounds may be paired to certain colors, or tastes with sounds, or colors with tactile sensations. Such relationships have occasionally been dismissed as idiosyncratic associations or as rare phenomena that have no bearing on the operation of the normal mind. Accumulated observations now suggest otherwise. Thanks to a recent review by Marks (1975), it is much easier to reach some conclusions.

Marks was concerned primarily with visual-auditory synesthesia, which is the richest source of published data. There are numerous reports of visual "photisms" associated with sounds, speech, or music. A trumpet's sound may be described as "scarlet" or as "bright red"; a flute's, as "bright blue." Or entire musical patterns or composer's works are described by color. Raines, (1909) for example, reported tendencies to describe Chopin's music as "purple," Wagner's as "red," and so forth. Idiosyncrasies do, of course, enter into these subjective pairings. But overall they are systematic and consistent. One of the most rudimentary synesthesias is the relation between imagined visual brightness and auditory pitch. This is illustrated in Figure 22 for the case of speech sounds.

Sensations or sensory dimensions that are linked to one another must be linked by something. Thus, all explanations of synesthesia that have been put forward are essentially theories of mediational processes. More specifically, there may be certain reactions that are general to all sensations and that are primitive and affective in character. The various senses can then be interrelated via these central "feelings." Hornbostel (1927) and Werner (1934) even argued that sensory stimulation first arouses a central emotional reaction before differentiating into specific, modal perception.

If stimuli from all senses evoke central affective qualities in a consistent way, as well as evoking the more specific sensory experiences, and if there is one central affective system, then it should not be surprising that individuals will pair a certain color with a certain sound, smell, or other sensation.

In general, the stronger the central affective reactions are for an individual, the more of a "synesthete" he or she will be. In the more primitive nervous system of infancy, where the primordial central affective structures are relatively more dominant, synesthesia is much more

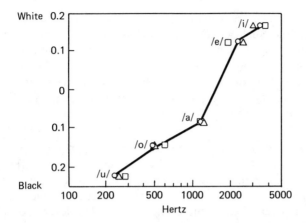

Figure 22. Relation of brightness to pitch in visual-auditory synesthesia (from Marks, 1975). The ordinate shows scores on a dimension of visual brightness, derived from probabilities of synesthetic responses to vowel sounds. The abscissa gives the sound frequencies of the pitch of the vowels as determined by Köhler, 1910 (circles), Modell and Rich, 1915 (squares), and Delattre et al., 1952 (triangles). The vowels are, in order of rising sound frequency, /u/, /o/, /a/, /e/, /i/. (Copyright, 1975, by the American Psychological Association; reprinted by permission.)

pronounced (Werner, 1948; Marks, 1975). As individuals mature, the primitive affective reactions are more likely to be masked by the complex verbal associations and imagery of later development.

Osgood's (1962) data, however, show that people in diverse cultural communities make similar synesthetic judgments. For instance, Anglo-Americans, Navajos, and Japanese all agreed that *heavy* is "down," "thick," "dark," and "near"; that *white* is "thin" and "calm"; and that *fast* is "thin," "bright," and "diffuse." This observation opposes the popular hypothesis of cultural relativity (the Whorfian hypothesis). Yet a cultural diversity obviously can still emerge at more complex levels of linguistic or symbolic mental impressions that are socially determined.

The Experience of Pain

The more we learn about that quality of experience known as pain, the more we must place its determinants squarely in the central cognitive processes. Pain is a powerful source of observations on emotion for the simple reason that it is a sharp, demanding experience and that there is, needless to say, relatively good observer agreement about its characteristics. Such agreement would be something to the effect that pain is highly unpleasant and highly arousing. Yet the conditions that cause pain vary from moment to moment, and from individual to individual. Those conditions are strongly influenced, even controlled, by an individual's reactions at a central cognitive level, or by that individual's "state of mind" at the moment, rather than solely by some external noxious stimulus.

Clinical abnormalities. One excellent source of information about pain comes from the occasional individual who shows an extreme lack of pain experience. People who have suffered damage to the frontal lobes of their brains are often left with a lack of emotional reaction, which is especially noticeable for stimuli that should evoke severe pain (Freeman and Watts, 1948; Melzack, 1973). This brain damage does not disrupt sensory pathways or sensory experience. In fact, sensory thresholds often appear to be *lowered* in this condition. For example, such persons might describe very accurately the sensory characteristics of sharp pin pricks as "burning" and "sharp," but still the aversive emotional quality of this stimulus is missing for them. A similar condition is congenital insensitivity to pain, or *pain asymbolia.* Here the sensations evoked by normally pain-inducing stimuli are intact, but the emotional quality is again missing.

The converse situation is that of "psychosomatic pain," the experiencing of severe pain in the absence of any noxious stimulus. One example of this is the occurrence of "phantom limbs" in amputees (Melzack, 1973). An individual may experience pain in a missing foot or hand. Such cases have at times been treated surgically by severing afferent nerve tracts in the remaining portion of the arm or leg or even in the spinal tract; yet even after those radical measures, the pain in a phantom limb may persist. There is a central cortical schema, or "body image," that apparently has pain reactions associated with it and that has become relatively independent of peripheral conditions. (These central schemata are described in Chapter 8.)

All the above clinical observations are biological abnormalities. Analogous situations, however, occur as transient conditions and might be experienced by anyone. Beecher (1959) observed the actions of soldiers severely wounded in combat. Only one of every three extensively wounded soldiers complained of pain or desired morphine. Most of these men denied having any pain at all, and as Beecher observed, they were not in a state of shock. At the same time, they were quite capable of feeling pain—they complained vehemently of pain that arose from inept vein punctures in the course of medical treatment. Civilians who had wounds similar to those of the soldiers claimed to have severe pain, and they pleaded for morphine injections.

Beecher's conclusion was that the soldiers' exhilaration at having escaped death effectively blocked their cognitive reaction to pain, though it did not block peripheral sensory experiences. A wounded soldier's response to injury was one of relief to escape the battlefield with his life. For the civilian, injury or surgery was a horrifying and calamitous event.

Compare some related observations originally made by Pavlov (1927, 1928). In certain of his classical conditioning experiments, dogs were repeatedly given food immediately after a shock was delivered to one of their paws. The shock would ordinarily elicit a violent pain-reaction. Eventually, however, the dogs responded to the shock delivered to a certain paw as a signal for food, and they salivated without showing signs of pain. In fact, after the shock the dogs would wag their tails and turn eagerly toward a food dish. Yet when the same shock was applied to other paws or to other parts of their bodies, they howled in an ordinary reaction to pain. This shows how one immediate psychological reaction (expectation of food) can color and change an emotional reaction.

Hypnosis and acupuncture. Melzack (1973) has described cases of clinically induced pain-blockage in individuals who suffer chronic pain. His work is largely an attempt to identify locations of neural control that determine pain experience, and it may lead to a better understanding of the psychological anesthesia produced through hypnosis and acupuncture. In these anesthesias, attention is brought under some extreme external control or distraction. With acupuncture, for instance, anesthesia is induced by the bizarre affective experience of needles inserted into one's body surface at sensitive points. Just as in the cases of abnormal pain deficit described above, the acupuncture patient has full and normal cognitions of the sensory experience of ordinarily painful stimuli, such as a knife penetrating the skin; but the aversive emotional quality is somehow masked. It is as if the central emotional reaction-system is deflected by its reactions to the input from the acupuncture needles.

Not as well understood as it should be, considering its enduring notoriety, hypnosis is directed especially at central control processes. In particular, it involves relaxing of attentional control and the narrowing, or dissociating, of attentional processes (see Hilgard, 1969). To emphasize the central cognitive basis of acupuncture and hypnosis, we must observe that personality characteristics, or "cognitive styles," which reflect different habitual patterns of self-control, render some people more susceptible and some less susceptible to these techniques. (Differences in cognitive style are described in Chapter 9.)

Reactions to Music

Music presents a realm of affective experience that is clearly different from that of pain, yet reflects some of the same underlying principles. Attention and anticipation are as important for the integration of emotion in the case of music stimuli as they are with pain stimuli. Traditionally, music is considered a form of "pure affective communication" that evokes emotion by means of a rule-governed system of auditory signs. However, music is fundamentally different from most other communication systems, in that it does not rely on signs or symbols directly associated with external events or objects. Thus, it differs from the communicative systems of literature, representative painting, physics, or biology.

Of course, music can be made to have explicit external reference, as when a pattern of tones produced on a trumpet is associated with the specific command "charge," or "retreat." But such music is simply being reemployed as a linguistic signal; unlike other musical phrases, these can be translated directly into natural language. Some poetry and abstract styles of painting may also directly evoke affective experience through formal properties alone, without having any other referential function. But historically and psychologically, music is the most pervasive example of affective communication.

Musicologists ask how combinations and patterns of tones produce the experience of emotional qualities. Most musicologists, however, study the formal rule structures (the "grammars") of musical creations rather than the cognitive process of emotion. The study of musical structure per se provides no direct explanation of the psychological mechanism of the affective process (just as the concerted study of the structures of language provides no explanation of the psychological mechanisms of language comprehension).

Time and music. Music exists because certain biological rhythms and temporal processes exist. Music is fundamentally a temporal phenomenon—it is vibration rates, temporal patterns, and pulsations. And its ranges of pulsations, rhythms, and periodicities are not arbitrary; they cover the narrow spectrums of the same temporal intervals involved in the microgenetic cognitive processes that were reviewed in Part II of this text. Music thus seems to play directly upon the temporal processes of consciousness. Most events in our experience flow through time, yet the multilevel temporal patternings of music apparently throw the temporal pulses of central cognition into a greater resonance with external stimuli. By inducing this entrainment of the central processes, music manipulates their very temporal existence. This leads to affective experiences of uncertainty, tension, arousal, expectation, surprise, resolution, delight and so on. In other words, music evokes directly the emotional reactivity of central cognitive processes. Perhaps nothing shows the wonder and the subtlety of affective reactions more than these responses to music.

The resonance of central processes with the flow of patterned sound involves rapid integrations, fusions of sound, rhythms coordinated with buffer delays, and short-term-memory groupings of phrases. In addition to microscopic temporal events in the inner ear, which contribute to pitch discrimination, there are the central combinations of sounds and the fusion of notes into sound patterns (Bregman and Campbell, 1971). These seem controlled at the level of rapid attentional integration. Rhythm, as we noted in Chapter 4, is generally associated with the buffer intermittency. Melodic patterns and rhythmical phrases are associated with STM capacity. These are the structural components of music.

The pattern and flow of music provides an example of Gestalt principles (see Chapter 3). A melody is not merely temporal sequence. It becomes a unitary object in our experience. And the affective response to musical sequences is highly context-dependent; even simple judgments of consonance and dissonance are strongly influenced by preceding and following tones. Thus, a normally dissonant combination of pitches, when inserted between certain other harmonious combinations, can have a perfectly acceptable and compatible sound; it is experienced as a transition sound that is related structurally to the preceding and following combinations (Gardner and Pickford, 1943). Moreover, in some cases a sequence of tones may evoke either a sorrowful mood or a mood of gaiety, depending upon the larger musical phrase and rhythm in which it is embedded. The musical artist in effect plays upon the temporality of human consciousness. He plays upon those times and sequences to which the process of human cognition is tuned. The emotions experienced during this play are the immediate reactions resulting in arousal, attention, exhilaration, relaxation, and so forth.

The evolution of musical styles shows that certain learned techniques of temporal manipulation must be shared by the musical artist and his audience if effective communication of emotion is to take place. These techniques could be called rule systems—patterns of expectation and different types of temporal-integration strategies. Different styles of music represent different rule systems for the actions of central control processes in the perceiving of auditory stimuli. Each style of music requires a somewhat different attentional strategy in the parsing of rhythms, or the grouping and relating of tones. The emotional effects of music, as in other perceptual reactions, depend to a large extent on the listener's control of his attention. A listener who is "set" to hear Baroque music and is presented instead with a Romantic piece would likely not experience the reaction desired by the Romantic composer.

The first time an individual hears the music of Bach, he or she may not have the aesthetic experience that is possible after repeated exposure to Bach's style. After such exposure, however, one learns to attend in certain ways or to look for certain types of regularity in the sound pattern of the music. Music arouses expectancies of patterns. These in turn set up tensions that are resolved in the course of the syntheses, fusions, and constructions that constitute musical perception.

Some people, however, suffer *amusia,* an inability to produce or comprehend music. They do not integrate the musical stimulus in a way that produces the emotional reaction. This condition is somewhat analogous to congenital pain deficit, or pain asymbolia (reviewed in the previous section).

Dimensions of musical reaction. To conclude this description of reactions to music, we turn to the research of Wedin (1969, 1972) on the variety of these reactions. Wedin presented listeners with 35- to 40-second excerpts from a wide range of instrumental compositions spanning many styles and periods of musical composition. Listeners rated each piece on a scale of one to ten for each of forty emotion adjectives (one meant that the adjective did not apply; ten meant that it applied to a very large extent).

When the ratings were factor-analyzed, 87 percent of the variance in them was predictable from three underlying dimensions. The most prominent of these was the *arousal* factor (also called the *energy* factor or the *activation* factor), which accounted for about half of that variance. About 33 percent of the variance was in the *hedonic* dimension, which Wedin described as a "gaiety versus gloom" factor. A third factor, which Wedin compared to Osgood's *potency* dimension, accounted for the remainder of the variance. It is interesting that in these reactions to music, the *arousal* dimension emerges as predominant. In many other factorial studies of emotional reactions, the *hedonic* dimension is predominant.

Musical experiences, however, show the same emotion space that has appeared in studies of other sources of emotional reaction. Figure 23 is Wedin's characterization of his analysis.

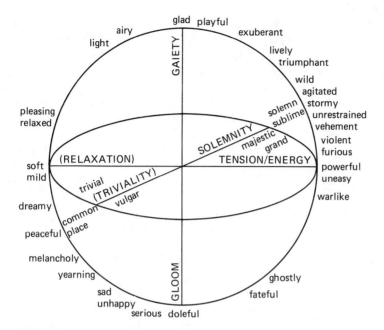

Figure 23. The tridimensional system in reactions to music. This system is the result of a factor analysis of listeners' ratings of musical compositions. With respect to the Wundt-Schlosberg-Osgood three-factor emotion theory (Figure 17), *gaiety-gloom* corresponds to the pleasure dimension, *relaxation-tension/energy* to the arousal dimension, and *triviality-solemnity* to the attentiveness dimension. (From Wedin, 1972; reprinted by permission.)

Visceral-Cognitive Integrations

Ever since the early proposal of the James-Lange theory that visceral reaction and emotion-experience interact, and ever since Wundt's attempts to find reflections of the three-dimensional descriptive system in distinct physiological reaction patterns, it has often been observed that there is no simple one-to-one correspondence between peripheral physiological manifestations and specific emotional experiences. Yet pulse, respiration, circulation, and other physiological phenomena do fluctuate sharply in the presence of strong emotional experience and appear to become a part of that experience.

Modern observations of these interactions began with the investigations by Schachter and Singer (1962), who manipulated independently both the physiological reaction pattern and the emotion-arousing information in their subjects' environments. The former manipulation was achieved by injections of adrenalin, after which the subjects were either informed or misinformed of the reaction that would result. This reaction was a bodily state resembling one usually experienced during strong emotion. The latter manipulation was achieved by placing subjects in environments in which other persons were acting out emotional behavior or in which emotional situations were displayed on film.

The unexpected input of emotionlike bodily reactions to the central assembly of experience may be integrated with any emotional component already present, and so may amplify that part of experience. Schachter and Singer's unsuspecting injected subjects were exposed to environmental situations arranged to suggest either *anger* or *euphoria* and, accordingly, they had emotional experiences matching those suggested by their environments.

Control subjects, who were injected with placebos, experienced no amplification of emotional experience when in the same environments. Adrenalin-injected subjects who were correctly informed about the effects of the adrenalin also felt no exceptional emotional experience, and went about their business regardless of emotion-provoking environments. Although emotionlike sensations occurred in these informed subjects, attentional integrations included additional information—namely, the explanation of the adrenalin reaction, which led them to ignore or to separate those sensations from attention.

The emotionally aroused subjects, it should be stressed, did not merely "label" reactions as emotions after some deliberation and analysis. Rather, their experiences were immediate and impulsive. According to the testimony of these individuals, their experiences were no different from any other naturally occurring state of anger or euphoria in their experience.

Enhancement and Repression

Descriptions of emotion as the central and primary quality of experience suggest that the smallest changes in experience can be felt emotionally even when other elements of that experience are not localized or identified at all (Goldstein, 1951; Krueger, 1928; Wundt, 1896). We can have "feelings of familiarity" or "feelings of knowing" that some event has occurred or that some familiar object is present, yet we are not able to identify that event or object other than to acknowledge our vague feelings about it.

Emotion and memory. Consider the "tip-of-the-tongue" phenomenon (so named by James, 1890). It is most likely observed during the attempt to recall a forgotten name; the rememberer "draws a blank" yet asserts that the name would be recognized if heard, and that wrong names would instantly be recognized as such. In the course of reconstructing a sought-for name, it will often be noticed that some specific, identifying affect arises first. In his classic studies of the process of remembering, Bartlett (1932) spelled out the significance of this affective reaction for acts of remembering in general. He summarized a series of experiments by pointing out how the rememberer begins with a "general impression" or a subjective general "attitude"; the details of the item to be recalled are then reconstructed from this basis. Bartlett then continued:

> Ask the observer to characterise this general impression psychologically, and the word that is always cropping up is "attitude." I have shown how this "attitude" factor came into nearly every series of experiments that was carried out. The construction that is effected is the sort of construction that would justify the observer's "attitude." Attitude names a complex psychological state or process which it is very hard to describe in more elementary psychological terms. It is, however, as I have often indicated, very largely a matter of feeling, or affect. We say that it is characterised by doubt, hesitation, surprise, astonishment, confidence, dislike, repulsion and so on. . . .when a subject is being asked to remember, very often the first thing that emerges is something of the nature of attitude. The recall is then a construction, made largely on the basis of this attitude, and its general effect is that of a justification of the attitude. (1932, pp. 206-7)

Wenzl (1932) provided systematic studies of James's tip-of-the-tongue effect by presenting descriptions of obscure words or names to subjects, who then attempted to produce the names and to convey whatever reactions they experienced in their generally unsuccessful attempts at recall. Often, they could report a certainty of having previously used the word but could still not reproduce it. Also, reports of various qualities associated with the forgotten word were often made. As well as reporting linguistic qualities (number of syllables, rhyming words, and so on), Wenzl's subjects also reported their affective and synesthetic reactions. Forgotten words were described as having such qualities as "bright," "sonorous," "sad," "gloomy," "pleasing," "banal," "cozy," and "exotic," and in one case as provoking an imagined sensation of color.

Later investigators have provided other observations of the tip-of-the-tongue effect (Hart, 1965, 1967; Brown and McNeill, 1966; Freedman and Landauer, 1966). In particular, Hart has analyzed such occurrences as reflections of a "memory monitoring process" which is the arousal of elemental reactions that facilitate recognition. In the present terms, these reactions are affective enhancements of certain directions of the attentional activity in its search of memory. Hart states the value of this process to memory as follows:

> If people were computers with relatively infallible memories, they would have no need to use feeling-of-knowing indicators. A memory item in storage would be retrieved; failure to retrieve an item would mean that it was not in storage. A fallible memory system requires an additional process that assesses storage states when retrieval failures occur. (1967, p. 685)

Emotion and perception. If the affective component of experience has some initial or early temporal status in the individual acts of remembering, perceiving, and thinking, then affective reactions may have a determining influence on the subsequent direction and form of those acts. Pleasant, arousing, or attention-heightening reactions can enhance, augment, or exaggerate certain impressions in the attentional integrations of perception and memory. This is widely described as cognitive or perceptual *vigilance*. In the opposite case, unpleasant, depressing, or attention-relaxing affects may lead to the avoidance, repression, masking, or inhibition of components of experience. This has often been described as cognitive or perceptual *defense*. Such observations formed the basis of a vigorous and often controversial line of research in the 1940s and 1950s now known as the "new look" in perception research, or as "directive-state theory." The following are some classic original examples of that research:

A starving man is extraordinarily quick to pick up some component of sensation or some concept that suggests food. Levine, Chein, and Murphy (1942) presented ambiguous visual stimuli to hungry men, who then frequently claimed to perceive these configurations as items of food.

Schafer and Murphy (1943) paired ambiguous stimuli with a series of rewards and punishments. The stimuli were drawings consisting of an irregular line running vertically through a circle so that each half of the circle could be seen as the profile of a face. The two profiles were then cut apart and presented separately. In a training series, each time one profile was shown, a reward (a small sum of money) followed; after the other profile, a punishment (loss of money) followed. In a later test session, the two profiles were rejoined to again form a circle divided by an irregular line, which was now presented to subjects in very brief tachistoscopic flashes. The subjects showed a marked tendency to attentionally integrate ("to see") only the profile that had been associated with reward. Presumably, the conditions of the experiment had set up a directive affective reaction in the attentional-integration process.

In other experiments, brief presentations of emotion-generating stimuli at exposure intervals too brief for complete perceptual identification would still provoke an emotional reaction that can be detected through some physiological response pattern. McCleary and Lazarus (1950) demonstrated this phenomen with emotionally conditioned nonsense syllables as stimuli. Five of the meaningless letter combinations were previously associated with a disturbing emotional condition (one-second presentations accompanied by an electric shock). A reliable indicator of emotional reactions is an increase in the electrical conductivity of the skin—the galvanic skin response. After a series of shock-accompanied presentations, the galvanic response became conditioned to the five nonsense syllables so as to occur in their presence regardless of the presence or absence of shock. In a subsequent test the syllables appeared individually in brief tachistoscopic exposures, ranging from a few milliseconds up to durations necessary for correct identi-fication. Galvanic skin responses were measured between the presentation of each stimulus and the subject's report of what he saw. The skin responses reappeared following the syllables previously associated with pain, even when the presentations were not long enough to permit full perceptual identification.

To restate, with events that are too brief for their full microgenetic development in rapid attentional integration, a preliminary emotional reaction is still set off as part of the initial stage of perceptual identification.

Controversies over emotional influences. Observations such as these touched off considerable controversy, for they made human experience seem much more vulnerable to the whims of emotion than some theorists would have supposed. And then there was a prolonged controversy over the methodologies and interpretations of these experiments. As a result, interest in the whole area of research faltered. The directive state research had also suffered from a lack of any strong or consistent notion of cognitive processes; in general, there were confusions concerning the location of internal control processes, problematical distinctions between perceptual processes and response process, and uncertainties about the nature of selective attention.

However, with advances in the study of human information processing and with the development of general descriptions of central cognitive processes, a basis for explaining emotional, or directive-state, influences upon immediate cognition became available. Reviews by Dixon (1971) and Erdelyi (1974) were significant first steps in bringing these two areas together. Erdelyi, in particular, reviewed the earlier controversies and showed how they have been discounted by subsequent discoveries of the microgenetic cognitive processes and of characteristics of selective attention.

Much of the controversy had revolved around a claimed logical paradox: If perceptual repression is truly perceptual, then how can the perceiver selectively defend himself against a particular stimulus (that is, prevent his own perception of it) unless he first perceives it? This paradox lost its force with the delineation of several components in the central control process of cognition. Impressions may reach consciousness at the level of buffer storage but not be integrated further. Or, if two events are both part of one rapid attentional integration, one may be aborted (or masked) in favor of the other. Or, impressions may reach storage in short-term memory but not be refocused and transferred to permanent memory, and may thereby be lost. Chapters 3, 4, and 5 illustrated these occurrences in numerous ways. In brief, perception or cognition is not an all-or-none process and cannot be described as a single response.

Further examples. Consider now an enhancement effect that appears in dichotic listening situations—situations in which two independent auditory inputs are presented, one to each ear. Previously shock-associated words presented to the nonattending ear will "capture" attention (Corteen and Wood, 1972). Or, if a listener's name should occur in the nonattended channel, it will "enter consciousness" significantly more than other words of no special importance (Moray, 1959). The "cocktail-party phenomenon" is likely a familiar instance of this finding. In a room crowded with several groups of conversing people, a person's own name, when uttered in a separate, unattended conversation, may suddenly leap into his or her awareness.

Strong enhancement of one event is likely to entail repression of others. The item of a personal or high-priority nature in a sequence of rapid inputs can cause a lessened awareness of neighboring items. (This has been called "induced amnesia," "cognitive masking," "repression," and "momentary forgetting.") Rehearsal and consolidation processes are apparently monopolized here by the high-priority event (Saufley and Winograd, 1970; Schulz, 1971; Tulving, 1969). Such occurrences were first mentioned above in Chapter 5 in the section on decay of impressions.

To study momentary forgetting, Luborsky (1973) searched through hours of tape recordings of psychiatric interviews for instances in which patients paused and then said, "I forgot what I was going to say" (or some synonymous phrase). Luborsky then analyzed the dialogue surrounding each of these points of momentary forgetting. Every 50-word segment in the preceding and following 500 words was rated by an independent judge according to a rating form concerning patterns in the patients' utterances. Some ratings assessed "attentional difficulties" (also called "cognitive disturbances"); these were ratings of the patient's uncertainty about thoughts, unclarity or confusion in expressing thoughts, and similar difficulties. All ratings were then converted to a numerical score for each 50-word segment. The level of attentional difficulty was found to increase rapidly just prior to the instant of momentary forgetting (see Figure 24). Other ratings indicated a similar prior increase in content that was personally difficult for the patient—in particular, content that included references to problematical relationships between patient and psychiatrist. Thus, repression does not necessarily implicate memory per se, but rather can be a central control effect, a distraction of attention (as has been argued by Klein, 1967).

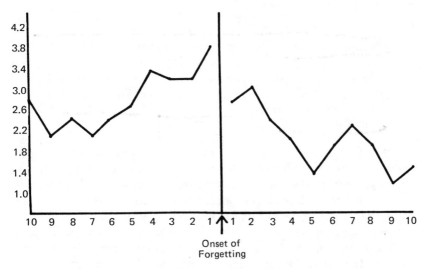

Figure 24. Levels of cognitive disturbance (attentional difficulty) before and after momentary forgetting. Averages are for 10 individuals. (Reprinted by permission from *Psychoanalytic Research*, Chapter 2, by L. Luborsky. Copyright 1973 by International Universities Press, Inc.)

CONCLUSIONS

Emotional experience appears to arise from elementary reactions of the central integrative processes in the course of their construction and integration of consciousness. In this way, emotion constitutes a primitive core in cognitive operations. It augments and directs attentional process-es. It influences the retrieval of memories, the structuring of thoughts, and the formation of perceptions. It may depress certain types of experience, and it may heighten others.

According to certain evolutionary viewpoints, all forms of organized experience are thought to have split off from, or developed out of, primitive emotional reactions. The remaining emotional core helps integrate our diverse experiences and lends them some continuity. Hence, different sensations, thoughts, and memories may be linked together because they share common "affective tones."

Earlier in this chapter, two summary generalizations were advanced to help organize the large body of data on emotional experience. Those generalizations are again as follows:

Emotion arises from reactions of the rapid-attentional integration process in the course of its integrations of immediate experience.

There are at least three systems (or dimensions) of fundamental reaction that form emotional experience. These have been called, among other terms, "the hedonic," "the arousal," and "the attentiveness" systems.

Most of the descriptions in this chapter of repression and enhancement phenomena could just as well have been included in the chapter on cognitive control, the final chapter of this text. Emotional qualities in cognition—the elementary affective reactions of attentional integrations—give rise to actions of self-control, or to feelings of volition, will, and purpose, which in turn support longer temporal integrations of human experience. Before considering cognitive control, the text now turns to the issue of longer temporal integrations in general.

8

LONGER TEMPORAL INTEGRATIONS

The central control processes of consciousness develop habitual patterns of integrating experience and action. In some cases these patterns develop rapidly; in others they develop over the lifetime of the individual. The microgenetic components of cognition (described in Part II) define the psychological present—the integrative capacities of, and the limitations on, the flux of immediate experience. The longer temporal integrations (described in this chapter) are habits that develop in the central nervous system with recurring experiences and actions over any time span.

In Figure 2, p. 19, longer temporal integration is shown as a separate aspect of psychological function—namely, as *long-term memory*. Other more specialized topics concerning this aspect of cognitive functioning include: "concepts," "schemata," "images," "abstractions," "plans," "expectancies," "habituation," "perceptual constancies," "attentional sets," and "pattern recognition." All refer to a longer integration of experience, one that brings continuity to human actions.

GENERAL PRINCIPLES

Longer integrations of experience are another form of the summation of temporally separate impressions. At any given moment, these summations are reflected as unitary reaction patterns or, more specifically, as stereotyped patterns in the sense that they are persistent, organized, and often automatic ways of perceiving, thinking, feeling, and remembering. Longer integrations are likely an integral part of, or at least a context for, almost every instance of thought, memory, perception, and emotion. And so the diagrammatic separation of long-term memory in Figure 2 may be too extreme. That is, immediate attention is itself continually influenced by and composed of habitual patterns and can thus reflect summations of experience that trace well back into an individual's history. This was implied in many observations in previous chapters. One such example was described in Chapter 3, in the section on apparent movement: the movement illusion arising from intermittent stimuli is determined partly by prior knowledge of those stimuli; the motion of the figure of a runner, for example, is integrated more readily than the motion of an abstract stimulus.

The conversion of a sequence of experiences and memories into a simultaneity yields images, concepts, schemata, and symbols—items of experience that can be dealt with at once as unitary experiences themselves. This results in an enormous savings in time and attention, for each previous related experience need not be recalled individually. "Perceptual constancies" are an example of this savings: a "new" perception generally arises by means of its relation to some preexisting schema of cognitive activity, not by an exact matching with previous, individual perceptions.

Longer temporal integrations may develop from what are at first deliberate, selective summations of experience—the bringing together of separate thoughts, memories, and perceptions at one moment, a moment at which the short-term-memory capacity holds them simultaneously and thereby permits further fusions and integrations by attention. The summation that results is just that aspect of attentional integrative activity that is common to each of the separate experiences. And when an integrative activity becomes habitual, it may become functionally autonomous—that is, become a concept, symbol, schema, or rule that is largely independent of the original sensory or memory patterns that initiated it. Then this integrative action may enter into relations with, or influence the course of, other mental formations, which may occur in the learning of a complex principle of physics or in the simple assumption that the object one is looking at is an apple.

The constructivist view. Well-established patterns of attentional activity are, then, as the above discussion implies, the perceiver's, thinker's, or rememberer's contribution to the flux of events that form his experience. This implication appears in a long tradition of psychological analysis that finds the structure of experience to be fundamentally the creation of the perceiver (Wundt, 1896; Bartlett, 1932; Bruner, Goodnow, and Austin, 1956; Neisser, 1967). Shepard summarizes some of this analysis as follows: "...the dependence of perception upon some internally applied constraints appears to be an unavoidable implication of behavioral experiments (Bower, 1966, 1967; Fantz, 1965; Ganz and Wilson, 1967; Hebb, 1937), physiological evidence (Hubel and Wiesel, 1963, 1968), and logical considerations (Minsky, 1961; Shepard, 1964)" (1975, p. 115). It seems clear, in much of this work, that we make use of well-established nervous system schemata for the generation of experience. The working of these schemata can be inferred when, for example, we see bizarre human faces in pansy flowers or the profile of an elderly man in the quarter moon.

Yet even to perceive the pansy as a flower, or the moon as a moon, we must surely rely on some established perceptual schemata. For logically, it is only when sensory input is organized and elaborated by an internal integrative pattern that a percept, image, memory, or idea can be recognized at all.

The nativist view. If an act of assimilation to a preexisting internal pattern is necessary to perception, then even if most of our prior internal representations and schemata are the product of learning, the infant must be equipped with some inborn predispositions upon which perceptual and memory development can begin. Piaget's developmental psychology is largely the investigation of how such schemata are progressively elaborated and extended through maturational stages (cf. Flavell, 1963). Life starts, according to Piaget's studies, with innate sensory-motor schemata that show themselves immediately as stereotyped behavior in the newborn—looking, grasping, sucking, smiling, frowning, and so on. With the assimilation of experience, these inborn schemata evolve and elaborate, and in turn the ability to perceive, to remember, and to think grows apace.

The status of language. A claim is often made by social scientists that language is the distinguishing characteristic of humans, and that language has brought about the greater powers of human thought and mental life in general. This assertion may be somewhat superficial. Having investigated human cognitive processes, we can see that human language is but one reflection of the special characteristics of human mental processes, and that what might have appeared to be unique or special skills for language use are actually the same skills that are found in all manner of human activity. Humans can also produce more sophisticated and enormously more varied forms of music than can other animals; humans establish more elaborate kinship systems; the architecture of human dwellings is infinitely more varied; the human capacity for artistic expression is not found in other species. These are not reflections of linguistic capacity. They are all reflections of a more general, underlying capacity.

Some theorists have claimed that language appeared first and that other cognitive skills were derived from it. Other theorists claimed that tool use appeared first and other skills followed. Still other theorists claimed that artistic expression came first. But many psychologists, including Gregory (1970), Lenneberg (1969), and Shepard (1975), now argue that all these skills were made possible at the same time by the development of the human brain and structural changes within it, which led to the superior integrative capabilities of the central cognitive processes. That superiority, as now seems likely, is the capacity to summarize, to categorize, and to schematize experience and action, as described above. We must look further, then, into what special benefits that superiority bestows.

Automatization. Once any pattern of experience becomes a well-established schema, attentional effort is freed, to varying degrees, from the mechanics of integration that were originally applied to that pattern. This move toward automatization of mental processes is fundamental for any developed cognitive capacity. If an act did not become easier and even automatic after being performed many times, if careful attention to details continued to be necessary for the performance of the act, the entire activity of a lifetime might well be confined to one or two deeds. No mental development or progress could take place. The tying of a shoelace or the adding of a few numbers would, on each occasion, demand as much attention of an adult as it would of the inexperienced child.

Automaticity bears a certain kinship to *habituation*, the lessening or the "streamlining" of reactions when stimulating conditions are frequently repeated. Habituation is a biological observation that is reflected in all forms of life—from humans to protozoa. Whether the reactions are those of an individual learning to read written language or those of Pavlov's dog in the conditioning experiment, with time and experience, reaction patterns become progressively more efficient, parsimonious, and simplified. Harris (1943) and Thompson and Spencer (1966) point out—and this is important to note—that habituation is not the same as fatigue in effector responses, nor is it the same as receptor adaptation. In habituation, a process does not disappear, but rather becomes simplified and more automatic. Schwartz and Schiller describe the range of developed automatizations in humans as follows:

> Motor automatization is exemplified by such simple skills as walking and hand-eye coordination, and by the more complex achievements of the athlete, the artist, and the industrial worker (see Broadbent, 1958). Automatization of thought is exemplified by the effortless use of grammatical structure in everyday speech and by the ability to perform arithmetic computations (Rapaport, 1957). Automatization of perception is exemplified by general perceptual styles (Gardner, et al., 1959) and by the dulling of one's ordinary perceptual world, with the consequent desire for new experience, be it in the form of a vacation or a hallucinogenic drug (Deikman, 1963). (1970, p. 84)

The Würzburg observations. Shortly after the turn of the century, a group of psychologists at Würzburg University led by Külpe called attention to the significance of automatization in the highest mental processes. Their work began with a controversy over the question of imageless thought: with familiar mental activity, such as solving familiar problems or answering familiar questions, mental content or imagery often seems to drop away, and, paradoxically, thinking then occurs automatically, "without content."

The Würzburgers observed automaticities in a variety of mental performances, but most of these observations were introspective and naturalistic rather than truly experimental. Among the Würzburgers, Ach (1905) observed the introspections of problem solvers and pointed out that people are able to use the knowledge necessary for reaching a conclusion without bringing that knowledge to full consciousness. Perhaps, he suggested, some sensation or image comes to consciousness and stands as a symbol for a large range of other mental habits or material. He concluded, "We designate this recession of the content of awareness as the *automatization* of the process" (1905; translated by Rapaport, 1951, p. 25). He goes on to argue that most of our mental life is automatically predisposed, adjusted, or set to receive certain impressions.

In another Würzburg study, Messer (1906) made similar observations and concluded that the actual psychological processes involved in an explicitly formulated thought may run their course in all sorts of abbreviated forms, telescoping into one another. And further, according to Messer, "This relief of consciousness, the gradual mechanizing by practice of processes that at first demanded effort of attention and consideration from various points of view, is one of the most firmly established results of psychology" (1906, translated by Titchener, 1909, pp. 124-25).

Titchener summarized Wundt's earlier and very similar observations on automaticity as follows:

> At this point reduction sets in; choice and deliberation give way to secondary impulses, and active attention gives way to secondary passive attention. The ground is thus cleared for further growth; new formations appear in the state of active attention, to be simplified in their turn, and the cycle recurs, with constant alternation of habit and acquisition. . . . (1908, p. 314)

The value of automatization. The mental automatism—the well-established concept, abstraction, schema, or symbol—is a central integration that occurs with a minimum of attentional effort or activity. It is a cognitive activity that had, at some earlier time, been more effortful and painstaking, and that had likely involved repetition, refocusing, or rehearsal. But later, attentional activity became better organized and more efficient in the integration of the recurring pattern of experience.

Thus, automatization brings about a decrease in the information, the time, and the effort necessary to construct a cognitive event or action; the result is that awareness of that event is progressively reduced. Eventually, a particular pattern of integration may require only a "blip" of attentional activity in order to be reconstructed. Or, perhaps, habituated schemata and cognitive-control programs can operate from short-term memory and require only occasional attentional monitoring.

We may now ask whether automatization ever frees attentional capacity completely. At present there is little certain data on which to answer this question. Kolers (1975), however, argues that the skilled performance does not consist of the same actions or integrations as the unskilled performance; it is not merely a more rapid, less attentive performance but a different kind of performance. More specifically, the skilled performance is better organized, so that attention is deployed differently and more efficiently.

In any case, with automatization the attentional capacity is freer to integrate newly developed skills with other actions. Thus, it becomes possible for a skilled organist to play one keyboard with the right hand, another with the left, and yet another with the feet. In our daily actions and cognitions, we all perform comparable feats. Consider driving a car and carrying on a conversation at the same time. Or, at a more abstract level, consider the mathematician who is able to solve difficult problems because he has automatized subsystems of algebra and does not have to think them out in detail to employ them.

Because human experience and action is restrained at every turn by limited capacities, the development of cognitive automaticity has enormous value. The greater significance of all this, the general benefits that this superior ability to develop automatic schemata bestows on humankind, is that we become more and more able to attend to the ends of our actions rather than solely to their means. Such a course of progress in human affairs once led the philosopher Whitehead to remark, "Civilization advances to the degree that we can perform important processes without thinking about them."

Liabilities of automatization. Automaticity results in a more stereotyped performance. Stereotyped action and thought is, of course, a double-edged sword: its value for psychological performance can always turn into a liability. This happens, for instance, when old linguistic habits, being well established, are a hindrance to the learning of a new language. Similarly, efficiency-enhancing automaticities are potential liabilities in all spheres of human experience and action. Habitual emotional reactions may become maladaptive, but being highly automatized they are very difficult to change.

The ability to "de-automatize" is the special hallmark of the creative individual who can break through established patterns of thought. Random word-association, hypnosis, meditation, and even sensory deprivation are techniques that people have employed to overcome the barrier of heavily automatized dispositions. These are all techniques that deflect attention from its habitual course.

Research on learning and memory. The way in which longer temporal integrations develop is a question that forms a large part of the research on learning and memory. That research has become so voluminous that it can scarcely be reviewed in any single volume; it is clearly beyond the scope of this one. We find, however, that learning theories are, in most cases, based on one or a very few principles, such as "repetition," "contiguity," "drive reduction," "reward," "feedback," and "response consequences that determine the likelihood of response recurrence." With the growth of modern cognitive psychology, the process of attention has emerged as another principle, sometimes as the fundamental principle, underlying learning (cf. Estes, 1970; Kimble and Perlmutter, 1970; Levine, 1971; Restle, 1962; Zeaman and House, 1963). This suggests that whoever controls and manipulates attention will also control learning. Repetition, contiguity, drive reduction, and post-response contingencies may all determine learning to the degree that they influence the direction of attention.

If this is so, one old and persistent problem of learning research, that of incidental or latent learning as a by-product of pure observation, is easily accounted for. When a human, a pigeon, or a rat learns a

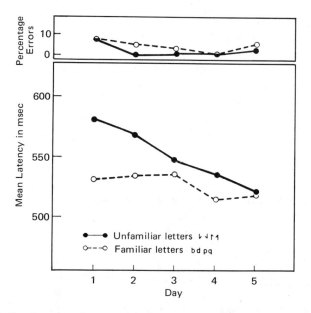

Figure 25. Development of automaticity in a visual-recognition task. The percentage of errors and the average latency times of matching responses for unfamiliar (Ⅴ ↲ ↑ ↲) and familiar (bdpq) letter patterns are shown. Automaticity, as indexed by decreasing recognition-time, continues to develop long after accuracy, as measured by decreasing recognition-errors, is at its best. Data are from 16 subjects. (From LaBerge and Samuels, 1974, based on data from LaBerge, 1973; reprinted by permission of Academic Press, Inc.)

response simply by observing another learner or by observing a situation, theorists have been forced to postulate, *post hoc,* some incipient response, secondary reward, or covert feedback that had escaped their experimental detection. There may be, however, only the action of selective attention, which integrates impressions with the established schemata of the organism. In other learning experiments, attention is provoked and directed by reward, stimulus frequency, or some other attention-getting event.

Learning, however, is not necessarily synonymous with automaticity. Learning may proceed to a level of perfect accuracy of response, and thereby appear to be a completed and stabilized process—but then automaticity continues to develop. Thus, two individuals may perform a learned task with equal accuracy, yet performance may be more automatized in one than in the other. Broverman and his associates (1966) have shown this to occur when one individual is less susceptible to distraction during a certain performance, is better coordinated in that performance, or is faster in reaction times for that performance. LaBerge (1973) and LaBerge and Samuels (1974) showed how reaction time continues to improve well after a criterion of maximum accuracy in a simple task of visual recognition has been reached (see Figure 25).

Summary generalizations. We can now summarize some of the general aspects of longer temporal integrations that will help explain the more specific observations that follow.

> Longer temporal integrations are fusions or extrapolations of similarities in attentional patterns that underlie separate experiences when those experiences are brought together in short-term memory.
>
> When an attentional pattern is repeated often, it can become automatized so as to require little effort—thereby freeing attentional capacity and facilitating assimilation of new experience.

OBSERVATIONS

The following five areas of psychological inquiry each constitute a broad aspect of longer temporal integration:

1. image formation
2. skilled performance

3. concepts and schemata
4. recognition
5. the self-concept

Image Formation

Imagery is cited first in this chapter because it has been held, in some quarters, to be especially fundamental to all cognitive activity. Arieti, for example, writes:

> Image formation is actually the basis for all higher mental processes. It enables the human being not only to recall what is not present, but to retain an affective disposition for the absent object. (1970, p. 138)

Neural processes associated with imagery tell us very little about the nature of any specific image. In Shepard's words:

> No amount of knowledge about the neural structure that, when activated, represents a certain external object can itself tell us which external object that may be. (1975, p. 92)

It is quite likely, as Konorski (1967) points out, that the neural processes associated with any given image are distributed quite widely throughout the tissues of the brain. When I say I see a triangle, or dream of a triangle, I am saying that what is going on in my brain has something in common with a cumulative, selective integration of a sequence of past experiences.

A clear example of this cumulative integration is the formation of images of objects through the sense of touch. Katz (1925), Révész (1950), and Gibson (1962) have described the *hand*, in this regard, as an exploratory sense organ. The identification of objects through touch depends on an exploratory sequence of touches that provides a series of mental impressions, which are integrated into a simultaneous internal representation (image). This act is one of transforming sequence into simultaneity.

Enduring schemata. Gibson has argued, however, that any explanation of this perceptual image as the mere summation of sensations fails to take account of the purposive character of the exploratory movement. The movements of the fingers in tactual perception, like the movements of eyes during visual perception, are not random. They follow a strategy, so to speak, and are directed systematically. Whenever a person explores any external event, some sense organ is under the direction of focal attention and is thereby adjusted continuously to register now this piece of information, now another, in order to verify a relationship or feature as part of a developing internal representation. Perceptual scanning is likely to be less systematic only when there is no expectation at all (or no prior schema) of what an object is.

But if always based on some prior schema, image formation would never be unsystematic. Kahneman observed this in his investigations of relations between eye movements and internal representations:

> Looking behavior is never random. When one's activities require the intake of visual information, the movements of the eye adjust to that function. In the absence of a specific task set, the control of fixation is handled by enduring dispositions and standard routines of "spontaneous looking." These routines, many of which are probably innate, tend to select stimuli that are ecologically likely to be significant. (1973, p. 51)

External motor activity, however, is by no means a perfect reflection of internal attentional activity. For instance, a person may look directly at one object while attending to another on the periphery of vision (Fraisse, Ehrlich, and Vurpillot, 1956; Grindley and Townsend, 1968).

The eyes, nevertheless, offer a good reflection of cognitive activity. Consider a study by Furst (1971), who recorded on film the eye movements of subjects who viewed photographs over a series of brief viewing sessions. As the sessions progressed, the rate and number of fixations habituated and became stereotyped, and the spatial distribution of fixations became very regular. This suggests that familiarity with the pictures was accompanied by the development of a perceptual schema that controlled the "looking behavior."

Like tactile images, visual images derive from a succession of stimulations. It is probably rare that a visual perception, in everyday experience, is based on only one retinal stimulation; more often, it is the result of a succession of retinal images being integrated into one impression. Lashley (1954) described how our visual perception of objects derives from a succession of scanning movements, the succession of retinal images being translated (or temporally integrated) into a simultaneous impression of a single form. Neisser added that "the individual 'snapshots' are remembered only in the way that the words of a sentence are remembered when you can recollect nothing but its meaning: they have contributed to something which endures" (1967, p. 140).

One very general and automatized internal representation occurs in what Head and Holmes (1911) and Paul (1967) have described as "the postural image" and others have discussed as "the body image." Through perceptual alterations in position we are always building up a postural schema of ourselves which likely undergoes constant change and development. Every new position or movement is recorded on this plastic model. Head (1920) inferred a "unified schema"—a continually evolving standard at a cortical level of representation, against which bodily movements are gauged. This integrative activity of the cortex brings every new set of postural sensations into relation with the central postural schema.

Such body-image schemata will often stay intact long after a limb has been amputated—hence, the phenomenon of the "phantom limb" that lingers long after amputation and that can even be localized in space. (This phenomenon was mentioned in Chapter 7, in the section on the experience of pain.) Head (1920) reported a case of phantom limb in which the patient later suffered cortical damage that destroyed his postural schema. The phantom limb then disappeared completely, but then accurate voluntary movement disappeared also.

Although mental imagery is usually discussed in terms of one sensory modality at a time (usually either visual, kinesthetic, or auditory), a given internal representation might be provoked by any variety of sensory input. With this in mind, Michotte and co-workers (1962) showed that mental imagery is often not uniquely identified with any one sensory mode. An object, for instance, is localized in space whether seen, touched, or heard. A sentence yields the same impression whether read, heard, or felt via Braille. Michotte and associates demonstrated experimentally that to have an internal representation of an object can mean to be equally prepared to identify that object through tactual sensations and through visual sensations.

Memory images. The above descriptions of imagery have concerned solely the perception of external objects. There is another sense in which the term imagery is widely used—that of memory imagery, which represents events or objects not present in the immediate environment. Oswald describes what may be a familiar situation in which this imagery arises:

> When we are awake we may become bored, our "attention
> wanders," we begin to day-dream, we may become drowsy

and lose contact with reality. We may then experience dream fragments or dream sequences in light sleep, going through vivid experiences, including visual and auditory experiences, in a world of fantasy, while often at the same time talking inwardly to ourselves with bizarre speech constructions. (1962, p. 66)

Consider a more extreme condition, perhaps related to the above one of boredom, that is also a rich source of such imagery—the condition of severe sensory deprivation (first described by Bexton, Heron, and Scott, 1954). In studies of this condition, volunteers are denied sensory stimulation to as great a degree as possible by being placed in special chambers in which all manner of stimulation is eliminated. Not only do individuals eventually begin to hallucinate, but their imagery can become extremely bizarre. If we assume a parsimonious system of cognitive processes, the same central processes should be at work in all types of imagery.

It is of little surprise to find that memory imagery can interfere with ordinary perceptions of external objects. Perky (1910) and Segal and Gordon (1969) showed how the ability to detect an external event can be diminished when individuals are engaged in forming independent internal imagery. In their demonstrations, observers were asked to form a mental picture of some object—say, an apple. Simultaneously, a faint visual stimulus was shown on a projection screen. The wholly internal image, if strongly formed, would prevent the detection of the ordinarily perceptible external stimulus. Such a finding should be rather familiar to the habitual daydreamer. It should even be fairly obvious to others not so inclined. Consider that a person engaged in trying to recall where he last placed his wallet may not "see" at all the picture on a television screen, even though his eyes are pointed directly at it.

Skilled Performance

The study of performance skill in human behavior has evolved into a specialized and highly technical area of research (compare the reviews by Welford, 1968; Pew, 1974; and Schmidt, 1975). The present section will offer only a few general observations from this research that are pertinent in the present context.

The term *skill* usually refers to one's level of proficiency in some performance activity. A characteristic of any such performance, whether piano playing, driving an automobile, or typing, is *automaticity,* which, to varying degrees, frees attention so that it can focus on performance goals while the skilled act is in progress. As a function of practice, automatic schemata are increasingly built up, enabling us to focus attention on higher-level goals and larger segments of action.

Most skill-acquisition research concerns sensory-motor performance and the coordination and timing of body movement. Bartlett (1958) and Fitts (1964) have pointed out, however, that many findings from skill research are general for any form of human activity, including patterns of abstract thought, and that motor skills and other cognitive skills should not be treated as separate topics. The investigations that began the tradition of skill research were those of Bryan and Harter (1899) on the progressive development of automaticities in the learning of telegraphic code.

Automaticity rarely appears in an all-or-none fashion. According to Fitts:

> As learning progresses, the subroutines [that is, the automatized parts of a skill] become longer, the executive routine or overall strategy is perfected, the stimulus sampling becomes less frequent and the coding more efficient, and different aspects of the activity become integrated or coordinated. (1964, p. 260)

Rather than viewing skilled behavior as a series of responses that lead to some goal, it is more profitable to conceive of it as an information-processing activity guided by some central plan or schema.

Variability in performance. The spatial-temporal organization of fully developed skills is relatively independent of specific sensory or muscular mechanisms. This gives highly developed skills their transferability, another important characteristic of skilled performance. For instance, when we have learned to walk, we can walk up hill or down, over smooth terrain or rough, though the specific foot and leg movements must be somewhat different in each case. It is probably true, according to Schmidt, "that the same response is never made twice when one considers the number of possibilities there are, for example, in shooting a basketball" (1975, p. 230). Language, of course, is a fascinating example of variability in performance. A thought may be expressed in language in a seemingly endless number of ways—through transformations of sentences, the reduction of sentences to clauses, the expansion of sentences, paraphrases, and so on. And when we recall human discourse, we seldom recall the specific words or their arrangement. Rather, we recall the general, underlying schemata which may be expressed in any number of ways. The particular words, syntactic arrangement, and style are matters of large variability.

The question of feedback. Only actions at a preskill level appear to be under the movement-by-movement control of specific stimuli. This type of stimulus control was, however, held for a long time to be the explanation of all instances of skilled behavior. The assumption was that the mechanism for skilled performance is stimulus-response chaining, the essential stimulus being, in the case of motor skill, continuous sensory feedback from the muscles and joints.

Initial support for this explanation came from an experiment by Mott and Sherrington (1895) performed on monkeys. The kinesthetic feedback was surgically eliminated from a single arm or leg of a monkey by the severing of the nerve tracts for that function. Mott and Sherrington found that the animals lost all fine control necessary for skilled movement in the affected limb. Continuous kinesthetic feedback was thereafter held to be necessary for all skilled motor behavior.

Lashley (1951) questioned that conclusion on logical grounds when he noted that in many highly developed skills, such as piano playing, the action and coordination of successive movements are executed so rapidly as not to leave enough time for the kinesthetic sensations to arise and travel through the necessary neural circuits. Even earlier, Lashley (1917) had reported clinical evidence that movement is centrally controlled. A patient suffering from a gunshot wound in his back had lost all sensation from his lower limbs, but had not lost the efferent nerve pathways that enabled movement. Coordinated walking and other leg capacities were retained!

Taub and Berman (1968) replicated and extended Mott and Sherrington's early investigation and reached a new conclusion. They again found, initially, that the surgical elimination of kinesthetic feedback inhibited a monkey's use of its limb. But then Taub and Berman restrained the remaining good arm with a straightjacket, whereupon the monkey began to use the surgically treated limb for all the same fine-control grasping and climbing movements that a good arm is capable of. This normal motor control, which was exhibited for lengthy stretches of behavior, was still present when visual feedback was cut off—showing that the lost kinesthetic feedback hadn't simply been replaced by visual feedback.

In a simple tracking task in which subjects manually tracked a visual point moving in a sine-wave motion, Magdaleno, Jex, and Johnson (1970) studied the effect of a sudden cutoff of visual feedback. Subjects are, they found, able to stay on course with their tracking movements for several seconds; then misalignments between manual control and target appear and gradually increase. The central-control schema thus seems to be a short-term-memory image that decays gradually if not periodically reinstated.

If continuous feedback is unnecessary for the execution of complex movement patterns, then these patterns must be controlled in the central nervous system by a motor program, plan, or schema. As central control processes, these schemata may be activated by attention but then, when well habituated, may perhaps operate as STM representations requiring only occasional monitoring by attention. In the case of motor skills, these are schemata for sending impulses from the central nervous system to muscle systems and for controlling the sequence, timing, and force of the resulting movements.

Skill acquisition. The acquisition of skills obviously demands much feedback and, in the initial stages, requires close attention to individual movements. Only as a result of close attention does one's rapid attentional control become routine, highly reduced, and eventually shifted to another level, perhaps short-term memory. This achievement allows us to talk, think, and use our hands while driving a car or walking. However, if we should begin to pay close attention to our individual walking or driving movements, not only will our ability to carry on a conversation simultaneously be reduced, but the walking and driving movements themselves are likely to lose some of their smoothness and coordination. For some deautomatization has then occurred.

Practice and repetition are obviously involved in the development of automaticity. If however, complex skills are controlled by central schemata, and if skill acquisition is essentially the establishment of such schemata, then perhaps there is a variety of ways to acquire a skill. For instance, a skill may be acquired hereditarily as is the song of some birds. Keele suggests another alternative:

> Perhaps, in learning some skills, the best approach is to *not* practice at all in early stages of development, or perhaps to practice only minimally.... it may be more fruitful to watch, listen to, or passively move with a model for extensive periods of time until the model becomes firmly fixed in memory. Then one can begin to practice movements and compare one's own performance to the internalized model. (1973, p. 131)

In support of this proposition Keele cited several examples from animal behavior, but more interesting in the present context is an example from human behavior—Pronko's (1969) description of the Suzuki method of teaching children to play the violin. With this approach, parents select a single piece of music and play it to their child every day, beginning soon after birth. When some weeks or months have passed, an infant will recognize the selection. Recognition is reflected in certain infant behavior patterns—generally reactions of relaxation and calming. In order for this recognition to occur, a model or schema of the music must be developing within the infant. When this has clearly occurred for one piece of music, a second piece is selected and again played repeatedly to the point of recognition. After several musical schemata are thereby established in the child, and when the child is old enough to have sufficient control over limbs and fingers, he or she is given a violin and begins lessons in playing the same music. The child can now, presumably, compare the produced sounds with an established internal musical schema and so can more easily make corrections in the sound-producing movements. The results of this procedure, as judged by musical and psychological investigators, is astoundingly successful.

✓Concepts and Schemata

Most of this chapter and some of the next chapter is concerned with concepts. This section looks further into the principle that concepts (or cognitive schemata) are active processes rather than object-like items.

Certain experiences can be described as representations of some concept because they share a constructive schema in their genesis as percepts, memories, or thoughts, as was noted in the generalizations at the beginning of this chapter. But studies of human concepts are often concerned with the analysis of the formal structures of concepts in order to list and categorize different types of concepts. Such an analysis, however, does not address the process of cognition—that is, the question of how concepts are developed, perceived, and used by the unique capacities of the human mental process.

A concept is often defined, though not necessarily correctly, as a collection of objects sharing a common attribute or several common attributes. An attribute may be a simple stimulus quality, a relation among parts, a function to which the objects may be put to use—indeed, anything we might dream up. And therein lies the criticism of this definition: a concept is not, in fact, a collection of objects; it is a psychological event, a mental process. And so concepts are not always found readymade; they are usually the constructive achievement, or invention, of the perceiver or the thinker.

In the associationist tradition of psychological theory, concepts were often described as some form of composite perception. The classic example of this is Galton's (1879) explanation of concepts by analogy to a composite photograph—a series of multiple exposures on a single film that preserves, in a composite image, only the most common features of the several objects photographed. An example of such a photograph is the composite face that represents all members of a family: the commonalities are intensified and the unique features of each individual are canceled out. Unfortunately this is a very fanciful analogy. Consider attempting to capture the generalized image of all triangles in a multiple-exposure photograph of all manner of triangles. Obviously, one would obtain only a blur—no image at all.

The true problem with this analogy is that it refers to a wholly passive process—the receptive medium of a plate of film. Concept formation, on the contrary, is an active and creative process. When a pattern of attentional integration becomes well established, we could say that the attentional actions that generate the impression of, say, a triangle conform to "generative rules" common to all triangles. ("Rules" here means a pattern of integration that specifies three-sided figures.) Such a stereotyped attentional pattern of integrating experience is a concept. And because it is highly automatic, it may lead us to see triangles when in reality no triangle is present—as in a dream, a hallucination, or a simple misperception.

As recurring patterns of attentional integration develop and become automatized, they form tools that simplify the burdens of thought and memory because they are summations of extended ranges of experience. A concept may stand for a potentially infinite variety of particular events—past, present, and future. In essence, it makes available simultaneously what would otherwise be available to experience only as a succession of unique impressions.

Some initial schema must always be invented, dreamed up, or guessed before features or instances of a concept can be perceived. These constructive actions have been examined by Bruner and associates (1956) in their studies of problem solving, which will be described in the next chapter. Logically, one could not first perceive defining attributes and then infer a concept from them, because there must be some criterion that specifies a defining attribute before it can be perceived as such. One must first have an hypothesis (a concept) directing attentional integration in order to be able to perceive at all.

Consider this introspective example: You see a dark shadow moving slowly under a chair in a dimly lit room. Given the lighting conditions, it is difficult to determine what, if anything, is there. While you stare at the meaningless shape, there comes from the same direction the auditory stimulus "meow." As anyone who has studied the perception of ambiguous stimuli would expect, the concept "cat" is now activated, and a highly automated integrational schema comes into play as a result. A pair of eyes, a furry coat, whiskers, and a tail—some or all might be "seen" suddenly, as an instance of this familiar concept. The same stimulus input (the shadow) was neither more nor less present earlier, but at that time there was no attentional strategy for organizing and integrating it in the above way. And all this might happen even when there is no cat present at all—only a moving shadow!

Knowledge. Highly automatized schemata are not tied to any particular event or stimulus but are generalized actions of attentional synthesis and integration. When cognitions have this independence, they can arise in almost any context. We speak of such cognitions as *knowledge.* Knowledge is traditionally described in terms of conscious content, such as semantic categories and long-term-memory contents. In the study of cognitive processes, however, this approach can lead to the fallacy of misplaced concreteness— the treatment of a process as though it were an object. In human performance, we find that yesterday's experiences are gone, never to return; all we have are processes and skills for generating similar experiences and actions.

Where, for instance, are a batter's home runs when he is not hitting them, and where is your concept "dog" or "triangle" when you are not thinking them? When the batter is eating dinner he is not carrying home runs with him; rather, he is carrying a home-run-hitting skill, which goes unexercised during dinner. The same may be said of your skill to recognize a triangle or a dog. It is not a triangle or a dog that is stored in the brain and carried around that makes recognition of those objects possible; rather, it is the skill to generate anew the experiencing of these objects.

Kolers summarizes this dynamic process of memory and recognition as follows:

> There is no deposit of information in some memory bank or store that is matched or referred to by a later encounter. Rather, the nervous system in its encounters with stimuli acquires and uses skills in encoding them; it does so by engaging in a "dialogue" with the stimuli of such a kind that repeated encounters modify the encoding operations. Memory then is not traces that are matched to a stimulus (or vice versa) but

procedures, operations, ways of encoding the stimulus that are used, and these change as a function of encounters with the stimuli. (1975, p. 700)

Semantic satiation. Meaningful symbols are generally linked to some automatized cognitive activity; when that bond is broken, meaning is lost, and a symbol becomes mere noise or random configurations. This can be shown in an experimental situation that causes attention to drift and wander so that the supportive schemata are lost from short-term memory for varying periods. This effect, often called *semantic or verbal satiation,* appears when a person simply repeats a familiar word or phrase over and over for an extended time; or the word or phrase may be recorded on a closed-loop tape and then played over and over (Messer, 1906; Bassett and Warne, 1919; Lambert and Jakobovits, 1960). If underlying organizational schemata then fade, as they often do in this situation, and if they are not reinstituted by attention, the person will experience a meaningful sound-symbol turning into a meaningless noise. For example, the repetition "canoe, canoe, canoe..." might at some point sound like "nooka-nooka-nooka..." With continued repetition it might even briefly cease to appear as human phonetic sounds at all. These effects are more likely to occur when a person is in a fatigued or drowsy state, a situation in which attention is more likely to wander.

Examples from Bassett and Warne show some of the different types of changes that may take place: The word "world" appeared to change into the word "whirl," and "skill" changed to "skillet." The word "port" appeared to fluctuate in meaning between the referents "harbor" and "wine." Bassett and Warne summarized their findings as follows:

> The experience of the word, when the meaning has dropped away, is generally reported as like that of a nonsense-syllable—a combination of sounds, neither familiar nor unfamiliar, which has no meaning other than that of mere verbal sound. Occasionally also a "feeling of blankness" is reported. In some instances, as a result of elision of the accentuation of a vowel or consonant in rapid pronunciation, words become strange, as if they had never before been experienced. (1919, p. 418)

Other dramatic examples of the fluctuations of conceptual schemata have come from research concerned with perceptual fragmentation. This effect, which is somewhat analogous to verbal satiation, consists of the fluctuations and partial fade-outs of visual experience that occur with the presentation of faint or defocused figures. Perceptual fragmentation also results from stopped retinal images, which presumably cause "fatigue" in the visual system. Under these conditions the role of the schemata that guide attentional construction is exaggerated, because of the poverty of the stimulus input relative to the central-process actions. Any fluctuation in the central process is then much more apparent: parts of objects or whole objects will either disappear or will change in meaning and familiarity (Pritchard, Heron and Hebb, 1960; Pritchard, 1961; McKinney, 1963, 1966).

Such disappearances and fluctuations in perceptual configurations are not random, but reflect schematic patterns. For example, when the image of a human head is the test stimulus in a perceptual-fragmentation experiment, unitary or self-contained parts of the image will fade in and out of experience. (See Figure 26.) The eyes in the figure of a head may disappear, or the hair may disappear, which suggests that there are recognition subschemata (an eye schema, a hair schema, and so on) that are components of the larger perceptual integration (see Pritchard, 1961).

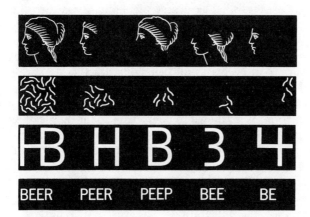

Figure 26. Perceptual fragmentation caused by stopped retinal images. Figures on the left are the stimulus patterns. Subschemata of the perceptual configurations fade in and out as units. (From "Stabilized Images on the Retina," by R. Pritchard. Copyright © 1961 by Scientific American, Inc. All rights reserved.)

Recognition

The preceding discussion of concepts involved the experience of recognition. A classic psychological puzzle is to explain how some experiences have more of a quality of familiarity than others. In the classical associationist tradition of psychological theory, recognition is generally explained as a process of image- or template-matching; the degree of familiarity is the degree to which a sensory input and an internal image or "trace" can be matched. But there is a persistent difficulty with this explanation: the sensory input is infinitely varied. We recognize letters of the alphabet even though different handwritings and printing styles present them in all sorts of shapes. Similar problems crop up in almost any type of object-recognition situation. It is the old problem of Galton's composite photograph: there is no one generic internal image that can represent all instances of a concept.

One attempt to escape this problem has been to reduce the task from whole-image-matching to feature- or attribute-matching. When this is done, only parts or qualities of a stimulus must be recognized, and these, in turn, lead to the recognition of the whole image (see Neisser, 1967). This, however, only pushes the problem of recognition back one level. It is just as much a problem to explain how part of a stimulus is recognized as to explain how the whole stimulus is recognized.

But recognition has also been described as "creative synthesis" or "analysis by synthesis." The degree of familiarity is then the extent to which habitual cognitive patterns are effective in integrating the new experience. It is this habitual integrative schema that forms the concept and that is applied to the constantly varying stimuli for the purpose of identifying a variety of events as all belonging together.

All these explanations still face the problem of the actual response of recognition—the feeling of familiarity. In the preceding chapter, affective reactions were shown to be relevant to the puzzle of recognition. If affects are fundamental reactions in all attentional integrations, then they may always underlie the "feelings of familiarity" that make up recognition (see the section in Chapter 7 on enhancement and repression). Accompanying the more facile integration of current information may be an affective experience of an intensity that corresponds to the ease and fullness of the integration. The early Würzburg psychologists described the sudden and full feeling of familiarity as "the aha-experience." This expression was meant to show that there are simultaneous affects of surprise, arousal, and release when recognition occurs quickly and strongly. In addition to affective reactions that are generated in this way, other unique affective patterns may be associated with each longer temporal integration of experience.

If affectivity plays a central role in recognition, it should not be surprising that relatively new experiences can evoke, by chance, some strong affect that makes these experiences seem familiar. This, of course, happens. It is called the *déjà vu* ("already seen") experience. A beautiful country village may suddenly impress a new visitor, who then tries in vain to recall some former encounter with that scene.

The feeling-of-familiarity reaction, however, may even have a necessarily prior status in attentional integrations underlying acts of recognition—just as affective attitudes may underlie the act of recall (according to Bartlett 1932; see Chapter 7 on enhancement and repression). Piaget has similarly given the following description of the onset of the experience of recognition:

> For recognition to begin, it is enough that the attitude previously adopted with regard to the thing be again set in motion and that nothing in the new perception thwart that process. The impression of satisfaction and familiarity peculiar to recognition could thus stem only from this essential fact of the continuity of a schema: the subject recognizes his own [affective] reaction before he recognizes the object as such. (Piaget, 1937; translation by M. Cook, 1954, pp. 5-6)

The Self-Concept

The identification of one's self, or the attainment of a self-concept, begins early in life and is surely one of the most important concepts that an individual ever forms. Self-preservation is meaningless unless the self is first delineated. The segregation of experiences into those belonging to the self and those that are not part of the self is a necessary one. Without it, we cannot evaluate events as threats to our existence, nor can we make the distinction between private events and public events. Awareness of self is surely central to all acts of self-control. Hands must appear as "my" hands, thoughts must appear as "my" thoughts before I can use them effectively.

The ultimate expression of the development of a living system is to maintain its spatial and temporal integrity and to maintain itself against the flux of the environment. Likely more than anything else, the self-concept contributes to this maintenance and gives a continuity to our experience throughout our waking hours.

In very early childhood, before self-awareness and self-identification have developed, we would expect, and indeed it is so, that attentional processes are not stable, that wholly private experiences (such as dreams) are not distinguished from other experiences, that memories are not readily secured. And, should the developed self-concept be radically changed or lost at any point in life, as sometimes happens, we witness the most extreme changes in human personality, including severe mental pathologies. Accordingly, the person with a highly integrated and stable self-concept may be less dominated than others by external events.

The self-concept must surely be one of the most automatized of all concepts because it begins early in life and is shaped continually throughout life. Koffka writes:

> It is probable that the Ego is first formed in organization which proceeds on the conscious level. But after it has been formed it becomes more and more stable, more and more independent of momentary conditions of organization, so that eventually it is a permanent segregated part of our total psychophysical field. This is, as I see it, the true justification of the various psychoanalytic theories which investigate the particular properties of this permanent Ego, the strains and stresses within it. (1935, p. 330)

In the same tradition as Koffka, Lewin (1935) proposed that the self-concept may be a complex schema consisting of many integrated subsystems. These subsystems are subconcepts that relate to different spheres of one's life but are nevertheless affected by the momentary condition of the whole self-system. Examples of such subconcepts are one's physical appearance, one's social role, and one's intellectual ability.

Head's "postural schema" (or body image), described in the section of this chapter on "Image Formation," may be one such subsystem of the self-concept. Thus, if a person has a poor opinion of himself, or a poorly integrated self-concept, his postural schema may be affected along with his entire self-concept. He may slouch in his posture, or his mannerisms or postural movements may become awkward.

Ego psychology. Obviously, many need systems develop out of the maturing schema of the self-concept because of its large contribution to the maintenance of the integrity and continuity of the organism. Certain events and experiences can then become necessary for the maintenance of the continuity of the schema (see Rapaport, 1957). If an individual's self-concept implies certain superiorities to other individuals, he or she might be geared automatically to seek appropriate recognition from others.

The investigations of the operations of this one human concept have come to occupy a large part of the study of human personality (see Loevinger, 1975). In addition, prominent developments in modern theoretical psychiatry derive from these investigations, which are now known collectively as the school of ego psychology, following Hartmann

(1939). However, the study of personality development has resulted in a voluminous literature that is beyond the scope of this book. The brief description of the self-concept that occupies this section merely serves as one point of connection between our survey of the process of cognition and the large area of study concerned with the self-concept. This connection is now well established in modern cognitive psychology by means of the issues of cognitive control. A good example of the connection is the following statement by Bower:

> Surely one feature distinguishing current-day information-processing theories of memory from the earlier S-R approaches of Hull, Guthrie, Skinner, etc., is this postulate of an executive monitor. That construct is necessitated by our recognition that the person is a complex machine having available several alternative methods for solving particular problems...To continue our harkening back to the Gestalt tradition, Köhler and especially Koffka (1935) assigned a very significant role to the "self" as an overseer or monitor controlling mental processes, assigning it a function very similar to those [of] the executive monitor. (1972, p. 108)

CONCLUSIONS

Longer temporal integrations of thought, perception, memory, or behavior bring constancy and guidance to experience. These integrations are made possible by the same biological capacities that give rise to all immediate experience. They can be understood as extrapolations from separate experiences and remembrances that have, at some time, been brought together in short-term memory. When in STM, separate experiences can be scanned together, fused, or integrated in a momentary focus of attention. Common attentional patterns that underlie separate experiences can then emerge as actions that are independent of the original experiences. As longer temporal integrations, these patterns are the internal creations of the thinker, perceiver, or rememberer, because they are based on the actions of selective attention. Concepts, for instance, are not presented to us—we construct them.

Repeated integrations of sets of experiences become automatized, which means that the amount of attentional effort or activity necessary to reproduce them is lessened. As automatic (or stereotyped) patterns, they become functionally autonomous. We then call them images, constancies, concepts, schemata, abstractions, or rules. A diversity of experiences is summarized or abbreviated in each of these automatized patterns. In this way, attentional capacity is progressively freed to concentrate on other experiences or to develop new experiences.

As an autonomous attentional pattern, a concept permits an infinite variety of behaviors or experiences to be recognized as instances of that specific pattern of attentional integration. The systems of longer temporal integrations that we use in this way in our thoughts and perceptions constitute internal models that represent our understanding of the world and of events.

Automatization of mental processes is of critical value for the growth and development of human knowledge. With the automatization of cognitive actions—so that they may operate without detailed attentional focusings—attention is free to concentrate on the goals rather than the means of performance. Previously complex patterns of attentional activity then become automatic tools in the construction of more complex mental formations. Our ability to learn may thus be limited to the degree that our attention is free and to the degree that it can be directed to the events to be learned.

Earlier in this chapter some generalizations were given that summarize longer temporal integrations. They are again as follows:

Longer temporal integrations are fusions or extrapolations of similarities in attentional patterns that underlie separate experiences when those experiences are brought together in short-term memory.

When an attentional pattern is repeated often, it can become automatized so as to require little effort—thereby freeing attentional capacity and facilitating assimilation of new experience.

In the next, and final, chapter of this text, the description of emotion and of longer temporal integration is extended to the pervasive problem of cognitive control.

9

COGNITIVE CONTROL

The final subject of this text has been an underlying theme throughout the previous chapters. It is the self-regulation of those central processes schematized in Chapter 2. The living organism's control of itself has been called "volition," "will," "intention," "choice," "effort," "self-generated activity," "executive routines," "vigilance," and "attention deployment." These are terms for the central events in mental function that lead to one course of thought, memory, or action rather than to others. But more important, cognitive control maintains the interacting components of cognition on one train of action, recycling one set of perceptions, memories, or motor activity, and cognitive control maintains coherence of thought during acts of making choices and pursuing goals.

Emotion and motivation are traditionally associated with the process of cognitive control. The fluctuations of emotional reactions constitute a motive force that directs the course of thought and action. Hence, cognitive control may always grow from some basis in the affective reaction-system.

GENERAL PRINCIPLES

Thoughts, perceptions, and remembrances are accompanied by innumerable pleasures and pains, excitements and depressions, tensions and relaxations that shape and direct the stream of experience (see Chapter 7). This affective influence surely manipulates attention and leads it in certain directions rather than in others. It is a directive force in the expansion or the constriction, the change or the fixation, of experience and behavior.

Cognitive control has from time to time been avoided by psychological theorists who assume it necessarily implies "free will." The problem here is analogous to psychologists' controversies about mind-body dualism, and it has been equally unproductive. Just as the study of mental processes does not imply acceptance of some nonmaterial mind-stuff, so the acceptance of central regulative processes in living beings by no means implies that organisms are free from natural law, or that their behavior is unpredictable.

Biological fundamentals. Because cognitive control is central to the whole question of the process of cognition, we must turn back to the initial biological and evolutionary fundamentals that were stated in Part I of this text. Cognitive processes are understood in terms of their adaptive function, or in terms of how they abet the organism in its struggle for consistency and survival. In modern biological theory, organisms are conceived as systems that maintain themselves against the flux of energies of the environment.

The biologist Haldane, for example, wrote that "biology must take as its fundamental working hypothesis the assumption that the organic identity of a living organism actively maintains itself in the midst of changing external circumstances" (1922, p. 391). Up to now we have examined this process of maintaining stability against changing events as a process of temporal integration—primarily, an integration of some sequence of present and past events. When we consider cognitive control, however, we must also observe that these integrations can include extrapolations into the future. This is accomplished by imaging, constructing, or synthesizing possible (and impossible) future states and manipulating them as items of consciousness. Such an achievement involves the normal operation of attentional integration, which can construct experiences that may not reflect at all the events actually present in the environment, as we have seen in many situations in previous chapters, and which is surely obvious in everyday experience.

Mandler, who has argued that control cannot be understood without first understanding consciousness, describes the value of these mental manipulations as follows:

> The first, and most widely addressed function of consciousness considers it as a scratch pad for the choice and selection of actions systems. Decisions are made often on the basis of possible outcomes, desirable outcomes, and appropriateness of various actions to environmental demands. Such a description comes close to what is often called "covert trial and error" behavior in the neobehaviorist literature. This function [of consciousness] permits the organism more complex considerations of action-outcome contingencies than does the simple feedback concept of reinforcement, which alters the probability of one or another set of actions. It also permits the consideration of possible actions that the organism has never before performed, thus eliminating the overt testing of possible harmful alternatives. (1975, pp. 243-44)

Indeed, the representation in consciousness of imagined future events has great survival value. It is a skill that any individual would do well to improve upon throughout a lifetime.

These mental processes involve choice and selection from among imagined future states, and they involve the initiation of actions to achieve them. This aspect of cognitive control is dramatically reflected by its extension to the control of the environment. The physical world in which we live today is largely the product of human mental processes. Although our ability to exercise control over the environment is partly limited by the material limits of that environment, it is more fundamentally limited to the degree that human cognitive processes are limited in their own functions.

Consideration of the nature of central cognitive control, however, is logically prior to that of our manipulations of the environment. We shall be more concerned in this chapter with the examination of the control of the central attentional mechanism that operates in perception, thought, and memory. As we have seen in the previous chapter, perception, under-standing, and manipulation of the environment are secondary to those processes of internal attentional control.

Motivational fundamentals. The fundamental biological assumption that the organism maintains itself in the midst of flux has been adapted and elevated to a psychological level by those who have postulated one basic motivational condition underlying mental processes. Goldstein (1940) called this condition "self-actualization." Allport (1955) called it the maintenance of integrity and the enhancing of the capacities of the experiencing organism. Heider (1958) described it as "the achieving of structure," and Festinger (1957) as the avoidance of "cognitive dis-sonance."

If, further, we follow the view that emotion, or affective reaction, is initial and primitive in an evolutionary sense (see Chapter 7), then we may consider emotion as the fundamental mechanism in the maintenance of this organic integrity. Goldstein (1951), who studied the question at some length, speculated that integration of momentary emotional tone gives direction to behavior and thought, and is the source of volition. Emotion, he says, "makes the individual feel that it is *he* who acts. . . . In 'emotionless actions,' on the other hand, the ego is more or less eliminated and activity more or less detached" (1951, p. 43). He thus suggests that the flow of experience, action, and longer temporal inte-gration be viewed as a sequence of episodes, or successions of integrated activity—each succession formed by and integrated by its own emotional tone.

Tomkins (1970) has pointed out a distinction between a need state, threat, or deprivation on the one hand and its cognitive "amplifier" on the other. The amplifier is the affective quality of experience and is a central aspect of cognitive control. The simple clarity of the biology of hunger, thirst, and anoxia has led to their prominence in most discussions of motivation; but in cognitive psychology, the orderliness, meaningfulness, simplicity, and consonance in our immediate experience are of more interest.

To motivate people, we need only arouse their affective experiences of joy, terror, surprise, shame, or whatever (see again Schachter and Singer, 1962, reviewed in Chapter 7 in the section on visceral-cognitive integrations). From the cognitive view, affects are the primary determi-nants of behavior, and are not governed strictly by environmental cir-cumstances, blood chemistry, or the contents of the stomach. Emotional experience can even stray "inappropriately" from any concordance with these peripheral realities. And the events that one person may integrate into a harmonious structure leading to pleasure may be experienced by another as a dissonance leading to displeasure. Tomkins has summarized the centrality of emotion as follows:

> The basic power of the affect system is a consequence of its freedom to combine with a variety of other components in what may be called a central assembly. This is an executive mechanism upon which messages converge from all sources, competing from moment to moment for inclusion in this governing central assembly. The affect system can be evoked by central and peripheral messages from any source, and in turn it can control the disposition of such messages and their sources. (1970, p. 105)

The self-concept. The individual differences that are so striking in the occurrence of emotional experience are doubtless linked to differences in schemata, or concepts, or longer temporal integrations, which have developed differently from individual to individual. These schemata, concepts, or integrations are, again, the standards, the constancies, the automatic attentional patterns that underlie our structuring and interpretation of experience. And probably the most important of these for the course of emotional reaction, and in turn volition, is the one that is most central—the self-concept.

As we noted in the last chapter, in early childhood, before self-awareness and self-identification have stabilized, attentional processes are not stable, wholly private experience (dreams) are sometimes not distinguished from public experience, and memories are not stored effectively for later retrieval or later reconstruction. But when identity of self is achieved and the subject-object distinction is stabilized, attention is controlled and deployed more effectively.

Dreaming is a situation in which these distinctions may be relaxed and in which volitional control is at a low ebb. Automatized patterns of experience then take over in often haphazard ways. Hence, most dreams unfold as mechanically and uncontrollably as if the dreamer were watching a motion picture. We remember night dreams only if we awake in the middle of them, while they are still reverberating in short-term memory; we can then control our scan of the fading images with voluntary attention and thereby store those images in longer memory.

Types of control. Kahneman (1973) has criticized attention research on the grounds that it overemphasizes attentional selectivity in the succession of experience and underemphasizes attentional effort, or intensity. In making this distinction, Kahneman in effect lends support to a classic distinction of two fundamental characteristics of attention deployment. In classical Wundtian psychology (Wundt, 1896), two aspects of deployment were distinguished. The first is Wundt's mental "clearness" process, which concerns the focusing or emphasizing of a single item of experience. This process was defined by Wundt as attentional synthesis, in which variations from broad to narrow syntheses (integrations) may occur. The other attention-deployment characteristic noted by Wundt is a mental "distinctiveness" process, which is the marking off of an item of experience from all others. Wundt described this as attentional analysis, a relating and comparing function; it is roughly equivalent to the later notions of attentional scanning and selection.

Benussi (1904, 1912), who was influenced by these notions, investigated variations in the perception of geometrical illusions. In these investigations, perceivers were set, by means of special instructions, to have either a global and unchanging attentional focus or a narrowly focused, actively scanning attentional pattern. While judging the lengths of lines, the former group experienced significantly larger illusional effects, which were caused by distracting lines (or biasing contexts) of the surrounding geometrical figures (see Figure 27). But these demonstrations suggested only one dimension of attentional action—the range from global and synthesizing attention to narrow and analyzing attention.

The specific character of the whole integration forces itself on its individual parts. Again following Gestalt psychology, "If that character is integral, simplicity is exaggerated; if divided, the division is emphasized" (Koffka, 1935). When stimulus information suggests a familiar figure, the perceptual organization of that input gravitates toward that figure according to the developed automaticities of attentional integration. Any such gravitation is likely to distort the true dimensions of the stimulus input.

An affective reaction may be the motive force behind this distortion, according to Woodworth's review (1938). Even when an observer looks at rather simple figures, an emotional or reactive impulse can be stimulated. Reactions of effort, strain, tension, or relaxation can thus influence the perceptual integration so that two equal lines appear dissimilar.

The rediscovery of these attention-deployment processes appeared within the "directive state," or "new look," movement in perceptual research in the early 1950s (reviewed in Chapter 7, in the section on enhancement and repression). It was found then that perception and performance are altered and shaped, not only by momentary transient emo-

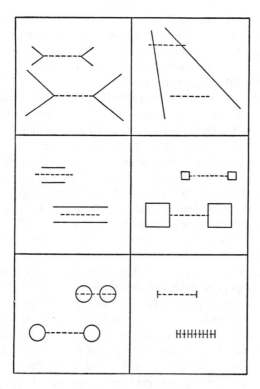

Figure 27. Typical geometrical illusions. According to Benussi, people who can narrow their attentional focus to the targeted dash-lines so as to close out the biasing contexts of other lines and figures will more likely see all dashed lines as equal, which they are. (From *Experimental Psychology* by R.S. Woodworth. Copyright © 1938 by Holt, Rinehart & Winston, Inc. Reprinted by permission.)

tion, but also by the habitual patterns of cognitive control that are acquired by individuals, patterns that lead to consistent styles of perception and performance. Eventually, two general and independent dimensions of attentional action emerged from these investigations. Gardner (1961) called them "field-articulation" and "scanning." The former refers to the degree of fidelity of the attentional focus, the ability to attend selectively to certain areas of experience and to shut out others. The latter refers to the degree of movement of the attentional focus from one item to another.

In their review of research on memory and cognition, which has been mentioned several times previously in this text, Craik and Lockhart

(1972) describe a similar dichotomy: two types of central cognitive control. The first is the focusing on the present item of experience. The second is "deeper-level" processing—again, a relating and comparing function in which an active search brings out connections of a given item of experience to related items in memory.

Gardner and his associates (1959) have provided the largest body of experimental data relevant to this now traditional distinction of two aspects of cognitive control. By means of factor analyses of a variety of perceptual-motor tests, they have shown these aspects of control (focusing and scanning) to be independent of each other. A person may focus attention in a very minute and constricted way—on narrow and well-defined areas of experience—and still scan rapidly from item to item, or may hold attention fixed on one small item without scanning other items. The extremities of these attentional patterns are typically induced by extreme emotional states, and are characteristic of mental pathology. Some of these extremities are described later in this chapter.

Two examples of the tests that Gardner (1961) employed are an embedded-figures perception test (developed by Witkin, 1950) and a size-estimation test (developed by Klein, 1954). Skillful performance on the embedded-figures tests is a good indication of "high field-articulation," or well-defined attentional focusing. Subjects in these tests receive a series of complex visual designs, each containing a familiar embedded figure. The dependent measure is the time required to find the figure. Some people are consistently better (faster) than others at this task.

In the size-estimation test—a good indication of individual differences in degree of attentional scanning—subjects adjust a circular light patch to be equal in size to hand-held disks. Again, there are consistent individual differences in the ability to perform this simple task, but this is not correlated with the ability to perform on the embedded-figures test.

Summary generalizations. We can now state some generalizations that summarize the above descriptions and help explain many of the observations that follow:

One dimension of cognitive control is attentional focusing, or field-articulation; this is the range of experience in a momentary attentional integration, from narrow to global integrations.

Another dimension of cognitive control is attentional scanning; this is the degree to which attention moves from one area of experience to another.

OBSERVATIONS

Cognitive control has not been easily brought under experimental scrutiny in recent times. It has even been avoided to the detriment of coherence in many experimental findings (see Newell, 1973). Part of the difficulty may lie in the stigma of the old "free will" controversy. The following areas of observation offer a variety of insights into the nature of self-control and into the general dimensions of attention deployment:

1. biofeedback
2. memory performance
3. manipulation of images
4. problem solving
5. language performance
6. schizophrenic malfunction

Biofeedback

We can control only those behaviors on which we are able to focus our attention, and our control will be only as precise as is our attentional focus. Thus, "high articulation" in the attention to some action is necessary for a high level of accuracy in the control of that action. Only when behavior has become routine and automatized, after a long period of precise control, may attention be lessened (or reorganized) in the control of behavior.

In complex organisms, there is a wide range of automatic actions that seem to be "wired in" at birth. The autonomic nervous system, for instance, controls many actions, such as those of the glands and the muscles of internal organs. All forms of automaticity, whether innate or learned, can be an enormous convenience, as we have seen. Attention is thereby not dominated by the many routine performances that must occur every day—breathing, walking, digestion, and so on. And again, there are also the negative cases in which automaticities have become maladaptive.

Several schools of psychological thought have acknowledged this distinction between voluntary and involuntary behavior. The distinction has led, in some cases, to the strict separation of two behavior systems, which are then said to obey entirely different laws. One has been called the "respondent" system, and is considered to involve only innate reflexes and reactions of the internal viscera. The other is the "operant" system, considered to involve only skeletal muscles that operate instrumentally upon the environment (Skinner, 1938).

As a result of experimental investigations, this sharp distinction between involuntary-respondent and voluntary-operant has broken down and is being replaced by a simpler principle: we can learn to control those actions upon which we can focus our attention (see Hilgard and Bower, 1975). Those actions may include any muscle or gland system. Since there is very little sensory feedback from most internal visceral reactions, there is for them very little input upon which to focus attention. Thus, special feedback supplementation or special attentive efforts are necessary if one is to learn to control these actions.

Similarly, certain external skeletal muscles provide little sensory feedback, so learning to control them may be equally difficult. The action of moving the ear voluntarily is, for humans, one example. In a pioneering study, Bair (1901) showed that the control of such groups of muscles is an attentional problem. Bair facilitated muscle control by electrical stimulation of a particular set of muscles so that learners would know just how that particular muscle action "felt." Another, less drastic way to learn to move your ears is to use supplementary visual feedback: watch your ears in the mirror as you struggle to move the muscles on the side of your head. When the ears by chance move, note what it feels like and work on reproducing that sensation. If you are diligent, you might become so adept at wiggling your ears that the behavior becomes highly automatized.

In the case of visceral responses, where one cannot have visual feedback, control has been made possible through modern electronic technology, which provides feedback through electronic sensors and amplifiers. By the late 1960s, it had become common to show that heart rate, intestinal action, blood pressure, vasodilation, and other internal processes could be brought under cognitive control by means of artificially supplied feedback. (Hilgard and Bower, 1975, and Schwartz, 1975, provide some introductory reviews.) Electronically detected action in these systems is simply amplified and converted into a light signal or a sound signal, which indicates the targeted event (say, an intestinal contraction) to an attentive subject. In effect, the signal supplements some slight visceral sensation, rendering that reaction more available to attentive consciousness. Then, just as in learning to control ear movement, one gradually learns to turn the electronic-visceral signal on and off. This area of research is now known as *biofeedback*, and in recent years it has become highly commercialized.

Memory Performance

As with the study of sensory phenomena, the study of human learning and memory is an area beyond the scope of this book. It is usually treated in a separate text. Nevertheless, some questions of human memory are central to the study of the process of cognition and provide another medium of evidence for the operations of cognitive control.

Modern investigations of memory include questions of the forms of storage of memory material, the separation of memory into different types or categories, and the distinction of different types of retrieval strategies. The greater part of this work is a conceptual extension of the British associationist philosophies of a century or two ago (well pointed out by Anderson and Bower, 1973). Those earlier analyses of mind described ideas or memories as being associated, organized, stored, and retrieved. But when we ask who or what does this associating, organizing, storing, or retrieving, we are thrust again back to the organismic questions of the *process* of cognition—to questions about the user of the information rather than about the information itself.

Basis of memory. When we speak of the contents of memory, we refer to what is largely, if not solely, the product of experience. As such, memory consists of predispositions to re-create certain experiences or actions. We can think of memory as "paths" over which mental activity retraces some former course of action in the construction of experience. Well-worn paths are trod more easily than new and poorly developed ones. Surely there are changes in cortical tissue that predispose that tissue to react in certain ways. We can only speculate about the "layer upon layer" of these subtle changes, interlocking in countless ways and diffused throughout the cortex.

Our different memories, or habits of thought and experience, are re-created more or less as they are needed at odd intervals. But our processes of cognition—the mechanisms of creating and re-creating those experiences—are in constant use, if to varying degrees, while we are awake. In fact, these processes are "wakefulness" itself.

Assimilation and clustering. One of the oldest truisms in memory research concerns the notion of *assimilation*. Information to be remembered must be assimilated by information already possessed. This suggests organic growth, in that any given new memory is an embellishment of some older memory. Assimilation is often observed as organizational factors in memory, particularly in situations of *free recall*. In the simplest demonstration of this organizational characteristic, a person is confronted with, say, a long list of words and is asked later to recall them in any order he can. People will then group words into categories, consistent with their past experience, even though these words were not organized in any way when first presented.

For instance, groupings may be simple semantic categories (plants, animals, cities, people). But they can just as easily be any idiosyncratic grouping that happens to be familiar to the individual learner. The words belonging in one of these categories will likely reappear together, in a "cluster," during recall (Bousfield, 1953). In this act of recall we observe in these clusters some indication of the preexisting knowledge that a person has brought to the memory task—the earlier memories into which, in this case, the list of words is assimilated. Cofer (1965) has summarized many of these observations.

The notion of assimilation in memory resembles another truism in perception. To perceive an event or object is to assimilate it into information already possessed (as described in the previous chapter). And the Gestalt principles of organization (see Chapter 3) are found in both of the mental operations of perception and memory. Because of this, it is natural to look for one central control mechanism that operates in both cases.

Importance of control actions. Neither time, effort, nor the content of experience wholly determines what will be recalled on any occasion. Rather, it is the type of central control actions of the attentional process that determines what we remember, or if we remember anything at all. And that process, as we have seen, is heavily subject to the whims of emotion.

One of the most productive recent series of memory investigations has come from Jenkins and his students (Jenkins, 1974). In their work, the effect on memory of cognitive control actions involves what Jenkins calls "semantic processing." For example, taking a list of words to be learned, subjects rated or placed each word along a semantic dimension, such as "pleasant versus unpleasant," "activity versus passivity," or "strong versus weak." On other occasions, subjects engaged in non-semantic tasks, such as identifying individual letters within each word, writing rhyming words, or identifying the part of speech of each word. The semantic processing resulted in far superior recall of the items, even when greater time, effort, and intention to learn were involved in the non-semantic processing. What Jenkins has called "semantic" was also called "affective" in Chapter 7. And so it seems that where the affective, or semantic, component of experience is emphasized, central control processes will establish memories much more effectively. Without that component, according to Jenkins, "variables such as time, effort, and 'intention to learn' seem to have little to do with remembering" (1974, p. 16).

Craik and Lockhart's (1972) theoretical paper has been especially influential with those who investigate the process rather than the content of memory. It presents the case for placing the primary emphasis on central control processes in theories of memory. Different types, categories, or strategies of memory representation, to follow their argument, are understood most clearly as by-products of the type of cognitive control actions at the moment of learning or of remembering. What one does during memorization by means of focusing attention and moving attention from one thought, perception, or image to another will determine memory. This kind of action may have been instigated to a greater degree in those of Jenkins' subjects engaged in the semantic rating.

Structure versus process. Some investigators of memory study the organizational patterns of long-term memory as underlying semantic systems. The semantic network diagrams of Collins and Quillian (1969), illustrated in Figure 9, p. 51, are now the best-known example. Their interpretation is that concepts such as fish, canary, animal, and tree are at functionally distinct locations or "nodes" of a semantic network. Lindsay and Norman (1972) have elaborated the idea that these nodes are linked by a variety of specific relationships (concept-attribute, theme-evidence, and superset-subset).

Although these models are descriptions of memory organization, they are not descriptions of how memory *works*. And as models of memory they may be rather too precise—like taking a well-made camera as a model of the human eye. Biological processes rarely conform to inorganic mechanical models. Tomkins has stated this problem as it confronts us in cognitive psychology:

> ...the central assembly is at best an untidy aggregate. It has none of the orderliness of our present-day computer programs. It is perpetually vulnerable to interference, drift, disassembly.... it is more like an information stew than it is like a program....As nature is said to abhor a vacuum, so psychologists have been loath to look entropy full in the face. (1963, p. 41)

A memory is likely never an exact copy of its corresponding original experience. Bartlett (1932) showed this well in studies of the changes, drifts, and disassemblies of memories over time. When he asked subjects to reproduce from memory simple drawings or simple stories, their reproductions on successive occasions strayed progressively away from the original. As the course of attention changes under the influence of changing needs, interests, or emotions, memories appear to change and drift, often in ways that are unique to the individual experiencing them. And so the associations among experiences that we rely upon as aids to memory can follow an idiosyncratic affective course, and thus not follow the abstract categories of, say, the English language, or the formalities of logic, at all. For the process-oriented psychologist, the problem of memory thus becomes one of studying cognitive styles, fluctuations, and levels of processing, rather than fixed, universal memory structures.

As shown in Chapter 3, Collins and Quillian (1969) tested their node-link description of memory storage by observing how quickly people could answer questions that contained terms either close or distant in semantic relatedness. They claimed that the more inter-node links that must be crossed, the longer it takes people to answer. Thus, "Does a canary sing?" and "Does a canary breathe?" required 1.3 and 1.5 seconds, respectively. The extra .2 seconds is seen as resulting from the memory search needed to bring together information located in nodes at different parts of the structure.

To translate this into a description in terms of cognitive processes, we could imagine the attentional integration creating an image of a canary—likely, it would simultaneously be the image of a *singing* bird because canaries are especially well known as singing birds. But representations of the act of breathing are not as likely to be an automatic aspect of images of canaries. And so the question about breathing would provoke one further, minimal act of attentional integration, and this act would require the additional time. We shall look further into questions of imagery in the next section.

Manipulation Of Images

One reason that mental imagery has at times been held as inaccessible to empirical research derives from naive attempts to treat it as though it were the very material of thought. Unfortunately, psychological processes are not that simple. The associationist philosophers of a century or more ago claimed that during the recall of a previously perceived object, the associative bonds between its name and its visual image would cause the appearance in consciousness of a revived copy of the original perception. Images, however, are far better treated as time-bound constructions than as stationary, fixed items that can be filed away and then retrieved on later occasions. Shepard (1968) reasons that when a person says, "I am imagining a red triangle," he is not claiming a red triangle to be inside his head. Nor are his words "red triangle" somehow directly attached to or associated with certain external objects. Rather, his words are directly associated with a functional mental process that we have in common and that might be provoked by any number of external objects or situations.

Thought, it seems, is fundamentally an imageless process, though images can be constructed as its accompaniment. Sometimes, the construction of that additional imagery is of great service to the effectiveness of thought and memory, as we shall see in this section. Memories are now often considered not as pictures in a file, but as programs, or some automatic routine, of the attentional reintegration of experience. In this sense, memories are "schemata" or "automatisms" of thought, as described in Chapter 8.

In the act of recall, it is only a special effort of attention that activates these schemata. Attention may also, with further effort, relate these schemata to neural centers for vision or for hearing; visual or auditory images are thereby produced. In the act of thinking, attention must therefore go an extra step to produce imaginary visualizations or imaginary sounds.

The alert, mentally healthy person with efficient attentional functioning distinguishes effectively between sensory experience and memory imagery. When, for instance, images are provoked in the course of recalling familiar objects, these impressions are not confused with perceptions. But when attention lags, when there is fatigue, or when an individual is on the threshold of sleep, that person is less able to make these discriminations (Oswald, 1962). At moments like these, memory images may be taken as immediately present environmental objects.

When sensory input is reduced to a minimum, attention is quickly directed to the sense modality that still receives a certain amount of stimulation, however faint. This stimulation will likely be radically elaborated into images, as a means of compensating for the poverty of other sensations. Generally, these experiences are hallucinatory. Vosberg, Fraser, and Guehl (1960) demonstrated this by presenting a faint input of unstructured noise to subjects undergoing sensory deprivation. All sorts of auditory hallucinations then occurred, as a result of the "magnification," or elaboration in consciousness, of this faint input.

Mnemonic techniques. Deliberate and voluntarily controlled imagery, however, is a powerful and efficient tool for improving thought and memory. Such uses of imagery are often called *mnemonic techniques.* Yet because imagery itself has occasionally been excluded from the topics of experimental psychology, the development of research in this area has been quite uneven. Careful empirical studies of mnemonic techniques and imagery manipulation are appearing today, but the most exhaustive investigations remain those of the German psychologist Müller (1911, 1913, 1917), which occupy three large volumes.

One of many conclusions that can be drawn from Müller's research is that the ability to construct images in the course of thought may, just like any other performance skill, become a highly refined and facile cognitive skill. And it might be attained to a high degree through dedicated practice. This conclusion contradicts certain views that hold superior memory ability to be a possession only of abnormal personalities.

The development of skill in imagery manipulation might be thought of as being analogous to the attaining of control over internal responses in the biofeedback situations cited in a previous section of this chapter. For the uninitiated, it may be difficult to begin developing the skill of imagery manipulation. Whereas a violin teacher can show you what finger movements you must learn in order to play the violin, no one can demonstrate exactly what you must do in order to manipulate an image. But it may be worth the effort to learn this skill because it has the potential of significantly improving human memory performance.

The mental action that one can learn and practice in order to improve memory is usually differentiated into several types. When these are closely examined, however, they may all resolve into the fundamental action of manipulating mental imagery. The following are four types of mnemonic technique:

1. *Simple Visualization.* In trying to remember the name of a new acquaintance, you might imagine a Mr. Carpenter as hammering his long, pointed nose into a wall.

2. *Method of Loci* (placing memories in imagined locations). You might remember a long shopping list by placing, in your imagination, each item on some object or piece of furniture in a room that is very familiar to you. When the time to remember arrives, again visualize the room and observe the items—the bananas on the desk, the milk on the television, and so forth. This device gives the attentional scan a structured point of entry into long-term memory.

3. *Pegword Method.* Here you commit a simple rhyme to memory in advance. The following has become the classic example: "One is a bun, two is a shoe, three is a tree, four is a door, five is a hive, six is sticks, seven is heaven, eight is a gate, nine is a dime, ten is a hen." Again, the final term in each phrase is an easily visualized object. As in the method of loci,

place one of each item of a list in, on, or beside one of these rhyme items. Later repetition of the rhyme prompts the memory of the list of items.

4. *Narrative Chaining.* This is the integration of a set of material to be learned into some sort of fanciful story. A list of words or items might be elaborated as a sequence of events that form a dramatic plot or episode. This technique may incorporate any or all of the above devices. The spinning of a story can be an especially effective mnemonic technique if you include yourself as a character in the episode.

Bower (1973) illustrated in a simple way the power of the narrative chaining procedure by giving two groups of subjects lists of words and instructions to memorize them. One group was also instructed to make up a story with the words; the other group could use any method of memorization they chose. Some time later the learners were tested; those who had constructed stories correctly recalled about seven times more items than did the others. Encouraging subjects to create mental pictures of verbally presented material and nothing more also significantly enhances retention of that material (Bower, 1970; Paivio, 1969).

Why is imagery an aid to memory? Imagery formation and manipulation demand the arousal of cognitive self-control. As we noted in the previous section, what a person *does* attentionally determines whether he will remember. This is true for remembering a shopping list, the names of people met yesterday, or the solution to complex mathematical problems. Mnemonic techniques facilitate the assimilation of new combinations of events or objects into some system of experiential predispositions that is already well established—that is already a part of the learner and that has qualities of familiarity and of affect.

In using mnemonic techniques, you must form mental images and then move them around somehow, or transform them, or bring them into relation with some other mental image. At first, it might seem that these techniques would not be accessible to controlled experimental study in a laboratory. However, a series of investigations by Shepard is one recent example of just such a controlled study.

Image rotation. Shepard devised indirect measures of *relationships* between memory images and other known perceptual images. He succeeded in making some precise inferences about nonobvious characteristics of these internal events. In one of many tests, Cooper and Shepard (1973) asked people to "rotate," in their heads, the mental images of individual letters or numbers in order to make them match the rotated position of some externally presented stimulus. Subjects were to say whether or not a letter was correctly printed or was a backwards mirror image. First, the subjects saw an upright letter on a screen for two seconds. Later, the same letter was shown again, rotated to some angle away from the upright position and perhaps also backwards (see Figure 28). The time to respond "same" or "different," indicating whether the rotated second presentation was in a correct or backwards orientation, was a function of the degree of rotation of the test stimulus away from the memory image of the first presentation.

This finding shows that mental images may be rotated and that the rotation may proceed at a certain rate and no faster. For one to perform this mental act, according to Shepard, "there may be no way to proceed but to impose small successive adjustments on the internal representation and, so, to pass through a 'trajectory' of internal representations that corresponds to the actual rotation of the external object" (1975, p. 105). (The average rotation rate is about 60° per second.) Shepard and Metzler (1971) found similar results in tests in which subjects were required to rotate mental images in the third dimension; that is, the top of a visual configuration was to be tilted forward and the bottom tilted away.

Before a person can compare a stimulus against an internal representation, or begin to rotate a mental image of it into a particular orientation, he must know both the identity and the orientation of that stimulus. As Cooper and Shepard showed, each such piece of information that the subject does not have in advance must be extracted from the

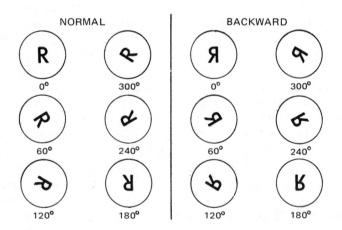

Figure 28. Normal and backward versions of a set of probe stimuli for comparison with a rotating mental image of the letter *R*. (From Cooper and Shepard, 1973; Reprinted by permission of Academic Press, Inc.)

stimulus itself at the cost of approximately an additional 100 msec in reaction time.

Shepard's experiments are empirical measures of the *voluntary* control of mental processes in a simple experimental situation that isolates those control actions.

Problem Solving

Were it not for the selective activity of attention that is exercised in the form of reasoning, we might never make any consistent mental advance; we might remain at the mercy of our sporadic thoughts and impressions. Neisser (1967) points out that "a hundred or a thousand 'thoughts' appear briefly and are gone again even when we are primarily engaged in purposeful activity" (1967, p. 298). The extent to which some thoughts are developed and recycled, while others are let go and forgotten, brings varying degrees of coherence to our momentary experience. Some lines of research on problem solving bear directly on this question of cognitive control.

Any approach a person takes when facing a problem is invariably influenced by expectations, hypotheses, rules, or any other automaticities of thought that are based on prior experiences in similar situations. Often deriving from those automaticities are emotional reactions, such as anxiety, eagerness, or the strain of incongruity, which may be the ultimate guiding force in the approach to a problem.

Frequently, the study of problem solving has been concerned with the description of problems per se—that is, with the analysis of the structure of problems and the categorization of various types of problems. This approach leaves the problem solver aside. The question for problem solving may then become, "How does the problem find its solution?" (Koffka, 1935), rather than, "How does the problem solver find a solution?"

Solutions to problems can be stated as a sequence of orderly steps. But it is likely that the human cognitive actions that arrive at solutions are not such a sequence; they may consist of false starts, daydreams, and idiosyncratic associations or images. Only when a person is trained so well in solving a particular type of problem that he performs it routinely are his thoughts and actions likely to follow the most efficient sequence of steps to a solution.

Span limits. People are always faced with a limited range of time, attention, and memory, and just as this limit constrains perception and learning, it also constrains problem-solving activity. Simon and

Kostovsky (1963) point out that short-term memory may assume special significance for problem solving, where the critical task is often that of trying to hold together all the impressions or images needed for solution while at the same time scanning, focusing, and combining them in various ways in the search for the solution. This is the familiar problem of "cognitive spans," described in Chapter 6.

Clearly, the "chunking" of impressions and the automatization of subskills is important here, as it is in other human performances. Bartlett (1958) even argues that problem solving should be conceived as fundamentally the same as achievement in perceptual-motor skills. To become an accomplished mathematician, for instance, one must learn many elementary mathematical systems (such as algebra and trigonometry) to the point of automaticity, so that attention will be free to concentrate on some further level of mathematical analysis.

In a classical discussion of problem solving, Maier noted, "It is obvious that the mere conscious presence of the necessary experiences or data is not sufficient to solve certain problems. Some other factor is necessary before the elements can be integrated into a unified whole, the solution of the problem" (1930, p. 133). Solutions are generally sudden integrations; it seems that the significant elements of a problem come together and are integrated in a unique way in one pulse of rapid attentional integration. This characteristic suddenness is usually described as the moment of insight. But for this to happen, attention must be free enough to go well beyond the raw data of the problem, without at the same time omitting that raw data from view due to overloading of the cognitive capacities.

Chess. Consider chess players, who relate current positions on a chessboard to past experience. This activity becomes automatized, and processing capacity is thereby freed up. De Groot (1965) tested chess players at three levels of skill development—"masters" (the most accomplished), "experts" (moderate skill), and novices. Each group was allowed a five-second look at a chessboard that contained pieces in positions occurring after the twentieth move in a game. Later, they were to reproduce the arrangement from memory. Of course, the novices could reproduce hardly anything at all; the masters made only a few errors; and the experts fell in between in their memory performance. The superior performance of the masters was not due to any superior memory capacity, because on memory tests not involving chess, they could perform no better than the novices. But chess masters automatically recognize whole patterns on a chessboard at a single glance, just as some skilled musicians recognize whole arpeggios or phrases at a glance when sight reading music (Wolf, 1976), or as the speed reader recognizes whole linguistic phrases at a glance.

In a first game of chess, the beginner faces the chessboard with uncertainty as to how the pieces are to be moved or in which way the play is to develop. Koestler has recorded some apt introspections of the development of chess-playing skill:

> After some practice it becomes impossible [for the new chess player] to move a rook diagonally without a feeling of aesthetic and moral revulsion, of having committed an obscenity or violated a sacred taboo: the rules have become automatized, encoded in the circuitry of his nervous system. At a still later stage he learns to apply certain stratagems just as automatically: to avoid "pins" and "forks," not to expose the king, to seek open rook files, etc. In games simpler than chess, the same type of situation will recur over and over again, and the appropriate stratagems will be codified in their turn. (1964, p. 156)

Note in Koestler's description the appearance of the emotional component in cognitive control.

Fixedness versus creativity. But again, there is a negative side to highly developed automaticities. It is what Duncker (1945) and Luchins (1942) named "functional fixedness." Well-developed automaticity may at times block creativity or blind us to new solutions for problems. Our patterns of attention can become too well set on particular schemes. Thus, the person engaged in serious problem-solving activity should heed the familiar advice of occasionally leaving the problem entirely alone, or putting it out of mind, as a technique for finding the answer! This may lead to the relaxation of old automaticities such that new patterns of thought have a better chance to appear. The creative person is the one who is able to de-automatize and also to apply old automatisms in new contexts.

McKeller (1957) describes many anecdotes from scientists who reported the importance of various bizarre fluctuations of mental imagery that suddenly brought about a transformation of their viewpoints and thus served as important steps in their finding of solutions to scientific problems.

Focusing and scanning principles. When examined experimentally, the activity of problem solving can reveal attentional patterns, or cognitive styles. Pioneering investigations of this were made by Bruner,

Goodnow, and Austin (1956). In most previous investigations, individuals had been presented with a certain puzzle item that they were to manipulate in order to find a solution. This was a "reception" situation, one over which the subject had little control. The innovation in the work of Bruner and his associates was to return that control to the subject so that the processes of active self-control (namely, focusing and scanning) were better revealed.

Bruner and his associates presented subjects with large arrays of stimuli, which they could manipulate in any manner they pleased in order to find some solution. This is a "selection" technique of studying problem solving, as opposed to the "reception" technique, in which the experimenter controls what the subject will see or what materials he or she will have to work with during every step of the problem-solving activity. Setting up a situation in which a subject is free to select items in order to test a problem-solving hypothesis makes it possible to observe what type of attentional pattern he employs.

Most of the Bruner and associates research required subjects to discover a predetermined set of attributes (size, shape, color) among a large array of visual patterns printed on cards (see Figure 29). First, the experimenter would point out one of the cards in this set as an instance of the "concept" to be determined. Subjects then asked questions by selecting further cards as possible other instances of the criterial set of features. This process continued until subjects were able to identify the set of features that the experimenter had in mind.

Two general characteristics of most problem solvers emerged. Bruner and co-workers described one as a tendency to emphasize focusing, the other as a tendency to emphasize scanning. Focusing strategy involves concentrating on a positive indicator of the concept and then comparing successive examples with this one example. For instance, the experimenter would designate a card containing the attributes *small, green,* and *square.* The subject might then select another card that contained *small, green,* and *triangle* in order to test the relevance of the shape feature (square versus triangle). If the experimenter answered that this second card was also an instance of the concept, the subject knew that shape was not relevant. The subject's hypothesis then was that the target category is all cards that contain small and green objects. This was tested by another choice. The focusing subject thus selected instances in which one attribute was focused and then varied, a strategy that allowed him to determine the relevance of one attribute at a time. The experimenters called this "conservative focusing." But sometimes subjects adopted a more reckless method: they varied two attributes at a time (a larger focus). Having been presented a *small green square,* the subject might

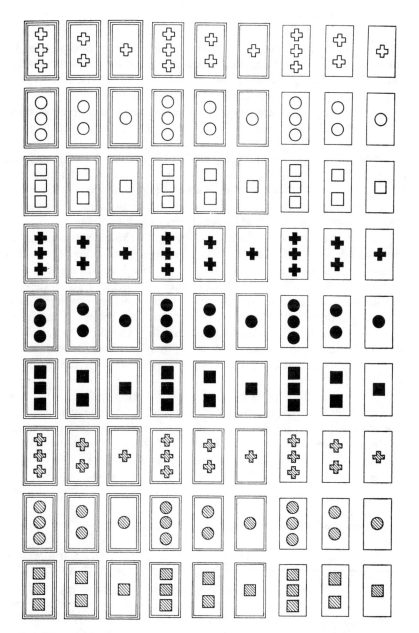

Figure 29. A stimulus array for studying problem solving in concept-identification tasks. The combinations of features on stimulus cards consist of four attributes, each exhibiting three values. Plain figures are in green, striped figures in red, solid figures in black. (From Bruner, Goodnow, and Austin, 1956. Reprinted by permission of John Wiley & Sons, Inc.)

select a *small red triangle* as a possible instance of the concept. This involved a greater pay-off in information if the subject guessed correctly. But it also entailed a greater risk—wasted time—if the hypothesis was incorrect. The experimenters called this "focus gambling."

The other general strategy that subjects sometimes adopted was that of scanning. Rather than focus on one item as an example of the category, some subjects formed a simple hypothesis about the solution—for instance, "all small squares"—and then tested it by searching out cards that fit this category. Some dealt with one hypothesis at a time (successive scanning); others dealt with several (simultaneous scanning). In the particular kind of problem presented in the Bruner and associates tests, focusing was a more effective strategy than scanning.

Some controversy has since arisen about the characterization of these strategies (see Laughlin, 1973). Primarily, the argument is that focusing and scanning are not mutually exclusive strategies; that is, a problem solver does not have to adopt one or the other. Rather, they are two dimensions of cognitive control that can operate simultaneously. Thus, the "conservative (one-at-a-time) focusing" strategy is similar to "successive scanning." Focusing and scanning, according to Laughlin, are not separate strategies as much as they are two dimensions of cognitive processing used in the testing of hypotheses by selection and integration of information.

Thus, various degrees of attentional focusing and scanning may determine levels of problem-solving efficiency in human performance. The crucial factor is the degree to which an individual gains information by the way he or she deploys attention to, say, isolate an item of experience, or to move attention around in order to make comparisons among several items of experience.

Language Performance

It is natural in this chapter to cite language as a supreme accomplishment of cognitive control. Humans have at times been so impressed with their ability to communicate via language that they have regarded this performance as the one characteristic that separates them from the other animals. Looking further into the matter through the study of cognitive processes, however, we realize that language is but one of several reflections of more basic mental capacities in which humans excel. These are the capacities of cognitive control that permit people to compose innumerable varieties of music, create endless types of tools, or devise mathematical systems.

The talking human is a creature that represents its own momentary states of consciousness (thoughts, images, and memories) in a sequential code. Such codes, or languages (for example, the grammar of English), are communally shared rule systems. If a sufficient variety of signals can be produced, any human behavior can take over the language-producing function that we usually associate with the vocal chords.That function could involve sounds produced by drums, visual patterns made by hand gestures, impulses from telegraph keys, graphic patterns printed on paper, and so on.

Control of linear sequencing. Any form of language production depends on an intricate hierarchy of skills, many of which are thoroughly automatized in the mature performer. The skills involve acts of transforming simultaneous mental representations into sequential outputs and also reintegrating sequences of signals into a mental representation. The necessary skills range all the way from patterns of the attentional analysis of configurations of thought to the rapid formation of a sequence of sounds or visual stimuli.

Certain automaticities in performance are necessary if fluent and articulate speech is to occur. That is, attention must be freed from the detailed mechanics of language production in order to control the *content* of speech and to proceed in a coherent way from thought to thought, concentrating on the purposes and goals of communication. To communicate our thoughts, we must analyze them attentionally into a sequence of components that can be converted almost simultaneously into a sequence of sounds. For example, we might focus first on a mental representation of an object, and then on some action or attribute of that same impression, and at the same time convert this sequence of two attentional focusings into a sequence of sounds, including certain signals that indicate the nature of the relations between these attentional formations. The most basic relational form is *predication,* which underlies any simple sentence. It is the elementary attribution of a quality or an action to some item of experience ("The barn is red" or "John ran away"). In everday speech, simple predications are compounded and organized into complex utterances.

Recent specialists in psycholinguistics, such as Garrett (1975) and McNeill (1975), contend that language performance skills may be divided into two fundamental levels. One concerns the analysis of the pattern of thought, and the other, the representation of this analysis in some sensory-motor channel. This account corresponds to two levels in the structural description of linguistic rules that have been postulated in linguistic theory: "deep structure" versus "surface structure" (Chomsky, 1957). When considering the psychological actions of formulating speech (in other words, language performance), we may refer to these levels as "central processes" versus "peripheral processes."

Underlying mental states. In early psycholinguistic studies, Wundt described each integrated segment of speech as reflecting an underlying holistic mental representation (Blumenthal, 1970). Similarly, Lashley (1951) suggested a simultaneous organizational schema at a central cortical level, a schema that is indirectly reflected in integrated sequences of language production. Boomer (1965) and Trager and Smith (1951) have described integrated sequences of peripheral processes as "phonemic clauses." Each such clause is a sequence of linguistic signals that reflect an integrated phase of performance. In general, the "clause"will have one primary stress, one terminal juncture, and a unified pitch pattern (which we might think of as a unified melodic pattern). The intonation patterning, timing, and other properties of fluent speech are thus tied together in sequences of action schemata.

Other sequential performance patterns were described in Chapter 5 as "speech rhythms," and were seen as reflections of the periodicity of short-term memory. Spans of speech fluency of fairly consistent duration suggest the unraveling of action schemata that are rooted in the momentary contents of temporary working memory (STM). In Wundt's descriptions, each fluent sequence corresponds to a sentence. But more recent empirical observation shows that spans of fluency in speech production do not necessarily coincide with sentence boundaries, and are perhaps more accurately related to performance capacities—everything from breathing rates to short-term-memory limits.

Two other recent psycholinguistic theorists, Kozhevnikov and Chistovich (1969), have given the name "syntagma" to the momentary mental contents underlying each fluent sequence of speech. In terms of the present description, the syntagma is the momentary configuration of thoughts, images, or memories that have been activated by attentional scanning and focusing and that are for a brief time immediately accessible in short-term memory. Momentary processes of language production are then a "mapping" of this central configuration, or parts of it, into the sequential ordering of linguistic signals: phonemes, words, and phrases.

This mapping may be "fine-grained," yielding a long and detailed utterance, or it may be simple and elliptical, yielding only a few words and forcing the listener to guess most of the intended message. The language-production problem, in any case, is one of rapid choice and arrangement—of which words are to precede, and which to follow and how relationships among words are to be indicated so that they accurately reflect the underlying pattern of attentional analysis. In this we are guided by the grammatical rules of particular languages, though we do not always follow them accurately.

Fluency. Confused speech does not necessarily indicate confused thought. A speaker may lack the skill or patience to formulate in words the insight and originality contained in some shadowy thought. Being articulate means being able to analyze such a momentary mental impression smoothly and rapidly, and being able to select words and word orders quickly and automatically. Severely inarticulate speech, in contrast, shows extreme hestitation, convulsive movements, and a grasping at suitable utterances, and the final product may be completely unintelligible; but even so, the speaker may have begun with perfectly cogent thoughts. Demands made on attention by the task of encoding these thoughts can cause performance to break down. Such demands might include an emotion, such as fear of an audience, or a conflicting thought, or fatigue.

When we drive an automobile, our attention can be overloaded by conversation or daydreams, and we might then go through a stop light or shift into the wrong gear. Similarly, when attention is overloaded during language performance, that performance may come apart at its linguistic seams. Speech errors are thus a rich source of information about the nature of cognitive control in language performance.

When control lapses. Many times, attention is subject to overload, distraction, or interference, and the structuring and organizing activity of language performance fails. Recorded observations are plentiful (Boomer and Laver, 1968; Fromkin, 1971; McKay, 1970; Merringer, 1908). The most exhaustive recent collection of these lapses of control is that of Garrett (1975), who categorized them into a variety of structural forms. The following examples illustrate the diversity of such lapses:

SOME PATTERNS OF SPEECH ERRORS

   a. Addition:
      "I don't see any many paddocks around here."
      (intended either *any* or *many* but not both)
   b. Deletion:
      "I'll just get up and mutter __ intelligibly."
      (intended *unintelligibly*)
   c. Substitution:
      "At low speeds it's too light."
      (intended *heavy*)

d. Complex addition:
   "The one exPosner experiment that...."
   (intended *Posner*)

e. Complex deletion:
   "That would be __ having like Harry."
   (intended *behaving*)

f. Shift:
   "That's so she'll be ready in case she decide __ to hits it."
   (intended *decides to hit it*)

g. Exchange:
   "Fancy getting your model renosed."
   (intended *nose remodeled*)

h. Fusion:
   "At the end of today's lection...."
   (intended *lecture* or *lesson*)

i. Double whammy:
   "He's a laving runiac."
   (intended *raving lunatic* or *maniac*)*

Summarizing his wide range of observations, Garrett found that interchanges of words or parts of words rarely involved items that occur in more than one phonemic clause or phrase. Any particular confusion thus seems to result from the imperfect unraveling of a single, central organizational schema. Further, the categorization of lapses according to the level of processing that fails is easily made. For instance, a lapse at a central semantic level yields, "At low speeds it's too *light*" (intended *"heavy"*). A lapse at a peripheral level of control concerned with sound patterning produces, "She decide to hit*s* it" (intended "decide*s* to hit").

Reading skill. In concluding this section, it is worthwhile to add a brief description of reading skill, for the act of receiving and comprehending language is by no means a less active process than that of language production. The act of reading demonstrates this well. Reading involves active search, perception, and concentrated attention. Perhaps the highest accomplishment in the receiving and understanding of language is the development of reading skills to their greatest level of facility and automaticity.

There are extreme individual differences in reading performance. On the one hand, an attentionally "inactive" reader who stares idly at the page may scan one word at a time and not fully receive the author's

---

*Garrett, 1975, p. 138. Reprinted by permission of Academic Press, Inc.

message. Because of syntactic structures, clauses and sentences are highly interconnected wholes and will not be fully understood if the strings of words aren't integrated as parts of a unified configuration. Indeed, the very meaning of many words is determined by their context.

An efficient reader, on the other hand, may read a text for meaning at a rate of 1,000 words per minute. This reader, of course, does not notice minor spelling errors or omissions; still, his comprehension of the text is far superior to that of the slow reader. But words per minute, we must note, may be a deceptive measure of the fast reader's accomplishment, because he is not reading word by word; he is probably reading phrase by phrase. And at many moments, when correctly anticipating the writer's thought or correctly guessing the directions that thought will take in succeeding passages, he may need to catch only parts of phrases here and there. Written language is highly redundant. If the fast reader misses some crucial item, it is likely that the same information can be inferred from some later parts of the text. If it isn't, an occasional look back for missing information is not very costly in time and effort.

The extremely efficient reader is a very active *thinker* when reading. Much less of the limited attentional capacity—the same limited capacity that a slow reader has—is devoted to letters and words. In these ways, good and poor readers deploy their attention differently (Kolers, 1975). The speed reader devotes much greater effort to constructing internal representations on the basis of rapidly scanned cues. The text is searched for verification of guesses and anticipations of its content—that is, for information to support the developing configuration held in short-term memory.

In summarizing a number of observations on efficient reading, Hochberg and Brooks state:

> This, of course, sounds more like what we think of as "skimming" than what we consider to be reading, but no hard distinction is really possible: "skimming" is much closer to what the subject has learned to do when he is listening to speech or when he is looking at scenes, long before he comes to the special task of learning to read....(1970, p. 305)

Most people do not develop reading skill to such high levels of proficiency, just as most people do not become concert pianists. And this is because, as we would soon discover, both of these skills require a large investment of time and effort—hour upon hour of practice at a forced rapid pace.

Schizophrenic Malfunction

For the last set of illustrations of cognitive phenomena to be described in this book, we turn to severe mental malfunction. Psychologists have often looked to malfunction as a source of insight into the operation of basic psychological processes. The most common form of mental abnormality is labeled very broadly as schizophrenia—meaning split from reality. Broen, a specialist in schizophrenia research, suggests how this malfunction may shed light on central cognitive processes:

> We "normals" sometimes feel overwhelmed by the pressure of human experience, not realizing how protected we are. We have amazing ability to ignore material that would be distracting to the task at hand. We can reduce our awareness of the world around us and within us to a miniscule fraction of the total pool of potential sensation, and the odds are that the fraction selected will include cues important for appropriate behavior.
>
> The degree to which selective attention enables us to live in shielded continuity and coherence is made obvious in the contrasting awesome experience called schizophrenia. (1973, p. 191)

Imagine not being able to control your attention and not being able to stop a continual fragmentation of experience, thought, or memories. When this loss of control becomes extreme, there may even be a dissolution of the sense of self. In describing their earliest symptoms of breakdown, schizophrenic patients have reported this awareness of a growing inability to control attention (Chapman, 1966; Freeman, 1965; McGhie and Chapman, 1961).

An extreme variety of abnormal behaviors has been placed under the label of schizophrenia. Yet since the turn of the century, many psychiatrists have noticed that schizophrenic individuals of all sorts show some form of deficit in attentional processes.

Schizophrenialike experience in normals. Any normal individual may have brief flashes of experience that resemble schizophrenia and that may give insight into what this malfunction is like. The most often cited of these experiences occurs on the edge of sleep, when attention may be relaxed, wandering, and somewhat out of control. Not everyone is familiar with such experiences, though they are common enough (Oswald, 1962).

When one is on the border of sleep, a state of experience and behavior known as "hypnagogic phenomena" can arise. This state involves an interlude that seems to lie between sleep and wakefulness, a time when events are fragmented and thoughts and images drift in nonsensical ways. The structuring activity of attentional integration would seem to be drifting and fluctuating as cerebral vigilance, or arousal, subsides toward sleep. A phenomenon that occasionally arises in this state is "sleepy speech" (Oswald, 1962)—nonsensical utterances by a drowsy individual. Typical of such utterances is the sentence, "Scramble the clock when the radio coughs." This sentence was intended as "Set the alarm clock when the radio program is over." In other cases of sleepy speech, the words may not even conform to a grammatical sentence pattern at all. This reflects a lack of cognitive control, or a failure to fully utilize short-term memory, or to scan longer memory, or to focus attention. Sleepy speech can bear striking resemblances to the continuous speech of many schizophrenic individuals.

Upon waking from sleep, one may have similar experiences (sometimes called "hypnopompic phenomena"). Occasionally, cognitive control will return very gradually. Shor has called this experience the return of a "generalized reality orientation," and describes it as follows:

> At the time I was neither conscious of my personal identity, nor of prior experiences, nor of the external world. It was just that out of nowhere I was aware of my own thought process- es. I did not know, however, that they were thought processes or who I was, or even that I was an *I*.... After a time, "wondering" started to fill my awareness.... In an instant, as if in a flash, full awareness of myself and reality expanded around me.... At one moment my awareness was devoid of all structure and in the next moment I was *myself* in a mul- tivaried universe of time, space, motion, and desire. (1959, p. 586)

The chronic loss of these orientations is another condition found in many schizophrenics.

Types of schizophrenia. Schizophrenic behavior falls into different, sometimes contrasting patterns. Each reflects extremes of mental functioning. Shakow (1962) has made a general distinction of these types that has become widely accepted. Some schizophrenic individuals seem compelled to move their attention about, to scan their experience to an extreme degree; it is as if the analyzing capacity of their mental processes has run wild as they overactively structure experience. Naturally enough, the result is complex and bizarre delusional systems; the individual may see in things an elaborate organization that others do not see. This general category is the *paranoid* schizophrenic type. In sharp contrast is the *nonparanoid* type, which includes many abnormal behavior patterns that all seem related to a fixed, or "frozen," attentional focus. Here, the individual scans experience minimally, if at all. A large body of experimental data, some of which is cited below, has accumulated in support of this distinction (see Silverman, 1964).

One other general dimension of schizophrenic abnormality was described by Arieti (1961)—problems of cognitive "holism." For instance, a schizophrenic's focus of attention may be narrowed so radically that he cannot perceive any large or complex configuration. In the most extreme form of this condition, an individual may be unaware that another person is present in his environment; instead, he may perceive now an isolated and detached hand, now one eye drifting about, and now a detached ear. Shakow described a case of this as follows:

> It is only when a patient develops a persisting aversion to food because the cafeteria menu lists a common item which we read as "soup" but which he can only see in its excretatory signifi- cance as "so-u-p," that we begin to realize how very many of the thousands of details of daily existence get by us ordinary normals. (1963, p. 303)

In other individuals, an opposite type of holism problem occurs: they are incapable of narrowing their focus of attention at all. For them, everything is one large configuration. Walking along a path, they are like- ly to wander off course and be unable to find their way back, simply because they cannot sharpen their focus of attention well enough to locate directions and objects.

Thus, the hyperactive attentional scanning of the paranoid schizophrenic can vary from narrow focusings to global focusings, because scanning and focusing are independent dimensions of attentional control. That is, although the paranoid schizophrenic always structures his experience overactively, because of attentional scanning, the units of the scanning activity may be either very minute or very broad attentional integrations.

When the schizophrenic suffers from both minimal scanning and minimal attentional focusing, that individual is, in effect, subjected to a kind of sensory-deprivation situation (see the section in this chapter on manipulation of images). No wonder that such individuals frequently have hallucinatory experiences, just as normals do when subjected to artificial sensory deprivation.

All of the above situations involve the same mental processes that nonschizophrenic individuals use every day. In schizophrenics, however, these processes are not operating in the "normal" range. They are either hyperactive, as in extreme scanning activity or extreme narrowing of focus, or they are extremely underactive.

Perceptual constancies in schizophrenics. The mechanism of perceptual constancy (described in Chapter 8) has been one of the most frequent objects of experimental study with schizophrenics (see Silverman, 1964). For instance, patients' reactions to geometrical illusions such as those in Figure 27, p. 157, distinguish general schizophrenic types. On the one hand, schizophrenics with highly fragmented thought and perception will not experience the illusory effect at all. For these individuals (the paronoids), perceptual constancies may even be exaggerated. It seems that the more intensively a person scans the perceptual field, the greater the tendency to overconstancy (Raush, 1952; Weckowicz, 1957). On the other hand, the nonparanoid schizophrenics will, in general, be wholly susceptible to the illusion. These individuals with inactive attentional scanning show very weak perceptual constancies; a familiar object that is far away may be judged to be a very small copy of that object.

The autokinetic effect. One diagnostic laboratory test employs a simple visual illusion, the autokinetic effect. This effect occurs when an individual confronts an isolated spot of light in an otherwise totally dark room. For most people, prolonged observation of the point of light will make it appear to move around in irregular patterns. The patterns of movement are not accounted for by eye movements (Royce, Carran, Aftanas, Lehman, and Blumenthal, 1966).

Voth (1947) was the first to discover that this illusion distinguishes certain types of schizophrenic individuals. Nonparanoids see much greater movement than paranoids, who rarely see any movement at all. Again, the continual attentional scanning and hyperanalytic attitude of the paranoid creates a highly structured world, which, consequently, has a high degree of stability. The autokinetic illusion is the result of a lack of structure and stability; this perceptual instability, the isolated point of light, leads presumably to an unstable cortical representation in most individuals. To stop the illusion, one must constantly construct an environmental frame of reference, concentrate on where the walls and ceiling are in the dark room, recall the dimensions of the room, or even imagine some objects to be near the light. The very undercontrolled attentional pattern typical of the nonparanoid schizophrenic is, conversely, highly conducive to this hallucinatory effect.

Emotion and defense. Emotion has a central role in the deformities of the central control process that produce schizophrenia. When unpleasant emotion becomes so strong that an individual can no longer bear or avoid it, then, according to Goldstein (1951), the severe stress placed on the operations of cognitive control may cause the attentional process to be distorted or to malfunction. Schizophrenia, according to clinical observations, is often precipitated by a period of overwhelming dread, failure, guilt, anxiety, pain, or stress (Bowers, 1968; Silverman, 1968). Some schizophrenics, in particular those who are chronically afflicted, seem to have abnormally low thresholds for disorganization under stress.

Whether a stress-influenced individual who experiences a schizophrenic breakdown will become a paranoid type or a nonparanoid type may depend on his or her previous normal personality characteristics. He or she may always have been rather analytically minded, tending toward a relatively high degree of attentional scanning, and the schizophrenic breakdown will lead to an exaggeration of these normal tendencies.

Schizophrenia is a last-resort adjustment of the cognitive system in defense against extreme emotional reaction. When many aspects of one's experience are extremely painful to focus upon, keeping the attentional processes "moving" constantly, as the paranoid usually does, and never stopping long to focus on one item of thought or memory, reduces the chance of being hurt by any particular experience. In another type of adjustment, the cognitive system swings radically to the opposite strategy— an extreme narrowing of the attentional focus, a freezing upon one spot of experience so that other, painful areas of experience are avoided.

CONCLUSIONS

In this chapter we have seen that human cognition is the embodiment of remarkable processes of cognitive control that not only ensure our survival in the daily flux of phenomena, but that also keep us well coordinated and on an even keel most of the time. A fundamental biological principle is reflected in those processes. Again, it is the act of temporal integration that maintains varying degrees of stability in the midst of flux. This integration includes not only the actual events of the present and the past that are perceived and represented in experience, but also it includes imagined and dreamed of events in the future. This extrapolation of events into the future leads to goals and choices that guide behavior.

A key mechanism in the control of these processes is the central emotional reaction. The central process of attention is aroused, directed, or inhibited by the emotional experiences it engenders. The emotional qualities of experience influence the operating characteristics of attention in at least two fundamental ways, which may be considered as two dimensions of cognitive control. One is attentional focusing, by means of which the range of experience in a momentary attentional integration can vary from narrow to broad. The other is attentional scanning, by which successive attentional focusings can move extensively from one area of experience to another, or can remain confined to relatively constricted areas, even recycling a single focus of attention for a considerable time.

Early in this chapter, some generalizations were provided to introduce the observations on cognitive control. They are again as follows:

> One dimension of cognitive control is attentional focusing, or field-articulation; this is the range of experience in a momentary attentional integration, from narrow to global integrations.
>
> Another dimension of cognitive control is attentional scanning; this is the degree to which attention moves from one area of experience to another.

Rather than a mechanical process with fixed elements, cognitive control is very much an organic process subject to drift, fatigue, constriction, or expansion.

RECAPITULATION

We have traveled a long path through psychological phenomena—all the way from the "microscopic" examination of time-intensity relations in the briefest pulse of attentional integration to the patterns of schizophrenic breakdowns that can affect the whole of an individual's life. In this array of observations, we have isolated basic mental processes, which all have at least one characteristic in common—utility for the survival of the human species.

Consider once more the illustration in the opening paragraph of this book: At many moments in the course of a day, you and I pass through and survive a rush of events, like engaging a friend in conversation, while at the same time dodging traffic on a street corner, struggling to remember items on a shopping list, being distracted by nude figures on a magazine cover, and scratching an itch. The process of cognition, which brings coherence and structure to this flux, reflects the most basic of biological principles—that life is a movement away from chaos and disorder and toward momentary stability and structure.

It appears that there is a general principle of temporal integration underlying mental processes. It is the transformation of sequences of events into simultaneities of perception, thought, or memory. The living organism's temporal integrations of the flux of events that occur in and around it generate consciousness. Primitive affective reactions, which these integrations evoke, then influence the course and character of that consciousness.

Many experimental psychologists over the last century have studied mental processes and have taken them apart piece by piece. Because these processes are fundamentally temporal in nature, this text has organized them into temporal categories and temporal functions, which have, in turn, been isolated and examined by means of selected illustrations as follows:

Rapid Attentional Integrations (RAI)

This class of microgenetic phenomena is perhaps the most fundamental for the construction of immediate experience. The following generalizations summarize numerous observations at this level:

> Rapid attentional integrations form immediate experience; the integration intervals vary from approximately 50 to 250 msec, with the most common observation being about 100 msec.
>
> Temporally separate events included in one integration are fused in experience to form a unitary impression; when those events are structurally different or incompatible, some may be omitted rather than fused.

As a central nervous system action, this process may reflect elementary excitability cycles or scanning mechanisms in the brain in which the mass of sensations and memories is summed, integrated, constructed, or elaborated—all at rapid speeds. In the research literature, many different terms are found that refer to this level of function. They include *scanning rate, psychological moment, central consolidation time, serial processor of information, identifier, integrator mechanism, attentional energy unit,* and *central assembly.*

Similar actions are observed in a wide variety of phenomena in the temporal range of these rapid attentional integrations. They include the following:

1. Time-Intensity Relations. Within the integration interval, there is a reciprocity of time and experience. A mental impression is integrated and formed over this duration. Several faint stimuli occurring within the interval may be summed to the mental impression of one intense stimulus. If events should somehow be cut off midway through the integration, our impression of them will be only partially or incompletely formed.

2. Central Masking. When two or more events that cannot be easily integrated occur within an integration interval, the process may develop or form impressions for some events and reject others.

3. Apparent Movement. Two spatially as well as temporally separate stimuli that fall within an integration interval may again be fused, or integrated, to a unitary impression. Because of their spatial separation, however, they will be experienced as one object in motion between the two locations.

4. Temporal Numerosity and Simultaneity. In any sequence of rapidly intermittent events, intermittency can be experienced at rates no faster than approximately 10 events per second. This is a limit on the rate of human cognitive performances in general.

5. Refractory Period and Prior Entry. Sometimes when two events occur in the same integration interval and are neither fused nor masked, one event will be delayed and integrated by a succeeding pulse of attention. It will thus appear to be displaced in time away from its true time of occurrence. If two responses must be made, one to each of two rapidly successive events, the second response is delayed for the duration of a rapid integration interval.

6. Memory Scanning. Impressions that are held in short-term memory can be scanned no faster than the rate determined by the attentional integration process. In searches of logically structured information held in long-term memory, the scan through chains of associations proceeds at the rate of the attentional integration process— about 75-100 msec for each node in the chain.

7. Stroboscopic Enhancement. In an otherwise unstructured stimulus environment, an intermittent stimulus (such as a flashing light) that pulses at a rate of about 10 per second can drive the rapid attentional integration process to exaggerated levels of constructive activity so as to produce hallucinatory phenomena.

Like all biological phenomena, there is a range of temporal variation in this integration process, which reflects momentary states of the organism or of environmental events. When greater energy is present, for instance, the process of integration is more rapid. Habituation, fatigue, or age may also cause the process to vary.

Basic Gestalt principles are observed in rapid attentional integrations. Most generally, with other things equal, attentional integrations develop in the direction that requires least energy or least effort.

Buffer Delays

Buffer delays are *pre*attentive delays of input to the central integration process. They constitute a mechanism of defense against information overload. Such mechanisms are necessary in any information-processing system whose capacity, or speed of processing, can differ from its capacity to receive information. A variety of terms have been used (but not always in a consistent way) to describe preattentive buffer delays. They include *iconic storage, echoic storage, stimulus trace, sensory store, channel capacity,* and *field of centration.* The following generalizations describe this delay process in human cognitive actions:

> Buffer delays are delays of inputs to experience at a simple or unstructured level of representation prior to incorporation into central attentional integrations; these delays vary from about a half a second to about two seconds, with the most common observation being three-quarters of a second (750 msec).
>
> In contrast to the one-track unifying process of rapid attentional integration, buffer delays maintain many separate events simultaneously.

The periodicity of this process was isolated in the following areas of observation:

1. Duration of Buffer Images. When an individual confronts a very briefly presented array of simultaneous events, they remain immediately available for about 750 msec at an unanalyzed or primitive level of experience. But they can be perceived or reported only as attention can focus on them while the buffer image lasts.

2. The Indifference Interval. Events that are slightly longer than the buffer delay may occasionally be experienced as attenuated in time, while those that are slightly shorter than the buffer delay may be experienced as slightly elongated in time.

3. Rhythm and Time-Order Errors. The experience of rhythm is confined to beat separations that fall within the range of the buffer delay process. Sometimes an interval between two rapid events may be experienced as slightly longer or shorter than it actually is, because of the intrinsic buffer delay action.

4. Anticipation in Performance. Events that fall together within one buffer image (or interval) are more readily associated in memory. Warning signals that precede other action signals are most effective if not separated in time by more than the buffer duration.

Short-Term Memory (STM)

There is also a *post*attentive delay that again serves a buffer function. It is a delay of events that have just been perceived, thought of, or recalled, and it has a longer duration than the *pre*attentive delay. STM provides a context for the stream of experience that is controlled by rapid attentional integrations. It holds a multitude of momentary goals, schemata, and ambient impressions. Those impressions decay over time or may be replaced by new items of experience. Other common terms for this process (though they are not always applied in a consistent way) include *active memory, temporary working memory, surface memory, operational memory, primary memory,* and *immediate memory.* The following generalizations summarize observations of this phenomenon:

> Short-term memory is a postattentive delay that holds impressions immediately accessible to consciousness for a limited period; unless attentionally reinstated, these impressions decay over an interval that varies from approximately 5 to 20 seconds, with the most common observation being about 10 seconds.
>
> Short-term memory provides a working background or directive context for the integrative operations of attention.

The periodicity of this process was isolated in the following sets of observations:

1. Decay of Impressions. Impressions that enter STM will decline in their recallability steadily over about 10 to 15 seconds unless they are refocused, or "rehearsed," by attention, in which case they may be recycled in STM indefinitely. Events that are not refocused in this way may slip away and then be very difficult to recall, even though they were in our thoughts just a short time before.

2. *Memorization and Retrieval.* The STM delay may be an important aid for the effective storage of impressions in long-term memory. It gives time for the assimilation of new experiences to the structures and schemata of memory. Similarly, it holds reference information in store to aid in the retrieval of memories.

3. *Speech Rhythms.* Spontaneous speech production shows cycles of alternate high hesitancy (frequent pauses) and low hesitancy (fluent) speech. When there are no other distracting events, these cycles may be fairly regular. Such cycles appear to reflect the duration of short-term memory. During the high-hesitancy phase, attention is largely turned inward to scan a set of impressions held in STM and to organize them in the planning of the next phase of fluent utterance. The duration of this planning activity is limited by the duration of the contents in short-term memory.

4. *Attention Waves.* In highly repetitive tasks, blocks or waves can sometimes be observed in performance, and those waves coincide with short-term memory periodicity. Threshold-level stimuli may appear to fade in and out at these same intervals.

Cognitive Spans

There are some very general limits on the capacities of human cognitive performance that derive from rapid attentional integrations, buffer delays, and short-term memory. They have been called *memory span, attention span, apprehension span, perception span, central computing space,* and *absolute judgment span.* They may be grouped into three types: simultaneity spans, sequentiality spans, and absolute judgment spans (a special case of sequentiality span). The following generalities summarize the nature of these limits:

> The number of simultaneous impressions that can enter consciousness is limited by the ratio of buffer-delay time to rapid-attentional-integration time.
> The number of sequential impressions that can be grouped together in momentary consciousness is limited by their duration in short-term memory.

Whatever is called an "impression," or "item of experience," or "memory item" is arbitrary—it is whatever is focused by attention as a unitary perception, thought, or memory.

The following are further descriptions of the three types of cognitive span:

1. Simultaneity Span. The ratio of a typical buffer-delay time of 750 msec to a typical RAI time of 100 msec yields a simultaneity span of 7.5. That means that only about 7 items can be identified from a single brief encounter with many simultaneous events. Those events are held in a buffer delay for about 750 msecs, and they are integrated (identified) at the rate of 100 msec each. This span of 7 will vary, of course, as the underlying temporal processes vary in their duration.

2. Sequentiality Span. A sequence of items can be immediately repeated or recalled only to the degree that they are retained in STM (unless some auxiliary mnemonic technique is used to extend memory). After one hearing of a sequence of related digits, letters, or words at an average rate of speech, a person generally repeats them back accurately only if they do not exceed about 6 or 7 in number. When there are more, they fade from STM before they can be repeated.

3. Absolute Judgment Span. This is the limit on the ability to identify qualities or magnitudes of simple isolated stimuli. People can make only as many discriminations of intensity, position, color, and so on, as they can maintain in short-term memory. The difficulty is that of holding many distinctions in mind long enough to scan and compare them.

Emotion

Emotional reactions may always interact with the attentional integrations of immediate experience. Elementary emotional components of experience give rise to actions of self-control and to feelings of volition and purpose. Emotion links enduring needs and dispositions to the psychological present. It can direct the retrieval of memories, the structuring of thoughts, or the formation of perceptions. The word "emotion" is used here in a broad sense that includes *affects, feelings, sentiments, moods, attitudes,* and *values.*

The following generalizations summarize a wide variety of observations on emotional phenomena:

Emotion arises from reactions of the rapid-attentional-integration process in the course of its integrations of immediate experience.

There are at least three systems (or dimensions) of reaction that form emotional experience. They have been called, among other terms, *the hedonic, the arousal,* and *the attentiveness systems.*

The following sets of observations describe the pervasiveness of the emotional component of experience:

1. Synesthesia. Common affective reactions occur for sensations from different sensory modalities. This leads to the association of certain sounds with certain colors, or of certain colors with certain tastes, and so on. This implies that there is one central affective system that may play a role in the organization of all experience.

2. The Experience of Pain. Pain research shows that extreme emotional experience can be entirely controlled by the actions of the attentional integration process.

3. Reactions to Music. Music, being a purely temporal phenomenon, manipulates rather directly the temporal processes of cognition, causing experiences of excitement, tension, anticipation, and so on. When varieties of music are rated on many descriptive dimensions, and when these ratings are factor analyzed, the traditional three-dimensional system of emotional quality emerges.

4. Visceral-Cognitive Integrations. Bodily reactions that are usually associated with emotion (for example, trembling, palpitations, and sweating) may enhance or exaggerate emotional experience, depending on how those bodily reactions are incorporated into attentional integrations. If interpreted as arising from a source unrelated to immediate emotional experience, they will have no effect on that experience.

5. Enhancement and Repression. The smallest changes in experience may evoke emotional reactions before that experience is fully localized and formed by attention. For instance, we can have feelings of familiarity with events we have not fully perceived or recognized. Memories, too, may be largely a reconstruction based on some initial affective attitude. It is thus not surprising that affect can direct, or even distort, our perceptions, thoughts, and memories; some may be enhanced, others repressed.

Longer Temporal Integrations

Habitual patterns of attentional integration develop throughout the lifetime of an individual. Separate thoughts, memories, and perceptions can be brought together in STM, and their common attentional patterns can then be isolated so as to become autonomous items of experience in themselves. These actions result in *concepts, schemata, abstractions, rules, expectancies, habituations, constancies,* and *sets.* The following generalizations describe some of the characteristics of these phenomena:

> Longer temporal integrations are fusions or extrapolations of similarities in attentional patterns that underlie separate experiences when those experiences are brought together in short-term memory.
>
> When an attentional pattern is repeated often, it can become automatized so as to require little effort—thereby freeing attentional capacity and facilitating assimilation of a new experience.

Longer temporal integrations illustrate how our experience is very much the product of our own internal construction. Many of these phenomonena are illustrated in the following areas of observation:

1. Image Formation. The images we construct are often cumulative integrations of many separate experiences. Images (such as the body image) can then have a guiding influence on our behavior and thought. Other internal imagery (such as daydreams) may interfere with our perceptions and operations in the external world.

2. Skilled Performance. Skills develop when patterns of behavior or of thought become automatized, leaving attention free to concentrate on the goals of performance, rather than on the means of performance. This occurs whether in learning to drive a car or in learning to solve a complex mathematical problem.

3. Concepts and Schemata. Much of our knowledge of the world is organized according to attentionally constructed concepts and schemata. These are not items we carry around with us in a mental file cabinet. Rather, they are action patterns for reconstructing experience. A concept stands for an innumerable variety of events, and so makes available as a simultaneity what was formerly available only as a succession of separate experiences.

4. Recognition. Longer temporal integrations maintain affective dispositions that direct the course of our perception. Some of these directive affects are broadly termed "feelings of familiarity" or "feelings of knowing." For recognition to begin, it may be sufficient for a certain affect to be set off to initiate the reconstruction of a certain attentional pattern.

5. The Self-Concept. Perhaps the most important longer temporal integration we ever form is that of the self-concept. Self-preservation is meaningless until the self is delineated.

Cognitive Control

Central to mental processes is the action of cognitive control, which has also been called *volition, will, intention, choice, effort, self-generated activity, vigilance, executive routine or monitor,* and *attention deployment.* It is largely synonymous with attentional integration, yet includes all the forces (primarily emotional reactions) that maintain cognition on one train of action, often recycling one set of perceptions, memories, or motor activities in order to maintain coherence of experience. Acts of cognitive control often involve the temporal integration of past and present events with future events—that is, with synthesized or imagined future events. In this way, goals are established and selected.

The following generalizations summarize a wide variety of observations of cognitive control actions:

> One dimension of cognitive control is attentional focusing, or field-articulation; it is the range of experience in a momentary attentional integration, from narrow to global integrations.
>
> Another dimension of cognitive control is attentional scanning; it is the degree to which attention moves from one area of experience to another.

Characteristics of cognitive control have been isolated in the following areas of observation:

1. Biofeedback. We can control only those behaviors that we are able to bring to the focus of our attention. Electronic amplifiers have made it possible to bring to attention the reactions of many internal organs. This in turn has made it possible for people to bring the actions of these organs under varying degrees of voluntary control.

2. Memory Performance. What we learn and remember is limited to the degree that we can bring events within the focus of our attention. Learning also depends on how attention then manipulates or integrates those events. The arousal of emotional reactions may lead to more effective memory than do other variables such as time, effort, or intention to learn.

3. Manipulation of Images. People are not only able to generate images; they can also rotate, transform, and manipulate them in systematic ways. Such actions of mental manipulation may be brought under individual self-control to the point of becoming a refined skill. In this way, memory performance can be improved considerably.

4. Problem Solving. The ability to solve problems and to create new bodies of knowledge depends on attentional flexibility, which allows individuals to break out of established automaticities of thought. In some problem-solving tasks, general dimensions of performance can be discerned: one is attentional focusing; another is attentional scanning.

5. Language Performance. Language production involves the transformation of a mental configuration (images, thoughts, perceptions, memories) into sequentially arranged elements. This is accomplished by the highly controlled attentional focusing and scanning of that mental configuration so as to analyze it into related parts and thus render its transformation into speech possible. A highly articulate person is one who is able to control his attention effectively in the course of this very intricate and subtle performance.

6. Schizophrenic Malfunction. The most common form of mental breakdown, schizophrenia, reflects severe distortions of attentional control. These are most likely brought on by extreme emotional states or by the inability to cope with stress. Attentional scanning can then run wild, becoming extremely and habitually overactive; or it may shut down and remain fixed on single areas of experience. Similarly, attentional focusing can become either extremely diffuse or extremely restricted and narrow, so as to render it nearly nonfunctional in either case. These different syndromes of schizophrenia may be demonstrated in numerous perceptual and psychomotor tests of the afflicted individuals.

In Conclusion. . .

Cognitive psychology began as a formal discipline when scientifically minded individuals first wondered about and asked testable questions about the regulation of the stream of consciousness. Now, with long traditions of psychological research behind us, we still confront many of the same questions; yet many more explicit answers can be offered today than could have been a hundred years ago.

This presentation of some of the answers has focused on the *process* of cognition in adult humans. As Hebb implied in the quotation at the beginning of this book, that process is the integrative activity of the brain, which can override reflex response and the flux of sensation, and which has the potential for freeing us to enjoy a world of our own choosing and of our own making.

REFERENCES

AARONSON, D. (1967) Temporal factors in perception and short-term memory. *Psychological Bulletin, 67,* 130-144.

ABELSON, R., & SERMAT, V. (1962) Multidimensional scaling of facial expressions. *Journal of Experimental Psychology, 63,* 546-554.

ACH, N. (1905) *Ueber die Willenstätigkeit und das Denken.* Göttingen: Vandenhoek & Ruprecht. Excerpts translated by D. Rapaport in D. Rapaport (Ed.), *Organization and pathology of thought.* New York: Columbia University Press, 1951.

AIKEN, L., & LICHTENSTEIN, M. (1964) Reaction times to regularly recurring visual stimuli. *Perceptual and Motor Skills, 18,* 713-720.

ALLPORT, D. A. (1966) Studies in the psychological unit of duration. Unpublished doctoral thesis, Cambridge University.

ALLPORT, D. A. (1968) Phenomenal simultaneity and the perceptual moment hypothesis. *British Journal of Psychology, 59,* 395-406.

ALLPORT, F. (1955) *Theories of perception and the concept of structure.* New York: John Wiley.

ALLPORT, G. W. (1955) *Becoming.* New Haven: Yale University Press.

ALPERN, M. (1952) Metacontrast: historical introduction. *American Journal of Optometry, 42,* 1-16.

ANDERSEN, J. R., & BOWER, G. H. (1973) *Human associative memory.* Washington D.C.: V. H. Winston (Distributed by John Wiley).

ARIETI, S. (1961) The loss of reality. *Psychoanalytic Review, 3,* 3-24.

ARIETI, S. (1970) Cognition and feeling. In M. B. Arnold (Ed.), *Feelings and emotions: The Loyola symposium.* New York: Academic Press.

ARNOLD, M. B. (Ed.) (1968) *The nature of emotion.* Baltimore: Penguin.

ARNOLD, M. B. (Ed.) (1970) *Feelings and emotions: The Loyola symposium.* New York: Academic Press.

ATKINSON, R. C., & SHIFFRIN, R. M. (1968) Human memory: A proposed system and its control processes. *The Psychology of Learning and Motivation 2,* 89-195.

ATKINSON, R. C., & SHIFFRIN, R. M. (1971) The control of short-term memory. *Scientific American, 225,* No. 2, 82-90.

ATTNEAVE, F. (1959) *Applications of information theory to psychology.* New York: Henry Holt.

AVERBACH, E. (1963) The span of apprehension as a function of exposure duration. *Journal of Verbal Learning and Verbal Behavior, 2,* 60-64.

AVERBACH, E., & SPERLING, G. (1961) Short-term storage of information in vision. In C. Cherry (Ed.), *Information theory: Proceedings of the fourth London symposium.* London: Butterworth.

BADDELEY, A. D., SCOTT, D., DRYNAN, R., & SMITH, J. (1969) Short-term memory and the limited capacity hypothesis. *British Journal of Psychology, 60,* 51-55.

BAIR, J. H. (1901) Development of voluntary control. *Psychological Review, 8,* 474-510.

BALDWIN, J. M. (1889) *Handbook of psychology: Senses and intellect.* New York: Macmillan.

BALES, R. F. (1970) *Personality and social roles.* New York: Holt, Rinehart & Winston.

BARTLETT, F. C. (1932) *Remembering.* Cambridge: Cambridge University Press.

BARTLETT, F. C. (1958) *Thinking.* London: Allen & Unwin.

BARTLEY, S. (1939) Some effects of intermittent stimulation. *Journal of Experimental Psychology, 25,* 462-480.

BASSETT, M., & WARNE, C. (1919) On the lapse of verbal meaning with repetition. *American Journal of Psychology, 30,* 415-418.

BEECHER, H. (1959) *Measurement of subjective responses.* New York: Oxford University Press.

BÉKÉSY, G. VON (1929) Zur theorie des Hörens. Ueber die eben merkbare Amplituden- und Frequenzänderung eines Tones. Die Theorie der Schwebungen. *Physik Zeitschrift, 30,* 721-745.

BÉKÉSY, G. VON (1931) Bemerkungen zur Theorie der günstigen Nachalldauer von Räumen. *Annals der Physik, 8,* 851-873.

BÉKÉSY, G. VON (1936) Ueber die Hörschwelle und Fühlgrenze langsamer sinusförmiger Luftdruckschwankungen. *Annals der Physik, 26,* 557-566.

BÉKÉSY, G. VON (1960) *Experiments in hearing.* New York:McGraw-Hill.

BÉKÉSY, G. VON (1967) *Sensory inhibition.* Princeton, N.J.: Princeton University Press.

BÉKÉSY, G. VON (1971) Auditory backward inhibition in concert halls. *Science, 171,* 529-536.

BENUSSI, V. (1904) Zur Psychologie des Gestalterfassens. In A. Meinong (Ed.), *Untersuchungen zur Gegenstandstheorie und Psychologie.* Leipzig: Barth.

BENUSSI, V. (1912) Stroboskopische Scheinbewegungen und geometrischoptische Gestalttäuschungen. *Archiv für die gesamte Psychologie, 24,* 31-62.

BENUSSI, V. (1916) Versuche zur Analyse taktil erweckter Scheinbewegung. *Archiv für die gesamte Psychologie, 36,* 59-135.

BERGER, G. (1886) Ueber den Einfluss der Reizstärke auf die Dauer einfacher psychischer Vorgänge mit besondere Rücksicht auf Lichtreize. *Philosophische Studien, 3,* 38-93.

BERLYNE, D. (Ed.) (1974) *Studies on the new experimental aesthetics.* New York: John Wiley.

BERTELSON, P., & JOFFE, R. (1963) Blockings in prolonged serial responding. *Ergonomics, 6,* 109-116.

BESSEL, F. W. (1823) *Astronomische Beobachtungen.* Königsberg: Academia Albertina.

BEXTON, W., HERON, W., & SCOTT, T. (1954) Effects of decreased variation in the sensory environment. *Canadian Journal of Psychology, 8,* 70-76.

BILLS, A. G. (1931) Blocking: A new principle in mental fatigue. *American Journal of Psychology, 43,* 230-245.

BILLS, A. G. (1935) Some causal factors in mental blocking. *Journal of Experimental Psychology, 18,* 562-573.

BLANKENSHIP, A. B. (1938) Memory span: A review of the literature. *Psychological Bulletin, 35,* 1-25.

BLISS, J., CRANE, H., MANSFIELD, K., & TOWNSEND, J. (1966) Information available in brief tactile presentations. *Perception & Psychophysics, 1,* 273-283.

BLOCH, A. M. (1885) Expériences sur la vision. *Comtes Rendues, Société Biologique,* Paris, *2,* 493.

BLOCK, J. (1957) Studies in the phenomenology of emotion. *Journal of Abnormal and Social Psychology, 54,* 358-363.

BLUMENTHAL, A. L. (1970) *Language and psychology: Historical aspects of psycholinguistics.* New York: John Wiley.

BLUMENTHAL, A. L. (1975) A reappraisal of Wilhelm Wundt. *American Psychologist, 30,* 1081-1088.

BOGGS, L. (1907) Studies in absolute pitch. *American Journal of Psychology, 18,* 194-205.

BOLTON, T. L. (1894) Rhythm. *American Journal of Psychology, 6,* 145-238.

BOOMER, D. S. (1965) Hesitations and grammatical encoding. *Language and Speech, 8,* 148-158.

BOOMER, D. S., & LAVER, J. D. M. (1968) Slips of the tongue. *British Journal of Disorders of Communication, 3,* 2-12.

BORING, E. G. (1942) *Sensation and perception in the history of psychology.* New York: Appleton-Century-Crofts.

BOTWINICK, J., & BRINLEY, J. (1962) An analysis of set in relation to reaction time. *Journal of Experimental Psychology, 63,* 568-574.

BOUMAN, M. (1955[a]) The absolute threshold conditions for visual perception. *Journal of the Optical Society of America, 45,* 36-43.

BOUMAN, M. (1955[b]) On foveal and peripheral interaction in binocular vision. *Optica Acta, 1,* 177-183.

BOURNE, L., & DOMINOWSKI, R. (1972) Thinking. *Annual Review of Psychology, 23,* 105-130.

BOUSFIELD, W. (1953) The occurrence of clustering in the recall of randomly arranged associates. *Journal of General Psychology, 49,* 229-240.

BOWER, G. H. (1970) Analysis of a mnemonic device. *American Scientist, 58,* 496-510.

BOWER, G. H. (1972) A selective review of organizational factors in memory. In E. Tulving & W. Donaldson (Eds.), *Organization of memory.* New York: Academic Press.

BOWER, G. H. (1973) How to . . . uh . . . remember! *Psychology Today,* October, 63-70.

BOWER, T. G. R. (1966) The visual world of infants. *Scientific American, 215,* 80-92.

BOWER, T. G. R. (1967) Phenomenal identity and form perception in an infant. *Perception & Psychophysics. 2,* 74-76.

BOWERS, M. B. (1968) Pathogenesis of acute schizophrenic psychosis: An experiential approach. *Archives of General Psychiatry, 19,* 348-355.

BOYNTON, R. M. (1957) Recognition of critical targets among irrelevant forms. In J. Wulfeck & J. Taylor (Eds.), *Form discrimination as related to military problems.* Washington, D.C.: National Research Council, 175-184.

BRADY, P. (1970) Fixed scale mechanism of absolute pitch. *Journal of the Acoustical Society of America, 40,* 883-887.

BRECHER, G. A. (1932) Die Entstehung und biologische Bedeutung der subjektiven Zeitenheit—des Momentes. *Zeitschrift für vergleichende Physiologie, 18,* 204-243.

BREGMAN, A., & CAMPBELL, J. (1971) Primary auditory stream segregation and perception of order in rapid sequences of tones. *Journal of Experimental Psychology, 89,* 244-249.

BRENTANO, F. (1874) *Psychologie vom empirische Standpunkte.* Leipzig: Duncker & Humboldt. Edited and translated by A. Rancurello, D. Terrell, & L. McAllister as *Psychology from an empirical standpoint.* New York: Humanities Press, 1973.

BROADBENT, D. (1958) *Perception and communication.* New York: Pergamon.

BROADBENT, D. (1971) *Decision and stress.* London: Academic Press.

BROCA, A., & SULZER, D. (1902) La sensation lumineuse en fonction du temps. *Journale de Physiologie et de Pathologie Générale, 4*, 632-640.

BROEN, W. E. (1973) Limiting the flood of stimulation: A protective deficit in chronic schizophrenia. In R. Solso (Ed.), *Contemporary issues in cognitive psychology.* Washington, D.C.: Winston.

BROVERMAN, D., BROVERMAN, I., & KLAIBER, E. (1966) Ability to automatize and automatization of cognitive style: A validation study. *Perceptual and Motor Skills, 23*, 419-437.

BROWN, J. (1958) Some tests of the decay theory of immediate memory. *Quarterly Journal of Experimental Psychology, 10*, 12-21.

BROWN, R., & MCNEILL, D. (1966) The "tip-of-the-tongue" phenomenon. *Journal of Verbal Learning and Verbal Behavior, 5*, 325-337.

BRUNER, J. (1964) The course of cognitive growth. *American Psychologist, 19*, 1-15.

BRUNER, J., GOODNOW, J., & AUSTIN, G. (1956) *A study of thinking.* New York: John Wiley.

BRYAN, W., & HARTER, N. (1899) Studies on the physiology and psychology of the telegraphic language: the acquisition of a hierarchy of habits. *Psychological Review, 4*, 27-53.

BUGELSKI, B. (1962) Presentation time, total time, and mediation in paired-associate learning. *Journal of Experimental Psychology, 63*, 409-412.

BURT, C. (1961) The structure of mind: A reply. *British Journal of Statistical Psychology, 14*, 145-170.

BURTT, H. E. (1917[a]) Tactual illusions of movement. *Journal of Experimental Psychology, 2*, 371-385.

BURTT, H. E. (1917[b]) Auditory illusions of movement—a preliminary study. *Journal of Experimental Psychology, 2*, 63-75.

BUSCHKE, H. (1967) Two kinds of short-term storage. *Psychonomic Science, 8*, 419-420.

BUTTERWORTH, B. (1975) Hesitation and semantic planning in speech. *Journal of Psycholinguistic Research, 4*, 75-87.

CANNON, W. (1927) The James-Lange theory of emotions: A critical examination and an alternative theory. *American Journal of Psychology, 39*, 106-124.

CARNAP, R. (1928) *Der logische Aufbau der Welt.* Berlin: Weltkreis. Translated by R. George, as *The logical structure of the world.* Berkeley, Calif.: University of California Press, 1967.

CAVANAGH, J. P. (1972) Relation between the immediate memory span and the memory search rate. *Psychological Review, 79*, 525-530.

CHAPMAN, J. (1966)The early symptoms of schizophrenia. *British Journal of Psychiatry, 112*, 225-251.

CHOMSKY, N. (1957) *Syntactic structures.* The Hague: Mouton.

COFER, C. N. (1965) On some factors in the organizational characteristics of free recall. *American Psychologist, 20*, 261-272.

COLEGROVE, F. W. (1898) The time required for recognition. *American Journal of Psychology, 10*, 286-292.

COLLINS, A. M., & QUILLIAN, M. R. (1969) Retrieval time from semantic memory. *Journal of Verbal Learning and Verbal Behavior, 8,* 240-247.

CONRAD, R., & HULL, A. (1966) The role of the interpolated task in short-term retention. *Quarterly Journal of Experimental Psychology, 18,* 266-269.

COOPER, L., & SHEPARD, R. (1973) Chronometric studies of the rotation of mental images. In W. Chase (Ed.), *Visual information processing.* New York: Academic Press.

CORTEEN, R., & WOOD, B. (1972) Autonomic responses to shock-associated words in an unattended channel. *Journal of Experimental Psychology, 94,* 308-313.

CRAIK, F. J. M. (1971) Primary memory. *British Medical Bulletin, 27,* 232-236.

CRAIK, F. J. M., & LOCKHART, R. (1972) Levels of processing: A framework for memory research. *Journal of Verbal Learning and Verbal Behavior, 11,* 671-684.

CROWDER, R. G., & MORTON, J. (1969) Precategorical acoustic storage. *Perception and Psychophysics, 5,* 365-376.

CUDDY, L. (1968) Practice effects in judgments of pitch. *Journal of the Acoustical Society of America, 43,* 1069-1076.

CZEHURA, W. S. (1943) The generalization of temporal stimulus patterns on the time continuum. *Journal of Comparative Psychology, 36,* 79-90.

CZERMAK, J. (1855) Weitere Beiträge zur Physiologie des Tastsinns. *Sitzungsberichte der weiner Akademie, 17,* 563-590.

DANIELS, A. (1895) Memory, afterimage, and attention. *American Journal of Psychology, 6,* 558-564.

DARWIN, C., TURVEY, M., & CROWDER, R. (1972) An auditory analogue of the Sperling partial report procedure: Evidence for brief auditory storage. *Cognitive Psychology, 3,* 255-267.

DAVIS, R. (1956) The limits of the "psychological refractory period." *Quarterly Journal of Experimental Psychology, 8, 24-38.*

DAVIS, R. (1957) The human operator as a single channel information system. *Quarterly Journal of Experimental Psychology, 9,* 119-129.

DAVITZ, J. (1969) *The language of emotion.* New York: Academic Press.

DAY, R. (1968) Fusion in dichotic listening. Unpublished doctoral thesis, Stanford University.

DE GROOT, A. (1965) *Thought and choice in chess.* The Hague: Mouton.

DEIKMAN, A. J. (1963) Experimental meditation. *Journal of Nervous and Mental Disease, 136,* 329-343.

DELATTRE, P., LIBERMAN, A., COOPER, F., & GERSTMAN, L. (1952) An experimental study of the acoustic determinants of vowel color: Observations on one- and two-formant vowels synthesized from spectrographic patterns. *Word, 8,* 195-210.

DIETZE, G. (1885) Untersuchungen über den Umfang des Bewusstseins bei regelmässig aufeinander folgenden Schalleindrucken. *Philosophische Studien, 2,* 362-393.

DIXON, N. (1971) *Subliminal perception: The nature of a controversy.* London: McGraw-Hill.

DOWLING, W., & ROBERTS, K. (1974) The historical and philosophical approaches to cognitive psychology. In E. Carterette & M. Friedman (Eds.), *Handbook of perception* (Vol. 1). New York: Academic Press.

DUNCKER, K. (1945) On problem solving. *Psychological Monographs, 58,* no. 5.

EBBINGHAUS, H. (1885) *Ueber das Gedächtnis.* Leipzig: Duncker & Humbolt. Translated by H. Krueger & C. Bussenius as *Memory.* New York: Columbia University Press, 1913.

EFRON, R. (1969) What is perception? In R. Cohen & M. Wartofsky (Eds.), *Boston studies in the philosophy of science.* New York: Humanities Press.

EISENDRATH, C., (1971) *The unifying moment: The psychological philosophy of William James and Alfred North Whitehead.* Cambridge, Mass.: Harvard University Press.

ENGEN, T., LEVY, N., & SCHLOSBERG, H. (1958) The dimensional analysis of a new series of facial expressions. *Journal of Experimental Psychology, 55,* 454-458.

ERDELYI, M. (1974) A new look at the new look: Perceptual defense and vigilance. *Psychological Review, 81,* 1-25.

ERIKSEN, C. W., & JOHNSON, H. J. (1954) Storage and decay characteristics of non-attended auditory stimuli. *Journal of Experimental Psychology, 68,* 28-36.

ESTES, W. (1970) *Learning theory and mental development.* New York: Academic Press.

EXNER, S. (1870) Bemerkungen über intermittirende Netzhautreizung. *Archiv für die gesamte Physiologie, 3,* 214-240.

EXNER, S. (1879) Physiologie der Grosshirnrinde. *Handbuch der Physiologie, 2,* 289-350.

FANTZ, R. (1965) Visual perception from birth as shown by pattern selectivity. *Annals of the New York Academy of Sciences, 118,* 793-814.

FECHNER, G. (1860) *Elemente der Psychophysik.* Leipzig: Breitkopf und Härtel.

FELLOWS, B. (1968) *The discrimination process and development.* Oxford: Pergamon.

FESTINGER, L. (1957) *A theory of cognitive dissonance.* Stanford, Calif.: Stanford University Press.

FIDELL, S., PEARSONS, K., GRIGNETTE, M., & GREEN, D. (1970) The noise of impulsive sounds. *Journal of the Acoustical Society of America, 48,* 1304-1310.

FITTS, P. M. (1964) Perceptual-motor skill learning. In A. W. Melton (Ed.), *Categories of human learning.* New York: Academic Press.

FLAVELL, J. H. (1963) *The developmental psychology of Jean Piaget.* New York: Van Nostrand.

FLAVELL, J. H., & DRAGUNS, J. (1957) A microgenetic approach to perception and thought. *Psychological Bulletin, 54,* 197-217.

FRAISSE, P. (1948) Rythmes auditifs et rythmes visuels. *Année Psychologique, 49,* 21-42.

FRAISSE, P. (1963) *The psychology of time,* translated by J. Leith. New York: Harper & Row.

FRAISSE, P. (1967) *Psychologie du temps* (2nd ed.). Paris: Presses Universitaires.

FRAISSE, P., EHRLICH, S., & VURPILLOT, E. (1956) Études de la centration perceptive par la methode tachistoscopic. *Archives de Psychologie Genève, 35,* 193-214.

FREEDMAN, J., & LANDAUER, T. (1966) Retrieval of long-term memory: "Tip-of-the-tongue" phenomenon. *Psychonomic Science, 4,* 309-310.

FREEDMAN, S. J., & MARKS, P. A. (1965) Visual imagery produced by rhythmic photic stimulation: Personality correlates and phenomenology. *British Journal of Psychology, 56,* 95-112.

FREEMAN, T. (1965) *Studies on psychosis.* London: Tavistock.

FREEMAN, W., & WATTS, J. (1948) Pain mechanisms and the frontal lobes: A study of prefrontal lobotomy for intractable pain. *Annals of International Medicine, 28,* 747-754.

FREUD, S. (1900) *Die Traumdeutung.* Vienna: Deuticke. Translated as, *The interpretation of dreams.* New York: Modern Library, 1938.

FRIJDA, N. (1969) Recognition of emotion. In L. Berkowitz (Ed.), *Advances in experimental social psychology,* Vol. 4.

FROMKIN, V. A. (1971) The non-anomalous nature of anomalous utterances. *Language, 47,* 27-52.

FURST, C. (1971) Automatizing of visual attention. *Perception & Psychophysics, 10,* 65-70.

GALLI, P. (1932) Ueber mittelst verschiedener Sinnesreize erweckte Wahrnehmung von Scheinbewegung. *Archiv für die gesamte Psychologie, 85,* 137-180.

GALTON, F. (1879) Composite portraits, made by combining those of many different persons into a single resultant figure. *Journal of the Anthropological Institute, 8,* 132-144.

GANTENBEIN, M. (1952) Recherche sur le développement de la perception du mouvement avec l'âge (mouvement apparent, dit stroboscopique). *Archives de Psychologie, 33,* 197-294.

GANZ, L., & WILSON, P. (1967) Innate generalization of a form discrimination without contouring eye movements. *Journal of Comparative and Physiological Psychology, 63,* 258-269.

GARDNER, P., & PICKFORD, R. (1943) Relation between dissonance and context. *Nature, 152,* 356.

GARDNER, R. (1961) Cognitive controls of attention deployment as determinants of visual illusions. *Journal of Abnormal and Social Psychology, 62,* 120-127.

GARDNER, R., HOLZMAN, P., KLEIN, G., LINTON, H., & SPENCE, D. (1959) Cognitive control: A study of individual consistencies in cognitive behavior. *Psychological Issues, 1,* Monograph 4.

GARNER, W. (1953) An informational analysis of absolute judgments of loudness. *Journal of Psychology, 46,* 373-380.

GARNER, W., HAKE, H., & ERIKSEN, C. (1956) Operationism and the concept of perception. *Psychological Review, 63,* 149-159.

GARRETT, M. (1975) The analysis of sentence production. *The Psychology of Learning and Motivation, 9,* 133-178.

GEYER, J. (1966) Perceptual systems in reading: The prediction of a temporal eye-voice span constant. Unpublished doctoral thesis, University of California, Berkeley.

GIBSON, J. J. (1962) Observations on active touch. *Psychological Review, 69,* 477-491.

GILSON, E., & BADDELEY, A. (1969) Tactile short-term memory. *Quarterly Journal of Experimental Psychology, 21,* 180-184.

GLADSTONES, W. (1962) A multidimensional study of facial expression of emotion. *Australian Journal of Psychology, 14,* 95-100.

GLICKMAN, S. (1961) Perseverative neural processes and consolidation of memory trace. *Psychological Bulletin, 58,* 218-233.

GOLDMAN-EISLER, F. (1968) *Psycholinguistics.* New York: Academic Press.

GOLDSTEIN, K. (1940) *Human nature in the light of psychopathology.* Cambridge, Mass.: Harvard University Press.

GOLDSTEIN, K. (1951) On emotions: Considerations from an organismic point of view. *Journal of Psychology, 31,* 37-49.

GOODMAN, N. (1969) *The structure of appearance.* (2nd ed.) New York: Bobbs-Merrill.

GREGORY, R. L. (1970) *The intelligent eye.* London: Weidenseld & Nicolson.

GRINDLEY, G., & TOWNSEND, V. (1968) Voluntary attention in peripheral vision and its effects on acuity and differential thresholds. *Quarterly Journal of Experimental Psychology, 20,* 11-20.

GUILFORD, J. (1927) Fluctuations of attention with weak visual stimuli. *American Journal of Psychology, 38,* 534-583.

HABER, R. (1970) How we remember what we see. *Scientific American, 222,* 104-115.

HALDANE, J. S. (1922) *Respiration.* New Haven: Yale University Press.

HALLIDAY, A. M., & MINGAY, R. (1961) Retroactive raising of a sensory threshold by a contralateral stimulus. *Quarterly Journal of Experimental Psychology, 13,* 1-11.

HAMILTON, W. (1859) *Lectures on metaphysics and logic.* Edinburgh: Blackwood. Vol. I, 254.

HARLOW, H., & STAGNER, R. (1933) Psychology of feelings and emotions. II. Theory of emotions. *Psychological Review, 40,* 184-195.

HARRIS, J. (1943) Habituatory response decrement in the intact organism. *Psychological Bulletin, 40,* 385-422.

HART, J. (1965) Memory and the feeling-of-knowing experience. *Journal of Educational Psychology, 56,* 208-216.

HART, J. (1967) Memory and the memory-monitoring process. *Journal of Verbal Learning and Verbal Behavior, 6,* 685-691.

HARTER, M. R. (1967) Excitability cycles and cortical scanning: A review of two hypotheses of central intermittency in perception. *Psychological Bulletin, 68,* 47-58.

HARTMAN, E. (1954) The influence of practice and pitch-distance between tones on the absolute identification of pitch. *American Journal of Psychology, 67,* 1-14.

HARTMANN, H. (1939) Ich-Psychologie und Anpassungsproblem, *International Zeitschrift für Psychoanalyse (Imago), 24,* 62-135. Translated by D. Rapaport as *Ego psychology and the problem of adaptation.* New York: International Universities Press, 1958.

HAYES, J. (1952) Memory span for several vocabularies as a function of vocabulary size. *Quarterly Progress Report* (Cambridge, Mass.: Acoustics Laboratory, M.I.T.) January-June, 1952.

HEAD, H. (1920) *Studies in neurology,* 2 vols. London: Hodder & Stoughton.

HEAD, H., & HOLMES, G. (1911) Sensory disturbances from cerebral lesions. *Brain, 34,* 102-254.

HEBB, D. O. (1937) The innate organization of visual activity: I. Perception of figures by rats reared in total darkness. *Journal of Genetic Psychology, 51,* 101-126.

HEBB, D. O. (1949) *The organization of behavior.* New York: John Wiley.

HEBB, D. O. (1974) What psychology is about. *American Psychologist, 29,* 71-79. Invited address, American Psychological Association convention, 1973.

HEIDER, F. (1958) *The psychology of interpersonal relations.* New York: John Wiley.

HENDERSON, A., GOLDMAN-EISLER, F., & SKARBEK, A. (1966) Sequential temporal patterns in speech. *Language and Speech, 9,* 207-216.

HERNÁNDEZ-PÉON, R. (1964) Psychiatric implications of neurophysiological research. *Bulletin of the Menninger Clinic, 28,* 165-185.

HILGARD, E. (1969) Pain as a puzzle for psychology and physiology. *American Psychologist, 24,* 103-113.

HILGARD, E., & BOWER, G. H. (1975) *Theories of learning.* New York: Appleton-Century-Crofts.

HOCHBERG, J., & BROOKS, V. (1970) Reading as an intentional behavior. In H. Singer & R. Ruddell (Eds.), *Theoretical models and processes of reading.* Newark, Delaware: International Reading Association.

HORNBOSTEL, E. VON (1927) Die Einheit der Sinne. *Melos, Zeitschrift für Musik, 4,* 290-297. Translated as The unity of the senses. *Psyche,* 1927, *7,* 83-89.

HOVLAND, C. I. (1938) Experimental studies of rote learning theory. *Journal of Experimental Psychology, 22,* 338-353.

HUBEL, D., & WIESEL, T. (1963) Receptive fields of cells in striate cortex of very young, visually inexperienced kittens. *Journal of Neurophysiology, 26,* 994-1002.

HUBEL, D., & WIESEL, T. (1968) Receptive fields and functional architecture of monkey striate cortex. *Journal of Physiology, 195,* 215-243.

HUNTER, W. S., & SIGLER, M. (1940) The span of visual discrimination as a function of time and intensity of stimulation. *Journal of Experimental Psychology, 26,* 160-179.

JACOBS, J. (1887) Experiments on "prehension." *Mind, 12,* 75-79.

JAMES, W. (1884) What is an emotion? *Mind, 9,* 188-205.

JAMES, W. (1890) *Principles of psychology.* New York: Henry Holt.

JENKINS, J. J. (1974) Can we have a theory of meaningful memory? In R. Solso (Ed.), *Theories in cognitive psychology.* Hillsdale, N.J.: Lawrence Erlbaum.

JEVONS, W. S. (1871) The power of numerical discrimination. *Nature, 3,* 281-282.

JONES, E. E., & BRUNER, J. S. (1954) Expectancy in apparent visual movement. *British Journal of Psychology, 45,* 157-165.

KAHNEMAN, D. (1968) Method, findings, and theory in studies of visual masking. *Psychological Bulletin, 69,* 404-425.

KAHNEMAN, D. (1973) *Attention and effort.* Englewood Cliffs, N.J.: Prentice-Hall.

KANTOWITZ, B. (1974) Double stimulation. In B. Kantowitz (Ed.), *Human information processing: Tutorials in performance and cognition.* Hillsdale, N.J.: Lawrence Erlbaum.

KAPPAUF, W., & SCHLOSBERG, H. (1937) Conditioning as a function of the length of the period of delay. *Journal of Genetic Psychology, 50,* 27-45.

KASAMATSU, A., & HIRAI, T. (1966) An electroencephalographic study on the Zen meditation. *Folio of Psychiatry and Neurology Japonica, 20,* 315-336.

KATZ, D. (1925) Der Aufbau des Tastwelt. *Zeitschrift für Psychologie, Erganzungsband,* No. 11.

KEELE, S. W. (1973) *Attention and human performance.* Pacific Palisades, Calif.: Goodyear.

KEPPEL, G., & UNDERWOOD, B. (1962) Proactive inhibition in short-term retention of single items. *Journal of Verbal Learning and Verbal Behavior, 1,* 153-161.

KIMBLE, G. (1947) Conditioning as a function of the time between conditioned and unconditioned stimuli. *Journal of Experimental Psychology, 37,* 1-15.

KIMBLE, G., & PERLMUTTER, L. (1970) The problem of volition. *Psychological Review, 77,* 361-384.

KLEIN, G. S. (1954) Need and regulation. In M. R. Jones (Ed.), *Nebraska symposium on motivation.* Lincoln: University of Nebraska Press.

KLEIN, G. S. (1967) Peremptory ideation: Structure and force in motivated ideas. *Psychological Issues, 5,* Monograph 18/19, 80-130.

KOESTLER, A. (1964) *The act of creation.* New York: Dell.

KOFFKA, K. (1909) Experimentelle Untersuchungen zur Lehre vom Rhythmus. *Zeitschrift für Psychologie, 52,* 1-109.

KOFFKA, K. (1935) *Principle of Gestalt psychology.* New York: Harcourt, Brace & World.

KÖHLER, W. (1910) Akustische Untersuchungen, II. *Zeitschrift für Psychologie, 58,* 59-140.

KÖHLER, W. (1923) Zur Theorie des Suksessivvergleichs und der Zeitfehler. *Psychologische Forschung, 4,* 115-175.

KOLERS, P. (1972) *Aspects of motion perception.* Oxford: Pergamon Press.

KOLERS, P. (1975) Memorial consequences of automatized encoding. *Journal of Experimental Psychology, Human Learning and Memory, 1,* 689-701.

KONORSKI, J. (1967) *Integrative activity of the brain: An interdisciplinary approach.* Chicago: University of Chicago Press.

KOSTER, W., & VAN SCHUUR, R. (1973) The influence of intensity of tone bursts on the psychological refractory period. In S. Kornblum (Ed.), *Attention and performance IV.* New York: Academic Press.

KOZHEVNIKOV, W., & CHISTOVITCH, L. (1969) *Speech, articulation, and perception.* Washington, D.C.: U.S. Department of Commerce, Joint Publication Research Service.

KRISTOFFERSON, A. B. (1967) Attention and psychophysical time. *Acta Psychologica, 27,* 93-100.

KRUEGER, F. (1928) Das Wesen der Gefühle. *Archiv für die gesamte Psychologie, 65,* 91-128. Translated by M. B. Arnold in abridged form as, The essence of feeling. In M.B. Arnold (Ed.) (1968) *The nature of emotion.* Baltimore: Penguin.

LABERGE, D. (1973) Attention and the measurement of perceptual learning. *Memory and Cognition, 1,* 268-276.

LABERGE, D., & SAMUELS, S. J. (1974) Toward a theory of automatic information processing in reading. *Cognitive Psychology, 6,* 293-323.

LAMBERT, W., & JAKOBOVITS, L. (1960) Verbal satiation and changes in the intensity of meaning. *Journal of Experimental Psychology, 60,* 376-383.

LANGE, C. (1885) *Om Sindsbevaegelser.* Copenhagen.

LANGER, S. K. (1967) *Mind: An essay on human feeling,* Vol. 1. Baltimore: Johns Hopkins.

LASHLEY, K. (1917) The accuracy of movement in the absence of excitation from the moving organ. *American Journal of Physiology, 43,* 169-194.

LASHLEY, K. (1951) The problem of serial order in behavior. In L. A. Jeffress (Ed.), *Cerebral mechanisms in behavior: The Hixon symposium.* New York: John Wiley.

LASHLEY, K. (1954) Dynamic processes in perception. In E. Adrian, F. Brenner, & H. Jasper (Eds.), *Brain mechanisms and consciousness.* Springfield, Ill.: Charles Thomas.

LAUGHLIN, P. R. (1973) Selection strategies in concept attainment. In R. Solso (Ed.), *Contemporary issues in cognitive psychology.* Washington, D. C.: Winston.

LAWRENCE, D. (1971) Temporal numerosity for word lists. *Perception & Psychophysics, 10,* 75-78.

LEEPER, R. (1970) The motivational and perceptual properties of emotion as indicating their fundamental character and role. In M. B. Arnold (Ed.), *Feelings and emotions.* New York: Academic Press.

LEIBOWITZ, H., & BOURNE, L. (1956) Time and intensity as determiners of perceived shape. *Journal of Experimental Psychology, 51,* 277-281.

LENNEBERG, E. H. (1969) On explaining language. *Science, 164,* 635-643.

LESHOWITZ, B., & GREEN, D. (1974) Comments on "absolute judgment and paired-associate learning: Kissing cousins or identical twins?" *Psychological Review, 81,* 177-179.

LEVINE, M. (1971) Hypothesis theory and non-learning despite ideal S-R reinforcement contingencies. *Psychological Review, 78,* 130-140.

LEVINE, R., CHEIN, I., & MURPHY, G. (1942) The relation of the intensity of a need to the amount of perceptual distortion. *Journal of Psychology, 13,* 283-293.

LEWIN, K. A. (1935) *Dynamic theory of personality.* New York: McGraw Hill.

LINDSAY, R., & NORMAN, D. (1972) *Psychology: An information processing approach.* New York: Academic Press.

LOEVINGER, J. (1975) *Ego development.* San Francisco: Jossey-Bass.

LORINSTEIN, B., & HABER, R. (1975) Perceived numerosity: An information processing analysis. *Canadian Journal of Psychology, 29,* 224-236.

LUBORSKY, L. (1973) Forgetting and remembering (momentary forgetting) during psychotherapy: A new sample. *Psychological Issues, 8,* Monograph 30, 29-55.

LUCHINS, A. S. (1942) Mechanization in problem solving: The effect of "Einstellung." *Psychometric Monographs, 54,* no. 6.

MCALLISTER, W. R. (1953) Eyelid conditioning as a function of the CS-US interval. *Journal of Experimental Psychology, 45,* 417-422.

MCCLEARY, R., & LAZARUS, R. (1950) Autonomic discrimination without awareness: An interim report. In J. Bruner & D. Krech (Eds.) *Perception and personality: A symposium.* Durham, N.C.: Duke University Press.

MCDOUGALL, W. (1908) *Introduction to social psychology.* London: Methuen.

MCDOUGALL, W. (1923) *Outline of psychology.* New York: Scribner's.

MCGEOCH, J. A. (1932) Forgetting and the law of disuse. *Psychological Review, 39,* 352-370.

MCGHIE, A. (1966) Psychological studies of schizophrenia. *British Journal of Medical Psychology, 39,* 281-288.

MCGHIE, A., & CHAPMAN, J. (1961) Disorders of attention and perception in early schizophrenia. *British Journal of Medical Psychology, 34,* 103-116.

MCGILL, W. (1961) Loudness and reaction time. *Acta Psychologica, 19,* 193-199

MCKAY, D. G. (1970) Spoonerisms: The structure of errors in the serial order of speech. *Neuropsychologica, 8,* 323-350.

MCKELLER, P. (1957) *Imagination and thinking.* New York: Basic Books.

MCKINNEY, J. (1963) Disappearance of luminous designs. *Science, 140,* 403-404.

MCKINNEY, J. (1966) Verbal meaning and perceptual stability. *Canadian Journal of Psychology, 20,* 237-242.

MCNEILL, D. (1975) Semiotic extension. In R. Solso (Ed.), *Information processing and cognition.* Hillsdale, N.J.: Lawrence Erlbaum.

MACRAE, A. W. (1970) Channel capacity in absolute judgment tasks: An artifact of information bias. *Psychological Bulletin, 73,* 112-121.

MAGDALENO, R., JEX, H., & JOHNSON, W. (1970) Tracking quasi-predictable displays: Subjective predictability gradations, pilot models for periodic and narrow band inputs. *In Proceedings of the Fifth Annual NASA-University Conference on Manual Control.* (NASA - SP215), 391-428.

MAIER, N. R. F. (1930) Reasoning in humans. I. On direction. *Journal of Comparative Psychology, 10,* 115-143.

MAIER, N. R. F. (1931) Reasoning in humans. II. The solution of a problem and its appearance in consciousness. *Journal of Comparative Psychology, 12,* 181-194.

MANDLER, G. (1975) Consciousness: Respectable, useful, and probably necessary. In R. Solso (Ed.), *Information processing and cognition.* Hillsdale, N.J.: Lawrence Erlbaum.

MARKS, L. E. (1975) On colored-hearing synesthesia: Cross-modal translations of sensory dimensions. *Psychological Bulletin, 82,* 303-331.

MASSARO, D. (1972) Preperceptual images, processing time, and perceptual units in auditory perception. *Psychological Review, 79,* 124-145.

MAYZNER, M. S., & TRESSELT, M. E. (1970) Visual information processing with sequential inputs: A general model for sequential blanking, displacement, and overprinting phenomena. *Annals of the New York Academy of Science, 169,* 599-618.

MELTON, A. (1963) Implications of short-term memory for a general theory of memory. *Journal of Verbal Learning and Verbal Behavior, 2,* 1-21.

MELTON, A. (1970) The situation with respect to the spacing of repetitions and memory. *Journal of Verbal Learning and Verbal Behavior, 9,* 596-606.

MELZACK, R. (1973) *The puzzle of pain.* New York: Basic Books.

MELZACK, R., & CASEY, K. (1970) The affective dimension of pain. In M. B. Arnold (Ed.), *Feelings and emotion.* New York: Academic Press.

MERRINGER, S. M. (1908) *Aus dem Leben der Sprache.* Berlin: Behr's.

MESSER, A. (1906) Experimentell-psychologische Untersuchungen über das Denken. *Archiv für die gesamte Psychologie, 8,* 1-224. Excerpts translated by G. Mandler and J. Mandler. In J. Mandler & G. Mandler (Eds.), *Thinking: From association to gestalt.* New York: John Wiley, 1964.

MEUMANN, E. (1894) Untersuchungen zur Psychologie und Aesthetik des Rhythmus. *Philosophische Studien, 10,* 249-322. 393-430.

MICHOTTE, A. (1963) *The perception of causality.* New York: Basic Books. Originally published as *La perception de la causalité.* Louvain: Publications Universitaires de Louvain, 1946.

MICHOTTE, A., THINÈS, G., & CRABBÉ, G. (1962) Causalité, permanence et réalité phénoménales. In A. Michotte & J. Nuttin (Eds.), *Studia psychologica.* Louvain: Publications Universitaires de Louvain.

MILLER, G. A. (1956) The magical number seven plus or minus two: Some limits on our capacity for processing information. *Psychological Review, 63,* 81-97.

MILLER, G. A. & HEISE, G. A. (1950) The trill threshold. *Journal of the Acoustical Society of America, 22,* 637-638.

MILLER, G. A., & TAYLOR, W. G. (1948) The perception of repeated bursts of noise. *Journal of the Acoustical Society of America, 20,* 171-182.

MINER, J. (1903) Motor, visual, and applied rhythms. *Columbia Contributions to Philosophy, Psychology, and Education, 9.*

MINSKY, M. (1961) Steps toward artificial intelligence. *Proceedings of the Institute of Radio Engineers, 49,* 8-30.

MODELL, J., & RICH, G. (1915) A preliminary study of vowel qualities. *American Journal of Psychology, 26,* 453-456.

MORAY, N. (1959) Attention in dichotic listening: Affective cues and the influence of instructions. *Quarterly Journal of Experimental Psychology, 11,* 56-60.

MORAY, N. (1967) Where is capacity limited? A survey and a model. In A. Sanders (Ed.), *Attention and performance.* Amsterdam: North Holland.

MORAY, N. (1970) *Attention: Selective processes in vision and hearing.* New York: Academic Press.

MOTT, F. W., & SHERRINGTON, C. S. (1895) Experiments upon the influence of sensory nerves upon movement and nutrition of the limbs: Preliminary communication. *Proceedings of the Royal Society of London, 57,* 481-488.

MÜLLER, G. E. (1911, 1913, 1917) Zur Analyse der Gedächtnistätigkeit und des Vorstellungsverlaufes. *Zeitschrift für Psychologie, Erganzungsband, 5,* 1-403; *8,* 1-567; *9,* 1-682.

MÜLLER, G. E., & SCHUMANN, F. (1894) Experimentelle Beiträge zur Untersuchung des Gedächtnisses. *Zeitschrift für Psychologie, 6,* 81-190, 257-339.

MURDOCK, B. (1972) Short-term memory. *The Psychology of Learning and Motivation, 5,* 67-127.

NEISSER, U. (1967) *Cognitive psychology.* New York: Appleton-Century-Crofts.

NEWELL, A. (1973) You can't play 20 questions with nature and win. In W. Chase (Ed.), *Visual information processing.* New York: Academic Press.

NEWELL, A., & SIMON, H. A. (1972) *Human problem solving.* Englewood Cliffs, N.J.: Prentice-Hall.

NORMAN, D. (1966) Acquisition and retention in short-term memory. *Journal of Experimental Psychology, 72,* 369-381.

NORMAN, D. (1968) Toward a theory of memory and attention. *Psychological Review, 75,* 522-536.

NORMAN, D. (1969) Memory while shadowing. *Quarterly Journal of Experimental Psychology, 21,* 85-94.

OATLEY, K., & GOODWIN, B. (1971) The explanation and investigation of biological rhythms. In W. Colquhoun (Ed.), *Biological rhythms and human performance.* New York: Academic Press.

O'FLANAGAN, P., TIMOTHY, J., & GIBSON, H. (1951) Further observations on the use of combined photic and chemically induced cortical dysrhythmia in psychiatry. *Journal of Mental Science, 97,* 174-190.

OLÉRON, G. (1952) Influence de l'intensité d'un son sur l'estimation de sa durée apparente. *Année Psychologique, 52,* 383-392.

ORNSTEIN, R. (1972) *The psychology of consciousness.* San Francisco: Freeman.

OSGOOD, C. (1962) Studies on the generality of affective meaning systems. *American Psychologist, 17,* 10-28.

OSGOOD, C. (1969) On the whys and wherefores of E, P, and A. *Journal of Personality and Social Psychology, 12,* 194-199.

OSGOOD, C., SUCI, G., & TANNENBAUM, P. (1957) *The measurement of meaning.* Urbana, Ill.: University of Illinois Press.

OSWALD, I. (1962) *Sleeping and waking: Physiology and psychology.* Amsterdam: Elsevier.

PAIVIO, A. (1969) Mental imagery in associative learning and memory. *Psychological Review, 76,* 241-263.

PAIVIO, A. (1971) *Imagery and verbal processes.* New York: Holt, Rinehart & Winston.

PAUL, I. H. (1967) The concept of schema in memory theory. *Psychological Issues, 5,* Monograph 18/19, 219-258.

PAVLOV, I. (1927) *Conditioned reflexes.* Oxford: Milford.

PAVLOV, I. (1928) *Lectures on conditioned reflexes.* New York: International Publishers.

PEPPER, R., & HERMAN, L. (1970) Decay and interference effects in the short-term retention of a discrete motor act. *Journal of Experimental Psychology, Monographs, 83,* Part. 2, No. 2.

PERKY, C. W. (1910) An experimental study of imagination. *American Journal of Psychology, 21,* 422-452.

PETERSON, L. R., & PETERSON, M. J. (1959) Short-term retention of individual verbal items. *Journal of Experimental Psychology, 58,* 193-198.

PEW, R. (1974) Human perceptual-motor performance. In B. H. Kantowitz (Ed.), *Human information processing: Tutorials in performance and cognition.* Hillsdale, N.J.: Lawrence Erlbaum.

PHILIP, B. (1940) Time errors in the discrimination of color mass by the ranking method. *Journal of Experimental Psychology, 27,* 285-302.

PHILIP, B. (1947) The effect of interpolated and extrapolated stimuli on the time order error in the comparison of temporal intervals. *Journal of General Psychology, 36,* 173-187.

PHILLIPS, W., & BADDELEY, A. (1971) Reaction time and short-term visual memory. *Psychonomic Science, 22,* 73-74.

PIAGET, J. (1937) *La construction du réel chez l'enfânt.* Neuchâtel: Delachaux et Niestlé. Translated by M. Cook as *The construction of reality in the child.* New York: Basic Books, 1954.

PIAGET, J. (1950) *The psychology of intelligence.* London: Routledge.

PIAGET, J., VINH-BANG, & MATALON, B. (1958) Note on the law of the temporal maximum of some opticogeometric illusions. *American Journal of Psychology, 71,* 277-282.

PIÉRON, H. (1914) Recherches sur les lois de variation de temps de latence sensorielle en fonction des inténsitiés excitatrices. *L'Année Psychologique, 20,* 17-96.

PODELL, H. (1958) Two processes of concept formation. *Psychological Monographs, 72,* no. 15.

POLLACK, I. (1952) The information of elementary auditory displays. *Journal of the Acoustical Society of America, 24,* 745-749.

POLLACK, I. (1952) Auditory flutter. *American Journal of Psychology, 65,* 544-554.

POLLACK, I. (1953) The assimilation of sequentially encoded information. *American Journal of Psychology, 66, 421-435.*

PORT, E. (1963) Ueber die Lautstarke einzelner kurzer Schallimpulsen. *Acustica, 13,* 212-223.

POSNER, M. (1973) *Cognition: An introduction.* Glenview, Ill.: Scott, Foresman.

POSNER, M. I., BOIES, S. J., EICHELMAN, W. H., & TAYLOR, L. (1969) Retention of visual and name codes of single letters. *Journal of Experimental Psychology, 7,* 1-16.

PRITCHARD, R. M. (1961) Stabilized images on the retina. *Scientific American, 204,* 72-78.

PRITCHARD, R. M., HERON, W., & HEBB, D. O. (1960) Visual perception approached by the method of stabilized images. *Canadian Journal of Psychology, 14,* 67-77.

PRONKO, N. H. (1969) On learning to play the violin at the age of four without tears. *Psychology Today, 2,* 52.

PURKINJE, J. (1823) *Beobachtungen und Versuche für Physiologie der Sinnesorgane I. Beiträge zur Kenntnis des Sehens in subjektiver Hinsicht.* (2nd ed.) Prague: Calve.

RAAB, D. H. (1962) Magnitude estimation of the brightness of brief foveal stimuli. *Science, 135,* 42-43.

RAAB, D. H. (1963) Backward masking. *Psychological Bulletin, 60,* 118-129.

RAINES, T. (1909) Report of a case of psychochromesthesia. *Journal of Abnormal Psychology, 4,* 249-252.

RAPAPORT, D. (1942) *Emotions and memory.* Baltimore: Williams & Wilkins.

RAPAPORT, D. (Ed.) (1951) *The organization and pathology of thought.* New York: Columbia University Press.

RAPAPORT, D. (1957) Cognitive structures. *Bulletin of the Menninger Clinic.* Reprinted in D. Rapaport, (1967) *Collected papers.* New York: Basic Books.

RAUSH, H. I. (1952) Perceptual constancy in schizophrenia. *Journal of Personality, 21,* 176-187.

RESTLE, F. (1962) The selection of strategies in cue learning. *Psychological Review, 69,* 11-19.

RÉVÉSZ, G. (1950) *Psychology and art of the blind.* New York: Longmans Green.

ROSNER, B. S. (1961) Neural factors limiting cutaneous spatio-temporal discriminations. In W. A. Rosenblith (Ed.), *Sensory communication.* New York: John Wiley.

ROSS, S., & FLETCHER, J. (1953) Response time as an indicator of color deficiency. *Journal of Applied Psychology, 37,* 211-214.

ROYAL, D., & HAYS, W. (1959) Empirical dimensions of emotional behavior. *Proceedings of the 15th International Congress of Psychology, Brussels, 1957,* 419.

ROYCE, J., CARRAN, A., AFTANAS, M., LEHMAN, R., & BLU-MENTHAL, A. (1966) The autokinetic phenomenon: A critical review. *Psychological Bulletin, 65*, 243-260.

RUCKMICK, C. (1917) Visual rhythm. *Studies in Psychology*. Titchener Commemorative Volume. Worcester, Mass.: Wilson.

RUCKMICK, C. (1936) *The psychology of feeling and emotion*. New York: McGraw-Hill.

SAUFLEY, W., & WINOGRAD, E. (1970) Retrograde amnesia and priority instructions in free recall. *Journal of Experimental Psychology, 85*, 150-152.

SCHACHTER, S., & SINGER, J. (1962) Cognitive, social, and physiological determinants of emotional state. *Psychological Review, 69*, 379-399.

SCHAFER, R., & MURPHY, G. (1943) The role of autism in visual figure-ground relationship. *Journal of Experimental Psychology, 32*, 335-343.

SCHENKEL, K. (1967) Die beidohrigen Mithörschwellen von Impulsen. *Acustica, 18*, 38-46.

SCHILLER, P. H. (1965) Monoptic and dichoptic visual masking by patterns and flashes. *Journal of Experimental Psychology, 69*, 193-199.

SCHILLER, P. H., & WIENER, M. (1963) Monoptic and dichoptic visual masking. *Journal of Experimental Psychology, 66*, 386-393.

SCHLEGEL, W. (1929) Die Abhängigkeit des Umfanges der tachistoskopischen Neuauffassung der Intensität des Reizes. *Archiv für die gesamte Psychologie, 70*, 463-520.

SCHLOSBERG, H. (1954) Three dimensions of emotion. *Psychological Review, 61*, 81-88.

SCHMIDT, R. (1975) A schema theory of discrete motor learning. *Psychological Review, 82*, 225-260.

SCHULZ, L. (1971) Effects of high-priority events on recall and recognition of other events. *Journal of Verbal Learning and Verbal Behavior, 10*, 322-330.

SCHWARTZ, F., & SCHILLER, P. (1970) A psychoanalytic model of attention and learning. *Psychological Issues, 6*, Monograph 23.

SCHWARTZ, G. (1975) Biofeedback, self-regulation and the patterning of physiological processes. *American Scientist, 63*, 314-324.

SEASHORE, C. (1938) *Psychology of music*. New York: McGraw-Hill.

SEGAL, S. J., & GORDON, P. (1969) The Perky effect revisited: Paradoxical thresholds or signal detection error? *Perceptual and Motor Skills, 28*, 791-797.

SHAKOW, D. (1962) Segmental set: A theory of the formal psychological deficit of schizophrenia. *Archives of General Psychiatry, 6*, 1-17.

SHAKOW, D. (1963) Psychological deficit in schizophrenia. *Behavioral Science, 8*, 275-305.

SHALLICE, T. (1964) The detection of change and the perceptual moment hypothesis. *British Journal of Statistical Psychology, 17*, 113-135.

SHEPARD, R. (1963) The analysis of proximities: Multidimensional scaling with an unknown distance function. *Psychometrica, 27*, 125-140.

SHEPARD, R. (1964) Attention and the metric structure of the stimulus space. *Journal of Mathematical Psychology, 1*, 54-87.

SHEPARD, R. (1968) Review of U. Neisser, *Cognitive psychology. American Journal of Psychology, 81*, 285-289.

SHEPARD, R. (1975) Form, formation, and transformation of internal representations. In R. Solso (Ed.), *Information processing and cognition.* Hillsdale, N.J.: Lawrence Erlbaum.

SHEPARD, R. & METZLER, J. (1971) Mental rotation of three-dimensional objects. *Science, 171*, 701-703.

SHEPARD, R., & TEGHTSOONIAN, M. (1961) Retention of information under conditions approaching a steady state. *Journal of Experimental Psychology, 62*, 302-309.

SHERRICK, C. E. (1968) Bilateral apparent haptic movement. *Perception & Psychophysics, 4*, 159-162.

SHERRINGTON, C. S. (1900) Cutaneous sensations. In E. Schäfer (Ed.), *Textbook of physiology.* New York: Pentland.

SHOR, R. E. (1959) Hypnosis and the concept of the generalized reality orientation. *American Journal of Psychotherapy, 13*, 582-602.

SIEGEL, J., & SIEGEL, W. (1972) Absolute judgment and paired-associate learning: Kissing cousins or identical twins? *Psychological Review, 79*, 300-316.

SIEGEL, W. (1972) Memory effects in the method of absolute judgment. *Journal of Experimental Psychology, 49*, 121-131.

SILVERMAN, J. (1964) The problem of attention in research and theory in schizophrenia. *Psychological Review, 71*, 352-379.

SILVERMAN, J. (1968) A paradigm for the study of altered states of consciousness. *British Journal of Psychiatry, 114*, 1201-1218.

SIMON, H. A., & KOTOVSKY, K. (1963) Human acquisition of concepts for sequential patterns. *Psychological Review, 70*, 534-546.

SINGER, J. L. (1966) *Daydreaming: An introduction to the experimental study of inner experience.* New York: Random House.

SINGER, J. L. (1970) Drives, affects, and daydreams: The adaptive role of spontaneous imagery or stimulus-independent mentation. In J. Antrobus (Ed.), *Cognition and affect.* Boston: Little, Brown.

SKINNER, B. F. (1938) *Behavior of organisms.* New York: Appleton-Century.

SMITH, M. C. (1967[a]) Theories of the psychological refractory period. *Psychological Bulletin, 67*, 202-213.

SMITH, M. C. (1967[b]) Reaction time to a second stimulus as a function of intensity of the first stimulus. *Quarterly Journal of Experimental Psychology, 19*, 125-132.

SMYTHIES, J. R. (1959[a]) The stroboscopic patterns. I. The dark phase. *British Journal of Psychology, 50*, 106-116.

SMYTHIES, J. R. (1959[b]) The stroboscopic patterns. II. The phenomenology of the bright phase and after images. *British Journal of Psychology, 50*, 305-324.

SMYTHIES, J. R. (1960) The stroboscopic patterns. III. Further experiments and discussion. *British Journal of Psychology, 51*, 247-255.

SOLLEY, C., & MURPHY, G. (1960) *Development of the perceptual world.* New York: Basic Books.

SPERLING, G. (1960) The information available in brief visual presentations. *Psychological Monographs, 74,* no. 11.

SPERLING, G. (1962) A model for visual memory tasks. *Human Factors, 5,* 19-31.

SPERLING, G. (1967) Successive approximations to a model for short-term memory. *Acta Psychologica, 27,* 285-292.

SPOONER, A., & KELLOGG, W. (1947) The backward conditioning curve. *American Journal of Psychology, 60,* 321-334.

STERNBERG, S. (1970) Memory-scanning: Mental processes revealed by reaction-time experiments. In J. Antrobus (Ed.), *Cognition and affect.* Boston: Little, Brown.

STEVENS, S. S. (1966) Duration, luminance, and the brightness exponent. *Perception & Psychophysics, 1,* 96-100.

STOTT, L. H. (1935) Time order errors in the discrimination of short tonal durations. *Journal of Experimental Psychology, 18,* 741-766.

STRINGER, P. (1967) Cluster analysis of nonverbal judgments of facial expression. *British Journal of Mathematical and Statistical Psychology, 20,* 71-79.

STROUD, J. M. (1955) The fine structure of psychological time. In J. Quastler (Ed.), *Information theory in psychology.* Glencoe, Ill.: Free Press.

STUDDERT-KENNEDY, M., SCHANKWEILER, D., & SCHUHMAN, S. (1970) Opposed effects of a delayed channel on perception of dichotically and monotically presented CV syllables. *Journal of the Acoustical Society of America, 48,* 599-602.

STUMPF, C. (1883) *Tonpsychologie.* Leipzig: Hirzel.

SULLIVAN, E., & TURVEY, M. (1972) Short-term retention of tactile information. *Quarterly Journal of Experimental Psychology, 24,* 253-261.

SWAN, W. (1849) On the gradual production of luminous impressions on the eyes and other phenomena of vision. *Transactions of the Royal Society of Edinburgh, 16,* 581-603.

TAUB, E., & BERMAN, A. J. (1968) Movement and learning in the absence of sensory feedback. In S. J. Freedman (Ed.), *The neuropsychology of spatially oriented behavior.* Homewood, Ill.: Dorsey.

TAYLOR, J. N. A. (1956) A comparison of delusional and hallucinatory individuals using field dependency as a measure. Unpublished doctoral thesis, Purdue University.

THOMPSON, R., & SPENCER, W. (1966) Habituation: A model phenomenon for the study of neuronal substrates of behavior. *Psychological Review, 73,* 16-43.

TITCHENER, E. B. (1908) *The psychology of feeling and attention.* New York: Macmillan.

TITCHENER, E. B. (1909) *Lectures on the experimental psychology of the thought processes.* New York: Macmillan.

TOLKMITT, F. (1973) A review of the psychological refractory period. *Acta Psychologica, 37,* 139-154.

TOLMAN, E. (1932) *Purposive behavior in animals and men.* New York: Appleton-Century-Crofts.

TOMKINS, S. (1962, 1963) *Affect, imagery, and consciousness,* 2 vols. New York: Springer.

TOMKINS, S. (1970) A theory of memory. In J. Antrobus (Ed.), *Cognition and affect.* Boston: Little, Brown.

TRAGER, G., & SMITH, H. (1951) *Outline of English structure.* Norman, Olka.: Battenburg Press.

TREISMAN, A. (1964) Monitoring and storage of irrelevant messages in selective attention. *Journal of Verbal Learning and Verbal Behavior, 3,* 449-459.

TRESSELT, M. E. (1944[a]) Time errors in successive comparison of simple visual objects. *American Journal of Psychology, 57,* 555-558.

TRESSELT, M. E. (1944[b]) The time errors in visual extents and areas. *Journal of Psychology, 17,* 21-30.

TULVING, E. (1966) Subjective organization and effects of repetition in multitrial free-recall learning. *Journal of Verbal Learning and Verbal Behavior, 5,* 193-198.

TULVING, E. (1968) Theoretical issues in free recall. In T. Dixon & D. Horton (Eds.), *Verbal behavior and general behavior theory.* Englewood Cliffs, N.J.: Prentice-Hall.

TULVING, E. (1969) Retrograde amnesia in free recall. *Science, 164,* 88-90.

TURVEY, M. T. (1967) Repetition and the preperceptual information store. *Journal of Experimental Psychology, 74,* 289-293.

TURVEY, M. T. (1973) On peripheral and central processes in vision: Inferences from an information-processing analysis of masking with patterned stimuli. *Psychological Review, 80,* 1-52.

UEXKÜLL, J. VON (1934) *Streifzüge durch die Umwelten von Tieren und Menschen.* Berlin: Springer. Translated by C. Schiller as, A stroll through the worlds of animals and men. In C. Schiller (Ed.), *Instinctive behavior.* New York: International Universities Press, 1957.

UNDERWOOD, B., & SCHULZ, R. (1960) *Meaningfulness and verbal learning.* Philadelphia: Lippincott.

UTTAL, W. R. (1971) The psychobiological silly season—or—What happens when neurophysiological data become psychological theories. *Journal of General Psychology, 84,* 151-166.

VENABLES, P. H. (1963) Selectivity of attention, withdrawal and cortical activation. *Archives of General Psychiatry, 9,* 74-78.

VIERORDT, K. (1868) *Der Zeitsinn nach Versuchen.* Tübingen: Laup.

VON FOERSTER, H. (1970) Thoughts and notes on cognition. In P. L. Garvin (Ed.), *Cognition: A multiple view.* New York: Spartan.

VOSBERG, R., FRASER, N., & GUEHL, J. (1960) Imagery sequence in sensory deprivation. *Archives of General Psychiatry, 2,* 356-369.

VOTH, A. C. (1947) An experimental study of mental patients through the autokinetic phenomenon. *American Journal of Psychiatry, 103,* 793-805.

WALTER, W. G. (1953) *The living brain.* New York: Norton.

WARD, J. (1918) *Psychological principles*. Cambridge: Cambridge University Press.

WAUGH, N., & NORMAN, D. (1965) Primary memory. *Psychological Review, 72*, 89-104.

WECKOWICZ, T. E. (1957) Size constancy in schizophrenic patients. *Journal of Mental Science, 103*, 475-486.

WEDIN, L. (1972) Evaluation of a three-dimensional model of emotion expression in music. *Psychological Laboratory Reports*, University of Stockholm, No. 349.

WEDIN, L. (1969) Dimension analysis of emotional expression in music. *Swedish Journal of Musicology, 51*, 119-140.

WELFORD, A. T. (1968) *Fundamentals of skill*. London: Methuen.

WENZL, A. (1932) Empirische und theoretische Beiträge zur Erinnerungsarbeit bei erschwerter Wortfindung. *Archiv für die gesamte Psychologie, 85*, 181-218.

WERNER, H. (1934) L'unité des sens. *Journal de Psychologie, 31*, 190-205.

WERNER, H. (1948) *Comparative psychology of mental development*. New York: Science Editions.

WERTHEIMER, M. (1912) Untersuchungen über das Sehen von Bewegung. *Zeitschrift für Psychologie, 61*, 161-265.

WEVER, E. (1927) Figure and ground in the perception of form. *American Journal of Psychology, 38*, 194-226.

WEYER, E. M. (1898, 1899) Die Zeitschwellen gliechartiger und disparater Sinneseindrücke. *Philosophische Studien, 14*, 615-639; *15*, 67-138.

WHITCHURCH, A. (1921) The illusory perception of movement on the skin. *American Journal of Psychology, 32*, 472-489.

WHITE, C. T. (1963) Temporal numerosity and the psychological unit of duration. *Psychological Monographs, 77*, no. 12.

WHITEHEAD, A. N. (1929) *Process and reality*. New York: Macmillan.

WICKELGREN, W., & NORMAN, D. (1966) Strength models and serial position in short-term recognition memory. *Journal of Mathematical Psychology, 3*, 316-347.

WIENER, N. (1948) *Cybernetics*. New York: John Wiley.

WITKIN, H. A. (1950) Individual differences in ease of perception of embedded figures. *Journal of Personality, 19*, 1-15.

WITKIN, H. A., DYK, R. B., FATERSON, H. F., GOODENOUGH, D. R., & KARP, S. A. (1962) *Psychological differentiation*. New York: John Wiley.

WITKIN, H. A., LEWIS, H. B., HERTZMAN, M., MACHOVER, K., MEISNER, P. B., & WAPNER, S. (1954) *Personality through perception*. New York: Harper.

WOLF, T. (1976) Attentional processes in musical sight reading. *Journal of Psycholinguistic Research, 5*, 143-171.

WOLFLE, H. M. (1932) Conditioning as a function of the interval between the conditioned and the original stimulus. *Journal of General Psychology, 7*, 80-103.

WOODROW, H. (1951) Time perception. In S. S. Stevens (Ed.), *Handbook of experimental psychology*. New York: John Wiley.

WOODWORTH, R. S. (1899) The accuracy of voluntary movement. *Psychological Review, Monograph Supplements, 3*, no. 13.

WOODWORTH, R. S. (1938) *Experimental psychology*. New York: Henry Holt.

WOODWORTH, R. S., & SCHLOSBERG, H. (1954) *Experimental psychology*. New York: Henry Holt.

WORDEN, F. (1966) Attention and electrophysiology. In E. Stellar & J. Sprague (Eds.), *Progress in physiological psychology* (Vol. 1.). New York: Academic Press.

WUNDT, W. (1874) *Grundzüge der physiologischen Psychologie*. Leipzig: Engelmann.

WUNDT, W. (1891) Ueber die Methoden der Messung des Bewusstseinsumfanges. *Philosophische Studien, 6*, 250-260.

WUNDT, W. (1892) Zur Frage des Bewusstseinsumfanges. *Philosophische Studien, 7*, 222-231.

WUNDT, W. (1896) *Outlines of psychology*, translated by C. H. Judd. Leipzig: Englemann.

WUNDT, W. (1899) Zur Kritik tachistoskopischer Versuche. *Philosophische Studien, 15*, 287-317.

WUNDT, W. (1903) *Grundzüge der physiologischen Psychologie* (5th ed., Vol. 3). Leipzig: Engelmann.

YOSHIDA, M. (1964) Studies in the psychometric classification of odors. *Japanese Journal of Psychology, 35*, 1-17.

ZAPPAROLI, G., & REATTO, L. (1969) The apparent movement between visual and acoustic stimulus and the problems of intermodal relations. *Acta Psychologica, 29*, 256-267.

ZEAMAN, D., & HOUSE, B. (1963) The role of attention in retardate discrimination learning. In N. Ellis (Ed.), *Handbook of mental deficiency*. New York: McGraw-Hill.

ZWISLOCKI, J. (1969) Temporal summation of loudness: An analysis. *Journal of the Acoustical Society of America, 46*, 431-441.

INDEX

SUBJECT INDEX